DEFINABLE TRACES IN THE ATMOSPHERE

Mike Marqusee (1953–2015) – journalist, political activist, and author – was born in New York City, and emigrated to Britain in 1971.

As well as his many books, Mike published articles in (among others), the *Guardian*, the *Independent*, the *Daily Telegraph*, the *Observer*, *Index on Censorship*, *BBC History Magazine*, *New Left Review*, *Race and Class*, the *Nation*, *Colorlines*, *India Today*, *Hindustan Times*, *Indian Express*, *Frontline*, and *Outlook*. He was a columnist for the Indian newspaper *The Hindu* and for the British left-wing magazine *Red Pepper*.

In addition to his writing, Mike was active for several decades in numerous campaigns for social justice. In the early 1980s he was a youth worker and trade union activist. For 20 years he was an active member of the Labour Party, and a long-time editor of and contributor to *Labour Briefing*. In 1995, he helped set up Hit Racism for Six, a campaign against racism in cricket. He helped establish both the Stop the War Coalition and Iraq Occupation Focus. On 15 February 2003, he was a speaker at the half million strong anti-war demonstration in New York City. In later years, he was a dedicated campaigner in support of the National Health Service.

In 2005, Mike Marqusee was named an Honorary Faculty Fellow by the University of Brighton in recognition of his 'contribution to the development of a critically-based form of journalistic scholarship in the social, cultural and political nature of contemporary global sport'.

Also by Mike Marqusee

Fiction
Slow Turn (1986)

Poetry
Street Music (2009)
Saved by a Wandering Mind (2012)

Non-fiction
Defeat from the Jaws of Victory: Inside Kinnock's Labour Party (with Richard Heffernan, 1992)
Anyone but England: Cricket, Race and Class (1994, republished 2016)
War Minus the Shooting: a Journey through South Asia during Cricket's World Cup (1996)
Redemption Song: Muhammad Ali and the Spirit of the Sixties (1999, republished 2016)
Chimes of Freedom: the Politics of Bob Dylan's Art (2003), republished as *Wicked Messenger: Bob Dylan and the Sixties* (2005)
If I Am Not for Myself: Journey of an Anti-Zionist Jew (2008)
The Price of Experience: Writings on Living with Cancer (2014)

DEFINABLE TRACES IN THE ATMOSPHERE

MIKE MARQUSEE

OR Books
New York · London

© 2018 Mike Marqusee

Published by OR Books, New York and London
Visit our website at www.orbooks.com

All rights information: rights@orbooks.com

All rights reserved. No part of this book may be reproduced or transmitted in any form or by any means, electronic or mechanical, including photocopy, recording, or any information storage retrieval system, without permission in writing from the publisher, except brief passages for review purposes.

First printing 2018

Cataloging-in-Publication data is available from the Library of Congress.
A catalog record for this book is available from the British Library.

ISBN 978-1-682191-63-7 paperback
ISBN 978-1-682191-64-4 e-book

Typeset by Lapiz Digital Services, Chennai, India. Printed by BookMobile in the United States and CPI Books Ltd in the United Kingdom.

CONTENTS

Egypt	1
Foreword: Mark Steel	3
Introduction: Liz Davies	9

**1: 'A man is worked on by what he works on' –
America and the 1960s** ... 23

- A victim of America: Muhammad Ali and the war against terrorism ... 23
- The politics of Bob Dylan ... 31
- 1968: the mysterious chemistry of social change ... 36

**2: Streets of the imagination – Thoreau, Paine,
Blake and Shelley** ... 49

- The voice within: a pilgrimage to Walden Pond ... 49
- Thomas Paine: restless democrat ... 53
- Streets of the imagination ... 59
- Time to talk utopia ... 64
- 1792: this is what revolution looks like ... 69

**3: Pathways of memory – nationalism, capitalism and
the love of a game** ... 75

- For love of the game ... 75
- Triumph and travail: the subcontinental story ... 82
- Pathways of memory ... 94
- Branding the nation ... 97
- The privatisation of cricket ... 101
- A level playing field?: global sport in the neo-liberal age ... 107

4:	**Wandering in the subcontinent – India and Pakistan**	113
	India's tryst with the death penalty	113
	Life-changing happenstance: discovering India	117
5:	**Behind many pious phrases – nationalism, imperialism and internationalism**	121
	Free speech and the war on terror	121
	Imperial whitewash	125
	Multi-culturalism and the politics of white identity	129
	A lovely, worldly quirk: Madeira's north coast	134
	Contesting white supremacy	139
	Small country, big struggle	144
	'The greatest nation on earth'?: Obama's victory speech viewed from overseas	149
	White supremacy alive and well in Britain	156
6:	**The long battle for Labour's soul**	161
	...And all those against	161
	All because he loves you: A Christmas tale	165
	Alternative campaign diary	172
	The sleep of reason breeds monsters	178
	Mistaken priorities	183
	Politics and 'the art of the possible'	186
	Riots, reason and resistance	190
	Politics, our missing link	196
	Success, failure and other political myths	201
	Thatcherism's resistible rise	206
	Why I am an unrepentant Bennite	212
7:	**The joys of art**	215
	Rocking for revolution	215
	A rasika's tribute	220

Matchless feast 223
Not pop as we know it: flamenco and the quest for authenticity 227
John Ford: melancholy democrat 232
My fantasy career (or why there is no such thing as world music) 237
'Life is possible on this earth': the poetry of Mahmoud Darwish 241
1200 BC: the world's first industrial action...rescuing the past for the future 246
Past visions, future dreams 250

8: Reflections on identity **255**
Some crucial distinctions 255
Echoes and analogies 259
Pathways across time and space 262
The real thing 265
Bible bashing (lessons for the rich) 269
'If not now, when?': on BDS and 'singling out' Israel 273

9: The last dance – a battle for healthcare, not for health **279**
As long as you've got your health 279
Equality: without ifs, ands or buts 284
The misbegotten 'war against cancer' 288
The cancer dance and the rites of positivity 294

Song of the besieged 299

Publishing history **301**
Acknowledgements **307**

EGYPT

First published in Street Music, *2012.*

These people filling the square on TV
are our friends and neighbours.
That's not a foreign language they're speaking
though it's an idiom we'll have to relearn.
Let's eavesdrop on their conversations,
see how they name things – freedom, oppression –
see how they tell the difference between names and things.

This is not a dream but like a dream
it's turbulent and calm, long wished for,
full of surprise. As in a dream
time is elided, elongated, hesitant then decisive...
exhausting and renewing. In the square
time is an art-form and space curves with it.

I know this is not a dream because it leaves
definable traces in the atmosphere, like incense.

I know this is not a dream because I have dreamed it before.
I know this is not a dream because like a dream
everything is changed in its wake.

FOREWORD

An earlier version was first published four days after Mike Marqusee's death on 13 January 2015.

We may all be unique, but few could be as unique as Mike Marqusee (1953 – 2015), as it's hard to argue that what the world has too many of is American socialist cricket fanatics. Usually described as 'writer and activist', for Mike this phrase was nonsense, as each activity was meaningless unless they combined with and enhanced the other.

His life as a glorious mix of disparate cultures began on his first day. Born in New York in 1953 to white Jewish parents, who became civil rights activists travelling to Mississippi to oppose segregation, one day he came home from school to find Martin Luther King in the living room. His attitudes were shaped partly by a youth spent in 1960s New York, when defiance of authority moulded every corner of culture. So as well as organising campaigns for civil rights and against the Vietnam War, he was embroiled in the battle for fun. He was captivated by the music, poetry and occasional spliff of the times, and developed a special affection for sport.

All aspects of this background landed with him, when he came to live in England in the 1970s. He joined the Labour Party, becoming a prominent supporter of Tony Benn, and more fundamentally became obsessed with cricket. One product of this fusion was a book that helped to transform sports writing, *Anyone but England: Cricket, Race and Class*, an account of the game that lauded its beauty while raging against the snobbery and racism that had spewed from those who'd controlled it throughout its history.

This was a blasphemy that must have burst a million arteries amongst those in charge of English cricket. Books about cricket were supposed to depict glorious summers and splendid figures and never stoop to ask grubby questions such as why the MCC supported apartheid, or why the odd England captain admired Hitler, because this was cricket. *Anyone but England* was cricket's equivalent of a scientific breakthrough that smashes all previous laws. And he was American! The impertinence!

The book was shortlisted for the William Hill Sportsbook of the Year Award, and praised around the world by figures such as Pakistan captain Imran Khan. But its greatest effect was in enabling thousands of cricket fans, who'd always felt uneasy about English cricket's imperial image, to proclaim a corner of their peculiar game.

For Mike, cricket was probably the ideal spectator sport, because it allowed time to dwell. A day watching cricket with him was an extraordinary education, as he'd discuss which province in India the batsman came from, then the role that region played in winning independence, its architecture, the poetry the batsman read, then why all this contributed to the reason he got out to spin bowling.

His next book on sport analysed the figure that did most to unite the defiant culture of his youth in both sport and politics. *Redemption Song: Muhammad Ali and the Spirit of the Sixties* ricochets between Vietnam, Alabama and knocking people out, each strand shaping the others, culminating in the thrilling scene in which Ali stands in a military office, refusing to cross a yellow line as his name is called out to be drafted into the army, declaring 'I ain't got no quarrel with the Viet Cong.'

He employed a similar combination of admiration and enquiry for *Chimes of Freedom*, on Bob Dylan's influence on the sixties. Then he confronted an institution arguably even more challenging than the cricket authorities; the state of Israel. *If I Am Not for Myself: Journey of an Anti-Zionist Jew* flashes between a personal account, and a history of the Middle East that manages to embrace the prophet Amos. It begins with his shock as a schoolboy at a Jewish Sunday School, when a young soldier who's fought for Israel in the 1967 war is introduced to the class.

'He told us the Arabs are ignorant people, who go to toilet in the street. I'd heard this language before, from bigoted white Southerners towards blacks. I raised my hand and said this seemed to me, well, racist. Angrily the teacher turned to me and said there would be no discourtesy to guests in the classroom.'

This incident began a lifelong tussle with Zionism, never as raw as when he was accused of being a 'self-hating Jew' for opposing the ethics of the Israeli regime. He enjoyed quoting the Jewish son of a friend who was accused of this, and replied, 'No, you misunderstand. It's you I hate, you bastard.'

Throughout each project he played prominent roles in campaigns such as Stop the War, and in local groups opposing cuts in his area of Hackney. In 2000 he left Labour, assessing the radical change he supported was unlikely to be advanced by an organisation led by Tony Blair.

But it now seems the timing of when Mike was lost to the world carries a dark and maybe comic irony. Because the part of Britain he came to was North London, and the local Labour Party he joined and helped transform was in Islington, which meant the figure at the centre of his daily political activities was the maverick, rebellious and nationally marginal Member of Parliament, Jeremy Corbyn.

Mike and Jeremy became friends and compatriots, to the extent Jeremy and I were co-hosts of the memorial event that took place a few weeks after Mike died, one week after Labour's disastrous defeat at the General Election of 2015. For Mike, Jeremy represented the spirit, intellect, principles and defiance he felt should drive the Labour movement. But eventually he also assumed Jeremy represented the hopelessness of the Labour Party. How could any organisation, especially a party designed to reshape the world for 'the many, not the few', promote figures who almost boasted of their lack of spirit, intellect and principles, while someone like Jeremy was derided and ignored?

In 2007 he was told he had multiple myeloma, a cancer diagnosis that created a new subject for enquiry. Amongst the articles he wrote on his illness was one called 'The bedrock of autonomy', describing the multitude of characters that led to his treatment being possible, written while on an IV drip. It includes 'all who contribute to the intricate ballet of a functioning hospital, the Irish physician Frances Rynd who invented the hollow needle, those who built and sustained the NHS... the drip flowing into my vein is drawn from a river with innumerable tributaries.'

One of his most frustrating times was when he was in a ward for three days with only one other patient, who appeared to have no interest in any subject at all. Eventually this chap noticed a headline in the newspaper about the Chinese army shooting at Tibetan monks and said, 'That's terrible.' Mike thought, 'At last I've got something to discuss with this bloke', until the other patient said, 'I mean, you can't just let monks run all over the place like that.'

After Mike's memorial I sat with Jeremy Corbyn, and the equally exorcised figure of John McDonnell, and I asked whether either of them was likely to stand for the vacant job of Labour leader, though this would obviously be a token gesture. 'We haven't decided yet', they agreed, and Jeremy mumbled it had been suggested it was his turn, said with all the enthusiasm of someone realising just as they're going to bed that it's their turn to take the bins out.

At every dramatic point in the Labour Party story, in the subsequent ridiculously unpredictable two and a half years, I have muttered aloud the words 'What on earth would Mike have made of this?' When Mike left us, it was accepted by every branch of respectable wisdom that Jeremy Corbyn and the ideas he represented were so absurd as to be barely worthy of a response. For those of us who have known Jeremy, every time we see him on the news at Prime Minister's Questions, there's a moment where we wonder what he's doing there, as if it's a strange dream in which your window cleaner is now the Pope.

To Mike, the idea that his old friend, carrying all those old values they fought for, is at the time of writing favourite to become Prime Minister, would be as much of a shock as it would be to Van Gogh, if he were told that while he may have died in poverty, every doodle he ever did is now worth millions. The story is not just a Hollywood tale of the rise of an underdog, it's a transformation that embodies all Mike stood for, that defiance, hope, principle and tenacity will always find a way of breaking through, as long as someone somewhere is battling to keep these ideas alive.

So throughout his illness Mike continued to write, speak about and be fascinated by William Blake, Kevin Pietersen, Indian poetry, the campaign against the Bedroom Tax, ways to confront UKIP and the corporate nature of the Indian Premier League, and how they all collide with and impact upon each other.

And he could convey his thoughts in a manner so inspiring they could make you thump the table and yell in public. Because what seemed to drive him above all was the idea that it makes no sense to have fun in this world if you're not prepared to insist that fun should be equally available to all of humanity. But there isn't much point in contending for a fairer world, unless in the process you're not prepared to have an enormous amount of fun.

Mark Steel
Britain, October 2017

INTRODUCTION

I guess I've been saved by a wandering mind,
Stretched out like a coastal path, thickening
And thinning, vagrant, an etcher's line,
Plunging to the sea, retreating uphill, zigzagging
To the safe haven beyond the false promontory –
Exhausting in its course but the view:
Pine-filled, erect, prismatic, you look
Three, four times, and still it's not enough....
– From 'Saved by a Wandering Mind', 2009.

I loved seeing Mike write. For the more than 24 years that we were together, it was part of my life. He banged away fiercely on his computer keyboard using four fingers and ignoring spelling errors on the first draft. The words and thoughts tumbled out, almost completely unrecognisable to an untutored eye. He would then return, going through word by word, cleaning up the spelling but much more importantly selecting exactly the right word. As he became more experienced, and more confident, he deleted and deleted, so that each sentence was beautifully concise. Mike's precision with language was constantly praised by reviewers. It was not just a gift, but something that he worked on, and shaped, all his life.

Writing would take over, no matter what we were doing, when deadlines loomed. I've sat in the kitchen desperate for dinner as the keyboard clattered away and he would 'be just ten more minutes'; I've gone to bed, and got up in the morning, to find Mike still in the same position, hunched over the computer. On holiday, he would sit in hotel rooms, banging out the words, and often swearing over the portable equipment he was having to use. As technology changed, so did the process of writing when we were travelling. Early on, he would write by hand, and we'd wander around Indian towns looking for a fax machine. Later, he'd write on a computer, but still have to send the copy in by fax, which required investing in a light, portable printer that would invariably break down. Come the web, but before ubiquitous Wi-Fi, he could write on a laptop, and then we would search for an Internet café. There generally followed some technological hitch (how to transfer the copy, did the USB port fit, what about a cable?). I often longed for the old-fashioned idea of reading copy down the telephone.

Writing didn't just loom large when Mike was up against a deadline. It was an essential part of his mind. He was never without a notebook. I've sat next to him on planes, in hospital waiting rooms, on railway stations, in cars, at other people's houses, watching him scribble down thoughts. He'd be developing a train of thought that would end up as a key theme in one of his articles or books, or articulating a reaction to a political or personal event, or working on a poem. Mike's response to everything was to write. I wasn't allowed to read anything until it was ready. Even now, over two years after his death, I'm nervous about delving into those notebooks.

Mike's great strength, sometimes lamented by him, was his eclecticism. He loved discovering new interests. And those new interests would then be connected to existing passions, producing insights unique to Mike. The world never divided itself into disciplinary compartments or categories. He would read into a subject intensely, buy associated music, watch movies, and follow through odd connections. As his ideas formed, he would clarify his thought process by talking: on walks, to friends sitting at our kitchen table, whilst watching cricket matches, late at night. There was something magical in his ability to grasp serious heavyweight ideas and recount them with a twinkle in his eye and a whimsical aside. Politics was a driving force, combined with a deep sense of history, a love of art and human creativity, and a vision of a better future. Although he bemoaned his wandering mind, saying he couldn't retain an audience because no one else wanted to read about cricket, Bob Dylan and the politics of anti-Zionism, he was also privately pleased by the depth and range of his knowledge. In reality, he acquired extra audiences as he published on different subjects. I – and the publisher – like to think that there is also a special audience out there, a Mike Marqusee audience, excited to read anything he's written, on any subject, because they appreciate the clarity, the political underpinning and the huge amount of knowledge he would share with his readers.

When we first met, in 1989, he was an authority on cricket, politics (the British Labour Party, the American labour movement, Civil Rights Movement and anti-Vietnam war protests), Renaissance art, racism and anti-racism, and Indian and Pakistani politics. During the following 25 years, he discovered flamenco and South Indian Carnatic music, developed a serious understanding of nationalism, imperialism and national identity, and developed theories about white supremacism and the inadequacies of multi-culturalism. In later years, he returned to earlier passions as he researched William Blake, Thomas Paine and the radical politics of the 1790s in France, America and Britain. He had always been an anti-Zionist and a supporter of Palestine's liberation, but he deepened that commitment as he explored his own Jewish roots and Jewish culture. He loved art in both its high and popular incarnations, and particularly enjoyed the explosion of popular culture that had occurred during his youth in 1960s America.

The selection of Mike's writing in this book reflects the eclecticism of his thought. The pieces here were selected by starting out with some basic categories: cricket, Jewishness and Israel/Palestine, high art and popular culture, India and the subcontinent, the British Labour Party and labour movement politics. But we soon realized that many pieces fell into more than one category whilst others fell into none. We started with subject areas in order to do justice to the broad sweep of Mike's interests – we didn't want to miss any of the more significant topics – but we didn't feel the pieces should be read within particular categories.

The earliest articles were published in what was then *Labour Briefing*, later to become *Labour Left Briefing*. Mike became a regular journalist on this small, left-wing, Labour Party oriented magazine in the mid-late 1980s, and he and I met through Labour Party activity and *Labour Briefing*. After a re-launch in 1990, Mike became the editor and later the political correspondent. During the 1990s, the main forum for his political writing was *Labour Left Briefing*, and sometimes the *New Statesman*. He also began to acquire a name for himself as a cricket writer, and published in various cricket magazines, as well as *Esquire* and, for a time, the *Daily Telegraph* where, improbable as it seems, he had a cricket column.

From 2005, Mike wrote regular columns for *The Hindu*, an Indian national English-language daily newspaper, and the British left magazine *Red Pepper*. He was also published in the *Guardian*. *The Hindu* column was titled 'Level Playing Field'. In *Red Pepper*, he wrote under the rubric 'Contending for the Living', a quote from Thomas Paine who, replying to Edmund Burke in *Rights of Man*, wrote: 'I am contending for the rights of the living against the manuscript-assumed authority of the dead.' Mike would want the pieces that appear here, and his writing more generally, not to be treated as 'manuscript-assumed authority' but rather to be shared, circulated, argued over, disagreed with, and used as inspiration for further thought and writing.

Many of these articles are about the British Labour Party, and must be read with the context in which they were written in mind. When Mike died in January 2015, his long-standing friend, Jeremy Corbyn, was a back-bench MP, representing Islington North and countless other causes assiduously, as he had done for the previous 32 years. Six months after Mike's death, Jeremy Corbyn ran for leadership of the Labour Party. His election radically changed the nature of the Labour Party, but was something that, until summer 2015, no one had contemplated. As this collection is published, Corbyn and the Labour Party have just fought a general election and emerged, against all predictions, gaining rather than losing Labour seats in Parliament. There is a real possibility that another general election could happen soon and that Corbyn could become Prime Minister.

Mike was a very active member of the Labour Party from the early 1980s to 2000. He was an enthusiastic and, as he later described it, unreconstructed Bennite. From the mid-1980s, and the defeat of the miners, the left in the Labour Party became ever more beleaguered. In 1994, after four successive general election defeats, the Labour Party elected Tony Blair as leader, and he immediately took steps to reshape the party politically. One of those steps was when Blair overturned my selection as Labour Party Parliamentary Candidate for Leeds North East, in a move against the socialist left of the Labour Party. For a brief period, Mike and I were in the public spotlight.

By 2000, three years into Blair's New Labour government, Mike had concluded that the old Labour Party alliance between socialists and social democrats no longer existed, and that Blair's neo-liberal economic politics, summed up by Peter Mandelson's quip that Labour was 'intensely relaxed about people getting filthy rich', was now the dominant ideology in the Labour Party. He left the Labour Party (I followed him a year later). After 9/11, as the war on terror developed, and Blair's government took Britain into the invasions of Afghanistan and Iraq, Mike was clear that Labour could not be supported. Had Mike lived, and seen Corbyn's election and the transformation of the Labour Party into a party of mass membership and action, I'm confident he would have been one of the first to re-join and would be an active, busy supporter of Corbyn.

Mike was born in New York City in January 1953 and brought up in Scarsdale, an affluent suburb of New York, until he emigrated to Britain in 1971. By his mid-teenage years, Mike was politically active: building the anti-war movement at his school, checking out SDS (Students for a Democratic Society) and the Black Panthers. Simultaneously, he was reading widely (Thoreau, Paine, Shakespeare, Milton, Ginsberg, Blake), watching movies, listening to Dylan, the Byrds, the Stones, Captain Beefheart, growing his hair long, and beginning to write. His first published work was 'Turn left at Scarsdale', an account of 1960s school students questioning their privileged upbringing (which appeared as a chapter in *The High School Revolutionaries*, Libarle & Seligson, Random House, 1970). In 1971, exhausted by political activity, he escaped to study English at Sussex University, where he concentrated on literature and (unlike almost every other student at Sussex at the time) ignored politics. He drifted into remaining in England. Mike thought England was a good place to be for a writer and hoped to make it his profession. He didn't manage that until later in his life. He did, however, at this time, discover and fall in love with cricket. By 1979, Britain was his home.

INTRODUCTION

In the early 1980s, Mike returned to political activity. He became a youth worker in Islington, and a Labour Party activist in Haringey, North London. Working at Highbury Roundhouse Youth Club changed his life and profoundly shaped his politics; he engaged with working-class kids, black and white, boys and girls, and became a trade union shop steward and negotiator. Around the same time, in 1979, he had made his first, and life-changing, trip to India, a place he loved. I used to think that there was a spring to his step whenever we arrived there. Travelling around India produced the novel *Slow Turn* (Sphere Books, 1986) which opens with probably the only – and certainly the best – description of a googly (a way of bowling a ball to the batsman) in print. By the mid-1980s, Mike gave up youth work to concentrate on writing. From that period, there is an unpublished novel, *Fugitive Red* (American Communist Party members on the run during the McCarthy era) and the beginnings of his prolific political journalism, initially for *Labour Left Briefing*.

Mike established himself as an authoritative writer in the 1990s. *Defeat from the Jaws of Victory* (Verso, 1992 with Richard Heffernan) is an account of Kinnock's battles with the Labour Party left, and the consequences for the 1992 general election. This came directly from the authors' own experiences as Labour left activists, and the network of left-wing members around the country whom they knew and had worked with. Mike then switched tack to write *Anyone but England: Cricket, Race and Class* (published 1994, re-issued 2016 by Bloomsbury). He and I talked about its themes for several years, and became regular spectators at Test and County cricket matches. However it was only when it was published, that I came to realize how significant were Mike's insights into national identity, the political context of sports, particularly internationally, and history. Mike's great hero was C L R James, and he could not have been prouder when one reviewer said

'C L R James started it. Marqusee is a worthy successor'. In a new edition (Bloomsbury, 2016), Rahul Bhattacharya's introduction starts 'Few cricket books are brilliant, fewer are iconoclastic, *Anyone but England* is essential.'

In 1996, Mike's *War Minus the Shooting* (Mandarin) was published. Its immediate subject matter was that year's Cricket World Cup, played in the subcontinent and climaxing with Sri Lanka beating Australia in Lahore. Mike had attended the World Cup as a journalist, found himself supporting Sri Lanka from early in the tournament, and was ecstatic when they won. But beneath the surface, *War Minus the Shooting*, like *Anyone but England*, was an early contribution to the political debate around globalisation, the role of multi-national corporations and the global media. In this respect they anticipated subsequent work such as Naomi Klein's *No Logo*.

Now, predictably, Mike changed tack yet again, this time to consider popular culture, sport and politics in 1960s America. As so often happened, a defining book emerged from a small commission which took hold of Mike's imagination. *Redemption Song: Muhammad Ali and the Spirit of the Sixties* (Verso, 1999) came from an essay written for the magazine *Race and Class*. Ali's life, and boxing, had been extensively written about, but Mike reclaimed the politics of the heavyweight's extraordinary career. Mike's interest in the Civil Rights Movement, Malcolm X and the Nation of Islam enabled him to recount Ali's involvement in those struggles and, as usual, he pieced together connections brilliantly. He detailed, for example, how Ali (then Cassius Clay), after he had won the heavyweight championship of the world in 1964, had spent the night discussing politics with Malcolm X, the singer Sam Cooke, and American footballer Jim Brown. The following day, Ali announced his support for the Nation of Islam and his change of name, declaring, 'I don't have to be what you want me to be'. In recounting these events Mike weaves together seamlessly sport, politics and black pride. Following Ali's death in 2016, *Redemption Song* was reissued with a new introduction by Dave Zirin (Verso, 2016). Zirin, whose writings Mike admired, wrote 'I'm a sportswriter because Mike Marqusee made me one. ... Not only did *Redemption Song* rediscover quotes, speeches and dimensions of Ali's politics and personality that had long been buried, but it revealed to me that sportswriting could be something different and even something dangerous.'

Chimes of Freedom: The Politics of Bob Dylan's Art (The New Press, 2003), later re-issued as *Wicked Messenger* (Seven Stories Press, 2005), similarly draws on another of Mike's early enthusiasms: his teenage excitement about Dylan's music, in particular an appreciation of its strengths both as poetry and as a way of connecting to 1960s American society. As he did for Ali, Mike reclaimed the politics in Dylan's work. Mike used to say that Dylan was like blotting paper in the way he soaked up lyrical and musical influences. Mike understood Dylan at a visceral level, sharing many of the singer's inspirations: Ginsberg, William Blake, the Old Testament, Woody Guthrie, Robert Johnson. *Chimes of Freedom/Wicked Messenger* explores the study of popular music, the politics of celebrity, and Dylan's complex relationship with left politics and anti-racism.

If I Am Not for Myself: The Journey of an Anti-Zionist Jew (Verso, 2008) might, at first glance, seem like another big jump in Mike's work. In fact, the Biblical references in Dylan's lyrics, and his Jewish origins, had sparked a train of thought in Mike, which coincided with his acquiring his grandfather's papers after his mother had died. The book tells two stories: his grandfather, a Jewish Communist Party fellow-traveller in the Bronx of the 1920s-40s who fervently believed in the establishment of the state of Israel, and Mike's own life, as a middle-class Jewish teenager who found himself at the age of 14 questioning first-hand an Israeli soldier who had visited his school and who referred to Arabs (the word 'Palestinian' was not then used) in terms that reminded Mike of racists talking about African-Americans. *If I Am Not for Myself* sets out a political anti-Zionist argument; it also delves into Jewish rabbinical theology and philosophy, explores the teachings of some of the Prophets in the Old Testament (Mike greatly admired the prophet Amos), and locates the struggle for Palestinian freedom in the context of the 21st century 'war on terror'.

A month before Mike finished the manuscript of *If I Am Not for Myself*, he was diagnosed with multiple myeloma (a type of blood cancer). The doctor postponed chemotherapy for one week so that Mike could finish writing the book. Mike and I lived with his cancer from that diagnosis in 2007 until he died in January 2015. In this period his writing took a different turn; he sought fewer commissions and faced fewer deadlines. He concentrated on what he wanted to write and relished the opportunity to write on numerous different subjects. He also resurrected and re-shaped poetry that he had started writing from the end of the 1990s. His first poetry collection, *Saved by a Wandering Mind*, was published in 2009. Subsequently, he grew more confident about working in this form and dedicated more time to it. *Street Music* (Clissold Press), a collection of poems written over the previous three years, was published in 2012. They deal with cancer, politics, music, living in Hackney, and love. I was immensely privileged to read these poems in various drafts. Other friends provided careful and constructive criticism. I was too overwhelmed to say much. In 2016, Jeremy Corbyn read the title piece at an event with writer Ben Okri.

Eventually and typically, Mike found the strength to begin writing about the disease that was killing him. Various articles on the topic, including several for the *Guardian*, appeared. Mike and I had always understood how politically significant the NHS is in British society, but now we understood it *emotionally,* and Mike became a passionate campaigner for the health service founded by the 1945 Labour government. In his pieces he railed against privatisation, PFI (government schemes requiring private finances of the NHS, at great long-term cost to the public purse) and Big Pharma. *The Price of Experience* (OR Books, 2014) is a collection of those articles, with an introduction by Mike explaining that while the last thing he had wanted to do was write about his illness, he had come to realize that doing so was inevitable.

One of his themes was his antipathy for the widely held notion that people with the illness were often involved in 'battling' against it. In 'A conscript in the "war on cancer"' he wrote: 'The emphasis on cancer patients' "bravery" and "courage" implies that if you can't "conquer" your cancer, there's something wrong with you, some weakness or flaw. If your cancer progresses rapidly, is it your fault? Does it reflect some failure of will-power? In blaming the victim, the ideology attached to cancer mirrors the bootstrap individualism of the neo-liberal order, in which the poor are poor because of their own weaknesses – and "failure" and "success" became the ultimate duality, dished out according to individual merit.' His defence of NHS staff on strike, published in the *Guardian*, was an expression of solidarity, a house-bound writer supporting the picket line. In the last six months of his life, Mike continued to write and think about cancer, and the politics of illness. He left notes for an unfinished article, 'Cancer Dance,' which Colin Robinson pulled together and edited, and which is published for the first time in this anthology.

It would be an omission to chronicle Mike's literary work without mentioning the great obsession of the last ten years of his life: William Blake, Thomas Paine and the politics of the 1790s, in Britain, France and America. Mike had been a disciple of both Blake and Paine since his teenage years. Blake's poetry and art, and Paine's political writing, had shaped him, and references to them appear in most of his books and many of his articles. For ten years, he researched their lives, their political activities and milieu.

Mike was fascinated by Blake's annotations to Richard Watson's *Apology for the Bible*. The Bishop of Llandaff, Watson had published his treatise in response to Paine's *The Age of Reason*. Blake scribbled in its margins, fuming against organised religion, but, during the repressive 1790s, was fearful of publishing his thoughts on the matter. Mike was planning to use the annotations as the foundation stone for a discussion of Blake and Paine's very different, equally radical, political outlooks, with reflections about politics and religion in the 21st century. He returned repeatedly to Blake's reclaiming of miracles, not as divine happenstance but as political activity, summed up when Blake responded to Paine's calm, rational demolition of the concept of miracles with the question: 'Is it a greater miracle to feed five thousand men with five loaves than to overthrow all the armies of Europe with a small pamphlet?' 'How could 'Paine "the worker of miracles" doubt their existence?' Blake asked. I have a treasure trove of Mike's notes and incomplete chapters on this topic. With friends, it may be possible to reconstruct enough to publish a forthcoming book.

The title of this volume, *Definable Traces in the Atmosphere*, is a quote from the poem 'Egypt', published in *Street Music* and reproduced at the front of this book.

One of the blessings that writers enjoy is that their writing lives on after them. Those who are already devotees of the writer can awaken old excitements by re-reading favourite books or poems. New readers can experience the thrill of discovering an unfamiliar body of work. We hope that this anthology can bring such pleasures to fans of Mike, both old and new. Some of these articles, along with more information about his books and other articles, can be found at http://www.mikemarqusee.co.uk/.

Liz Davies
London, June 2017

1

'A MAN IS WORKED ON BY WHAT HE WORKS ON' – AMERICA AND THE 1960S

A VICTIM OF AMERICA: MUHAMMAD ALI AND THE WAR AGAINST TERRORISM

First published in 2002.

When Hollywood bosses were asked by George W. Bush's administration to do their bit in the 'war on terrorism', they signed up eagerly – and came up with the notion of getting much-loved former heavyweight champion Muhammad Ali to promote US policy. According to the *New York Times*, studio executives are convinced that 'Mr. Ali will have special credibility with an audience believed to be deeply suspicious of the United States.'

The ironies here are many and intricate. It was precisely the damage allegedly wrought by Ali to 'the perception of America around the world' that piqued the CIA and FBI into subjecting him to years of surveillance. The day after he first won the heavyweight title, in February 1964, he stood before the press, with Malcolm X at his side, and announced that he was a member of what was then probably the most reviled organisation in the USA, the black separatist Nation of Islam. In so doing, the brash 22-year-old loudmouth was repudiating Christianity in a predominantly Christian country. He was repudiating the integrationist agenda of the Civil Rights Movement, then at the height of its prestige. Above all, he was repudiating his US national identity in favour of a global, diasporic one.

Having been taught by Malcolm that 'you are not an American, you are a victim of America', this young celebrity with the wealth of the world at his feet chose to throw in his lot with the despised 'Lost-Found Nation of Islam in the Wilderness of North America' – reaching out to the unknown masses who shared his grievance against the United States.

Soon Ali visited Africa, where he hobnobbed with Nkrumah and Nasser, both high on the State Department hate-list. Two years later, faced with the draft, he declared, 'I ain't got no quarrel with them Vietcong,' and was denounced as a traitor and coward by politicians, pundits and those paragons of public interest, the boxing authorities. He explained his thinking to a sympathetic reporter: 'Boxing is nothing, just satisfying to some bloodthirsty people. I'm no longer a Cassius Clay, a Negro from Kentucky. I belong to the world, the black world. I'll always have a home in Pakistan, in Algeria, in Ethiopia. This is more than money.'

In 1967, Ali refused induction into the US military, was stripped of his title, barred from the ring, convicted of draft evasion and given the maximum sentence of five years imprisonment. Released on bail appending appeal, and with his passport confiscated, he spent the next three and half years in a kind of internal exile – appearing at college campuses and talk shows, making his case for his right to conscientious objection, and to the heavyweight title.

At a time when popular perceptions in the USA are probably more divergent from popular perceptions elsewhere than in living memory, it's important to remember that, until the mid-1970s, Muhammad Ali was more reviled than admired in his native land, and enjoyed far more respect abroad. By refusing to 'go 10,000 miles from home and drop bombs and bullets on brown people,' he had put his money, and much more, where his mouth was. It was an act of solidarity and sacrifice that secured for Ali a uniquely international following. It is why Hollywood's patriotic moguls want him as their mouthpiece. Ali's totemic value lies precisely in the globally-known fact that he spectacularly defied the US establishment, risking jail in the process.

Since 11 September, members of an emboldened US right wing have repeatedly proclaimed the final defeat of their 1960s antagonists. The forces that made America 'weak' (in their view) have been purged from the body politic by the trauma of a massive terrorist attack and the apparent success of the military response. Yet strangely, in this moment of triumph, when they want to sell their freshly confirmed global domination to the populations they bestride, they turn to that archetypal figure of 1960s-style disloyalty, Muhammad Ali.

Of course, the genial Ali was long ago re-appropriated to the American fold as a depoliticised icon of personal courage. The makers of *Ali*, the $105 million biopic starring Will Smith, promised to restore the controversial edge to their hero. The film was in the can well before 11 September, and one can easily imagine the growing discomfort of studio bosses as they contemplated marketing this celebratory tale of a black American who converts to Islam and then refuses to serve his country in time of war.

Despite a strong opening on Christmas Day, the long-gestated epic soon foundered at the domestic box office, pushed aside by fantasy blockbusters and easily overtaken by the unblushingly jingoistic *Black Hawk Down*, the Boy's Own account of the grim 1993 US foray into Somalia. 'It's the biggest Martin Luther King opening weekend ever,' gushed Sony Pictures' marketing president, referring to *BHD*'s big takings over the national holiday named for the champion of non-violence and scorching critic of US foreign policy.

The customary absence of any hint of irony in the corporate cheerleading, as much as the success of *Black Hawk Down* itself, says a great deal about the current mood in the USA. An amnesiac culture is being exploited to generate popular enthusiasm for overseas military action. How much easier to channel national rage into aggression against little known and heavily demonized foreign enemies when the fine distinctions between image and substance, fictional recreation and historical reality, have been for so long persistently undermined.

In the half-light of this permanent present, commercial ill-timing is not the only problem facing the *Ali* film. Director Michael Mann has meticulously reproduced the surface veneer of the time and place, but has supplied so little explanatory context that viewers not familiar with the period may wonder what the fuss was all about. The care lavished on sets and locations, the attention to period detail, the rich array of sights and sounds are constant pleasures, but too often the only ones. Despite (or because) of the presence of five writers on the screen credits, the film is under-written, as is so much Hollywood product these days. Although the champ's refusal to fight in Vietnam is portrayed as heroic, there's a reluctance to scrutinize the politics of the war or the movement against it.

Received wisdom would have it that the way to 'popularise' a political subject like Ali is to focus on the personal drama and keep the arguments in the background. But in this case, at least, the received wisdom is wrong. The best way to have led inexperienced viewers into the political terrain would have been to let Ali speak for himself, as he did with such verve, wit, intelligence and uncompromising commitment in the 1960s. Some of the liveliest scenes in the film are those in which Smith carries off a note-perfect imitation of Ali's press conferences and TV interviews. These are funny, biting and surreal, both political and personal, and they were the only moments in the film to raise a laugh at the press screening. Apart from these scenes, and when he is doing his stuff (convincingly) in the ring, Smith's approach to the role is honourable but too solemn. The impish mischief that energized Ali's early years hardly appears, and the anger is mostly bottled up.

Despite some juggling of the sequence of events, *Ali* is largely faithful to facts. However, it engages in a telling sleight of hand when it comes to the detail of Malcolm X's break with the Nation of Islam. In the film, Malcolm (adroitly played by Mario Van Peebles) says that Elijah Muhammad suspended him from the organisation because of his desire to support the Civil Rights Movement in the wake of the murder of four children in the firebombing of a Birmingham, Alabama church. In fact, Malcolm was suspended because he chose to place the recent traumatic assassination of John F Kennedy in the context of US intervention in the Congo and Vietnam – and to describe it, to the shock of nearly everyone in the country at the time, as a case of 'the chickens coming home to roost.' Had that statement been included in the film, after 11 September, it certainly would have wound up on the cutting room floor. But well before then, it would seem, there were certain views of the United States' relation to the outside world that even more liberal elements in the American mainstream could not come to terms with.

The reluctance of *Ali* to engage with ideas, fear of hard-edged politics and preference for image over context may all be typically Hollywood, but they end up undermining the audience-engaging qualities the film-makers sought. The point is inadvertently confirmed by a comparison with a handful of scenes in William Klein's newly re-released documentary, *The Greatest*. For an intensely dramatic, translucent explication of what Ali meant in his early years, it will be hard to beat Klein's brief footage of Malcolm X talking direct to camera. Ali addicts, who relish any footage of the man in his prime doing almost anything, will feel compelled to see the film, but it's an amorphous, unkempt assemblage, and any unifying theme has to be supplied by the viewer. Even so, it re-emphasises the challenge that faced Michael Mann and his team. It's hard to improve on an original like Ali, whose raw reality as a confused young man wrestling haphazardly with huge issues is more complex, more political, more entertaining and more inspiring than the retrospectively revered hero of destiny Mann and Smith offer.

Both *Ali* and *The Greatest* find their inevitable and irresistible climaxes in the Rumble in the Jungle, which is the subject of the 1996 documentary *When We Were Kings*, still the best Ali movie. In 1974 Ali returned to Africa to face the formidable champion George Foreman in what was wisely assumed to be a futile last effort to regain the title that had been prised from him because of his political convictions. In all three films, the moment when Ali, after soaking up round after round of brutal punishment, unexpectedly turns the tables and dumps Foreman on the mat retains the power to make the hair on your neck bristle. No matter how many times I see it, in how many forms, the scene always makes me want to leap up and join in the jubilant celebrations that followed, in the stadium, on the streets of Kinshasa, and around the world. It was the kind of fairy-tale vindication – of an individual, the principles he stood for, and his myriad supporters everywhere – that would seem hopelessly contrived if it had been created merely to bolster a fiction, if one didn't know that the suffering and the ostracism and the world-churning events that led up to it were only too real.

Yet in that moment of supreme triumph, the causes and the constituencies Ali represented were being compromised and appropriated by alien forces. The Rumble in the Jungle was staged under the aegis of the tyrant Mobutu Sese Seko (only deposed in 1997), and ushered Don King into the heights of big-time boxing (he's still there). Both men indulged in 'black power' rhetoric to disguise their cynical exploitation of black people.

The social movements that had driven Ali forward – the African-American freedom struggle and the anti-war campaigns – were fragmenting and receding. Ali's embrace of his African patrimony was no longer controversial. Indeed, the Rumble in the Jungle helped alert the US-based entertainment industry to the potential commercial value of both 'blackness' and 'African-ness'. Ali's career had taught the corporate whiz-kids that it was possible to make big profits by commodifying rebellion. But as both *Ali*, the film, and Ali's planned role in the upcoming publicity blitz for the war on terrorism confirm, even the most magnificent images of resistance forfeit their power when severed from their moorings in history; torn from the context of social struggle that generates them, they lose their meaning and resonance.

In keeping with the culture of collective amnesia, no one is reminding anyone that this will not be the first rime Ali has consented to act as an overseas representative of the US government. In 1980, at Jimmy Carter's behest, he revisited Africa in a doomed attempt to drum up support for the US boycott of the Moscow Olympics, a protest against the Soviet invasion of Afghanistan.

Once upon a time, Muhammad Ali toured the world as a defiantly unofficial ambassador for a dissident America. He spoke for a nation-within-a-nation reaching out to and making common cause with others in foreign lands. But today, as in 1980, he is likely to have little impact as an official ambassador, and presumably apologist, for the White House, the State Department and the Pentagon. The American voices that have crossed borders and touched large global constituencies have been the passionately unofficial ones – earthy singers, demotic writers, political prophets or fast-talking heavyweight boxers. Muffle them in the Stars and Stripes, and the rest of the world soon turns off.

That US propagandists seem unaware of this reality (their 1950s forebears fighting the Cold War by cultural proxy, exporting jazz and abstract art, were more sophisticated) is another symptom of the narcissism of today's US elite – and of the national self-image they are currently selling, with such apparent success, to their fellow Americans.

THE POLITICS OF BOB DYLAN

First published in 2003.

Forty years ago, on 26 October 1963, Bob Dylan premiered 'The Times They Are A-Changin'', his generational anthem, to a sold-out house at New York's Carnegie Hall.

The song is founded on a conviction that the movement for social change is unstoppable, that history will conform to morality. In its second verse, Dylan issues a brash, enduring challenge to the punditocracy: 'Come writers and critics / Who prophesize with your pen / And keep your eyes wide / The chance won't come again / And don't speak too soon / For the wheel's still in spin.'

It was the unexpected achievements of the Civil Rights Movement, a grass-roots upsurge which transformed the American political landscape, that made this challenge and the song as a whole possible and even plausible. But it was Dylan's genius to articulate the universal spirit animating the specific historical moment.

The protest songs that made Dylan famous and with which he continues to be associated were written in a brief period of some 20 months – from January 1962 to November 1963. Influenced by American radical traditions (the Wobblies, the Popular Front of the thirties and forties, the Beat anarchists of the fifties) and above all by the political ferment touched off among young people by the Civil Rights and 'Ban the Bomb' movements, he engaged in his songs with the terror of the nuclear arms race, with poverty, racism and prison, jingoism and war. He also penned love songs that mingled delicate regret with brutal candour ('We never did too much talkin' anyway').

This creative firestorm gave us 'Let Me Die in My Footsteps', 'Blowin' in the Wind', 'A Hard Rain's A-Gonna Fall', 'Only a Pawn in Their Game' (class rule as the root of racism), 'With God on Our Side' (rejecting American fundamentalism), 'Masters of War' (taking on the military-industrial complex), the gleefully vindictive 'When the Ship Comes In' and the magnificent 'The Lonesome Death of Hattie Carroll', a clear-eyed account of a single injustice that becomes an indictment of a system and its liberal defenders.

Thanks to his sharp-edged radicalism and unique poetic gifts (as well as no little musical craft) Dylan renewed the protest genre and helped it reach a new mass audience. When *The Times They Are A-Changin'* album came out in January 1964, the 22-year-old from Minnesota found himself crowned as the laureate of a social movement, hailed as 'the voice of a generation'.

In the meantime, however, Dylan had decided that this was not what he wanted to be. The new Woody Guthrie was mutating into something else – something that made some of his early acolytes uncomfortable. For Dylan is not only the most renowned protest singer of his era but also its most renowned renegade. In mid-1964, he explained to critic Nat Hentoff: 'Me, I don't want to write for people anymore – you know, be a spokesman. From now on, I want to write from inside me... I'm not part of no movement... I just can't make it with any organisation...'

He was in the midst of recording a song called 'My Back Pages', a dense, image-crammed critique of the movement he had celebrated in 'The Times They Are A-Changin''. Here he sneers at 'corpse evangelists' who use 'ideas' as 'maps', who spout 'lies that life is black and white' and who fail to understand that 'I become my enemy in the instant that I preach.' Alarmed by the discovery of authoritarianism at the heart of the movement for liberation (and within himself), he rebels against the left's self-righteousness. He pours bile on the 'self-ordained professor / Too serious to fool'. He scorns what he sees as the dead culture of political activism: 'memorising politics / Of ancient history'.

'Equality,' I spoke the word
As if a wedding vow
Ah, but I was so much older then
I'm younger than that now.

This refrain – a recantation in every sense of the word – must be one of the most lyrical expressions of political apostasy ever penned. Ex-radicals usually ascribe their evolution to the inevitable giving-way of rebellious youth to responsible maturity. Dylan reversed the polarity. For him, the retreat from politics was a retreat from stale categories and second-hand attitudes. The refrain encapsulates the movement from the pretence of knowing it all to the confession of knowing nothing.

But in its assertion of youth's autonomy, 'My Back Pages' doesn't so much repudiate 'The Times They Are A-Changin'' as deepen and extend it. He was urging the young people of the sixties to reject categories inherited from the past and define their own terms. For Dylan, youth itself – that vast new social demographic – had become the touchstone of authenticity. A tremendously empowering notion for the generation whom it first infected, but also, as it turned out, a cul-de-sac, and less of a revolutionary posture than it seemed at the time.

Dylan's break with politics and the movement that had been his first inspiration unleashed his poetic and musical genius; it freed him to explore an inner landscape. His lyrics became more obscure; coherent narrative was jettisoned in favour of carnivalesque surrealism; the austerity of the acoustic folk troubadour was replaced by the hedonistic extravagance of an electrified rock n roll ensemble. The songs depicted a private universe – but one forged in response to tumultuous public events.

It's remarkable that so many of Dylan's left critics failed to see the politics that infuse his masterworks of the mid-sixties. 'Maggie's Farm' – booed by purists at the Newport Folk Festival – fuses class and generational rage in an uncompromising renunciation of wage labour. Here the power of the employers is propped up by ideology ('She talks to all the servants / About man and God and law') and the state ('the National Guard stands around his door'). The social order is experienced as intrusive, deceitful, inimical to the individual's need for self-definition. 'I try my best to be just like I am / but everybody wants you to be just like them.'

These themes were also explored in 'It's Alright Ma (I'm Only Bleeding)', Dylan's epic indictment of a society built on hypocrisy and greed ('money doesn't talk, it swears'). Here consciousness is the battleground; it's where the individual struggles to extract some autonomy from the all-pervading corruption of a society ruled by commodities.

> And if my thought-dreams could be seen
> They'd probably put my head in a guillotine

Although Dylan never dealt explicitly with Vietnam, its escalating madness can be felt in two of the major compositions he recorded in mid-1965, 'Highway 61 Revisited' and 'Tombstone Blues'. In the latter, Dylan portrays 'the Commander-in-Chief' (it was Lyndon Johnson, but might as well be George Bush) proclaiming:

> 'Death to all those who would whimper and cry!'
> And dropping a barbell he points to the sky
> Saying, 'The sun's not yellow it's chicken'

In these and other songs of the period, Dylan recoils with horror (and wit) from a public world poisoned by militarist patriotism and commercial hucksterism. Far from having jettisoned politics, Dylan was redefining its scope. In compositions like 'Visions of Johanna' or 'Desolation Row', great social themes jostle with intimate grievances. When a disappointed punter at the Albert Hall called out for 'protest songs', a frustrated Dylan replied: 'Oh come on, these are all protest songs.'

'To live outside the law, you must be honest,' Dylan wrote in 1966. This prophetic warning – to a generation, a movement, himself – leaps out of 'Absolutely Sweet Marie', a silly, swaggering song of sexual frustration. The next line is less well known, but telling: 'And I know you always say that you agree.'

For today's anti-war and global justice movements, Dylan's songs of the sixties offer both a bracing protest against enduring enemies and a salutary critique of some of our own worst habits.

1968: THE MYSTERIOUS CHEMISTRY OF SOCIAL CHANGE

First published in 2008.

1968 saw more young Americans drawn to the left than any time since the 1930s. In a Gallup survey of student opinion conducted in the spring (before the May events in France), 69 per cent considered themselves 'doves' on Vietnam, 16 per cent agreed that the war in Vietnam was 'pure imperialism' and eight per cent identified themselves as 'radical' or 'far left' (a 100 per cent increase in a year). In the autumn, a *Fortune* magazine survey revealed that half of all college students thought the US was a 'sick society' and 368,000 of them now considered themselves 'revolutionaries'.

The upsurges that convulsed the United States in 1968 were inextricably linked to global events, but shaped by factors peculiar to the national context. In this presidential election year, 500,000 US troops were in Vietnam, where a war that was supposed to have been won long before continued into its fifth year. At home, the country's racial hierarchy had been under challenge from the Civil Rights Movement for a decade. But socialist traditions were weak and there was no significant social democratic or communist party. This starting point accounts for many of the peculiar features of the American '68: its ideological and organisational chaos, as well as its willingness to experiment. Among young radicals there was a Year Zero mentality.

It was in the US that the global trends of media saturation and consumerisation were most pronounced at the time, which helps explain the importance assumed by images and gestures in the American movement. It was also in the US that the generational split, evident everywhere in '68, was most sharply divisive. In addition, activists in the US faced a degree of violent repression unknown in Western Europe.

The Civil Rights Movement's challenge to Jim Crow in the South had secured major advances, but had also exposed the intractability of US racism. Legal segregation had been destroyed, but economic inequality loomed larger than ever. In 1966, the Black Power slogan had signalled a new black nationalist consciousness among younger activists, who advocated building black-only organisations.

Martin Luther King stood in the middle of the tempest. In 1967, his opposition to the war had been denounced by mainstream civil rights leaders and liberal opinion-makers, including the *New York Times*. While he agreed with the militants that the movement had to enter a new, more ambitious phase, he continued to advocate nonviolence and inter-racial alliances. In early 1968, he launched a Poor People's Campaign, demanding a guaranteed income for all. He journeyed to Memphis, where black sanitation workers were on strike for union recognition and a living wage, supported by a tense but potent alliance between local black churches, white-led trade unions, students and ghetto youth.

King's assassination in Memphis on 4 April deprived the anti-war and black freedom movements of their most effective leader, perhaps the only one who could have resisted the tide of fragmentation. The civil disorder that followed was the most widespread in US history. Riots broke out in 125 cities; 70,000 US troops were called in to quell them. In Washington, DC, crowds 20,000-strong overwhelmed local police. Marines mounted machine guns on the steps of the Capitol. On 5 April, rioters reached within two blocks of the White House. In the end, 21,000 were arrested, 3,000 injured and 46 killed, all but five black.

One of those killed was Bobby Hutton, the 17-year-old treasurer ('Minister of Finance') of the Black Panther Party. The Panthers aimed to build an all-black ghetto-based cadre with a mission of self-defence against state violence. To this they added an anti-colonial perspective and a smattering of anti-capitalist rhetoric. Unlike most black revolutionaries at the time, they advocated building alliances with radical whites.

In the course of '68, the Panthers became icons for both black and white youth. They also became targets for the FBI. In September, J Edgar Hoover described them as 'the greatest threat to the internal security of the country' and launched a campaign to destroy them, fomenting violence between Panthers and street gangs, as well as splits and rivalries among the Panthers themselves. By the end of 1968, Huey Newton was in prison and Eldridge Cleaver had fled the country. In 1969, 27 Panthers were to be killed by police and hundreds more jailed.

Black Power politics took a multitude of forms. At the October Olympics, sprinters Tommy Smith and John Carlos gave the clenched fist Black Power salute on the winners' podium, and were promptly expelled from the games. That year also saw black car workers in Detroit forming the Dodge Revolutionary Union Movement, with an openly Marxist orientation. They enjoyed support in the community and from the white left, but earned the ire of employers, police and union leaders. The model spread quickly across the auto industry, and resulted in the formation of the League of Revolutionary Black Workers the following year.

For three years the anti-war forces had been gathering strength, challenging super-patriots and cold war shibboleths. 16,000 US troops were killed in '68, with an all-time high of 500 in the second week of February, casualties of the Tet Offensive, a military disaster but a political triumph for the Vietnamese. In its wake, establishment spokespersons came out against the 'unwinnable' war. But they were struggling to catch up with the movement.

The national leadership of the anti-war forces was fluid; the major demonstrations were coordinated by a shifting array of organisational alliances but the bulk of the action was initiated by grass-roots activists. In 1968 it took every conceivable form and spread to every corner of the country.

On 26 April, one million students took part in a nationwide anti-war strike, affecting a thousand colleges and schools. At the University of Arizona in Tucson, 11,000 students – half the enrolment – stayed out of class. A new wave of high school students joined the fray, with 200,000 staying out in New York City. On the following day, an anti-war march in San Francisco was led off by a contingent of 40 active duty GIs, one of the first signs of the GI rebellion that was ultimately to incapacitate the war machine.

During the course of '68, the anti-war movement came under pressure from opposite directions. Liberals wanted it to fold into the Democratic party, and radicals wanted it to become a multi-issue 'revolutionary' campaign. Neither offered much of substance to the rank and file.

The rebellion at Columbia University in New York City was triggered by a convergence of protests. The principal issues were the university's plans to build an exclusive gym on public parkland adjacent to Harlem (one placard read 'Gym Crow Must Go!') and its links with the Institute for Defence Analysis, a war think-tank. The local chapter of SDS – Students for a Democratic Society, the principal New Left youth organisation – called a protest on 23 April, which was joined by the Student Afro-American Society (SAS), and turned unexpectedly into a 1,000-strong occupation.

Shortly after the first building was seized, the SAS claimed it for black people and asked their white allies to leave. The white students deferred, and took over another four buildings. These soon became known as 'liberated zones', hosting meetings, performances, and non-stop informal debates. The students were joined by the Motherfuckers, an anarchist 'street collective' from the Lower East Side, and were visited by a succession of movement celebrities.

The logic of the occupation was summarised by one of the SAS leaders: 'There's one oppressor – in the White House, in Low Library [a university building], in Albany, New York. You strike a blow against the gym, you strike a blow for the Vietnamese people. You strike a blow at Low Library, you strike a blow for freedom fighters in Angola, Mozambique, Portuguese Guinea, Zimbabwe, South Africa.'

After eight days, the university called in the police. The black students surrendered en masse and in disciplined formation. Elsewhere, there was chaos. Some white students resisted arrest, some submitted passively, but all were beaten.

Plainclothes police swept through the campus attacking anyone who looked like a protester. Two hundred students were injured and 600 arrested. In response, nearly the entire student body and most of the faculty went on strike, closing the campus for a month. Leadership passed from SDS to the more broad-based Students for a Restructured University, which, with the aid of a $40,000 grant from the Ford Foundation, negotiated a compromise with the university administration.

SDS regarded Columbia as a triumph. Direct action had escalated the struggle, and repression had exposed the true face of the state. Tom Hayden called for 'Two, Three Columbias!' echoing Che Guevara's call for 'Two, Three Vietnams'. Thanks to the nationwide publicity attending the Columbia events (which preceded those in May in France), SDS ranks swelled to 100,000. But its leadership became entranced by revolutionary spectacle. By the end of the year, the organisation was mired in factional struggle, and it broke up in June 1969.

Political radicalism was joined with the counter-culture, not only in the minds of the media but in the minds of many millions of young people. Opposition to the war and to racism came to be associated with particular fashions and tastes in music, with the socially and sexually unconventional. Growing your hair long in 1968 was not just a fashion statement; it often meant family rows and harassment in the street. 'Underground newspapers' – several hundred of which appeared in 1968 – combined coverage of movement events with comments on music, sex and drugs. They gave people a taste of participatory journalism and, most importantly, the sense of belonging to an outlaw community.

The Yippies were the principal exponents of a marriage of the counter-culture and revolutionary politics. The name itself was an ironic parody, and the movement's leaders, Jerry Rubin and Abbie Hoffman, merrily exploited the media's appetite for sensationalist extremism. They were flippant, obscene, and sometimes daringly imaginative. They studded their manifestos with pop cult references and absurdist jokes. Jerry Rubin declared that 'Guerrilla war in America is going to come in psychedelic colors.' Abbie's book *Revolution for the Hell of It* was a best-seller.

One communist curmudgeon derided them as 'Groucho Marxists'. But the real problem with the Yippie leaders was that they were self-selecting and unaccountable. Their informal following was large; their antics struck a chord with many young people, while infuriating a much larger number of older people. The counter-culture inspired and energised, but it also fostered an an 'us versus them' construction of America; for some, the counter-culture was a way into politics, but for many others, not least many working class people, it was a barrier to participation.

The revolution in consciousness promoted by the counter-culture posed as a challenge to power, but it offered an easy get-out, in which personal lifestyle changes substituted for collective action. It was also a form of rebellion all too vulnerable to appropriation by the corporations and the establishment media. In the autumn of '68, Columbia Records placed a full-page advert in the underground press. It showed a bunch of long-haired protesters in a jail cell (but didn't indicate what they were protesting about) under the headline: 'But the man can't bust our music.'

1968 was the first time a mass social convulsion had been broadcast on television. In the absence of stable national organisations, the media selected the 'leaders', and the more outlandish your rhetoric (and your appearance), the more likely you were to be selected. The movement and the counter-culture were subject to non-stop attack from the mainstream media, which nonetheless played a key role in disseminating the message. A strange interaction grew up between the flesh and blood movement unfolding in different communities and the image of that movement that was projected back to us.

In reality, the youth movement was characterised by a spectrum of memory and experience, from neophyte teenagers to activists in their mid or late twenties who'd already gone through six to eight years of intense political struggle. People were moving at breakneck speed from earnest American idealism to embittered radicalism, going through liberalism and beyond, sometimes into Marxism, but mainly into a homespun anarchism. Throughout '68, the movement was prone to wild mood swings, from utopia to apocalypse and back in a matter of weeks.

This year's Democratic presidential primary has been dramatic, but it's a mere *The West Wing* episode compared to the full-blown tragic opera of the 1968 contest, which included the toppling of an incumbent president, the assassination of his leading opponent, and a riot at the nominating convention. Eugene McCarthy, a circumspect liberal, challenged Johnson in the primaries on an anti-war platform. His campaign drew in many students, and going 'clean for Gene' (cutting hair and shaving beards when canvassing for McCarthy) became a media-touted phenomenon.

Against all predictions, on 12 March McCarthy came a close second to Johnson in New Hampshire. Four days later, Robert Kennedy announced his candidacy, making a clear bid for the anti-war vote. On 31 March, Johnson bowed out of the race. Vice President Hubert Humphrey enjoyed the support of the party machine, but stayed out of the primary races, which became a contest between Kennedy and McCarthy, neither of whom actually called for US withdrawal from Vietnam. It was on the night of his victory in California – where the two 'anti-war' candidates split five million votes between them – that Kennedy was shot dead. His killer was a Palestinian, a people whose plight was raised in those days only by black radicals.

Humphrey was now assured the nomination. But the Democratic Party convention in Chicago was a debacle. The Yippies planned to organise a Festival of Life to counterpoint the Convention of Death. Other anti-war activists announced actions in the city. In the end, a modest crowd of 10,000 turned up, and were met with severe police violence, which spilled over into indiscriminate attacks on journalists and bystanders. For days, the images of confrontation were nightly TV fare. Many were radicalised by the spectacle, but many more thought (and told pollsters) that the police gave the protesters what they deserved. The federal government eventually indicted eight people on conspiracy charges, among them Hoffman, Rubin, Hayden and Black Panther Bobby Seale. Their 1969 trial became a notorious showdown between the movement and the establishment.

Nixon campaigned on a 'law and order' platform, bolstered by a secret plan to bring 'peace with honour' in Vietnam. He claimed to speak for 'the silent majority' – i.e., all those who were not protesting. In November, he edged out Humphrey. The Peace and Freedom Party, with Eldridge Cleaver as its presidential nominee, was on the ballot in 13 states and picked up just under 200,000 votes. Thirteen million votes went to the diehard segregationist George Wallace, who pledged to run over any demonstrators who got in front of his limousine and asserted that the only four letter words that hippies did not know were w-o-r-k and s-o-a-p. The white backlash was in full swing and out of it was born modern conservative Republicanism.

Many activists ended 1968 in despondency. A Nixon White House meant more war, more domestic repression. The movement appeared fragmented and stalemated. But the impetus of the year's rebellions was not spent. Although it is often presented as a series of climactic confrontations, 1968 was full of harbingers of the future.

Latino Americans, inspired by African Americans, formed their own militant organisations, notably the Young Lords and the Brown Berets. In September, second wave feminism made its first public splash when a group of radical women disrupted the Miss America contest. The next year, the Stonewall riots – whose participants included veterans of civil rights and anti-war struggles – kicked off the gay liberation movement. The white working class, quiescent for so long, began to stir; 1969 saw more days lost to strike action than any year since 1946; rank and file reform movements emerged in major unions. The peak of anti-war activity came in 1970, when three million students took strike action against Nixon's widening of the war into Cambodia. Six of them were killed at Kent and Jackson State universities.

The wave of insurgency washed into the most unlikely places, including the political backwater that was my home town, suburban, affluent and all-white. I turned 15 at the start of 1968 and I remember the events of that year more vividly than those of 1988 or 1998. After the Columbia rebellion, a small group of us resolved to form an SDS chapter. We got in touch with the national office, who sent a staff member to meet us; we pooled our allowances to pay her fare.

She must have been all of 21, but to us she was an elder. However, the line she took was that in SDS college students couldn't tell high school students what to do; she urged us to start with 'our own oppression'. It wasn't what we were hoping for; we wanted someone to tell us how we could take part in 'the revolution'. We did, however, produce one issue of our own 'underground' newspaper, printed at the SDS offices in New York's Union Square.

In the autumn, two young men working for the federal government turned up and made contact with our little group. They were not FBI agents but employees in the Volunteers in Service to America (VISTA) programme. Often referred to as a 'domestic Peace Corps', VISTA ordinarily focused on projects in disadvantaged communities. But within VISTA radicals argued that the problem with America was not the poor but the rich, and that VISTA should therefore be working with young people in affluent areas.

Soon they had us reading Marcuse's *One Dimensional Man*, a text we found largely incomprehensible. More usefully, they helped us organise a picket of a local grocery store in support of the United Farmworkers' Union's epochal campaign against California grape-growers. Still, the emphasis was more on 'addressing our own oppression' than solidarity with people more obviously oppressed. In our school, pressure to get good grades was intense. So we decided to turn the tables by distributing a 'teacher evaluation form' ('How boring is your social studies teacher; rank from 1 to 10 ...') For this crime we were suspended from school for a week. This seemed anything but a punishment and

I remember spending much of that week watching Godard films in Manhattan.

Late in the year, we learned by word of mouth that Abbie Hoffman and Eldridge Cleaver were speaking at a Catholic community college in a neighbouring town. We drove over and found thousands of young people milling around, excited just to be there. The revolutionary rhetoric was laced with impudent humour. Abbie performed yo-yo tricks and told us how he'd got so fed up with seeing pictures of himself in the *New York Times* that he had taken to writing FUCK on his forehead: 'Let them print that if they want!' It was amazing that so many youth would put aside their other concerns to turn up to hear visceral calls for the destruction of the system of which they were supposed to be the beneficiaries. But after hearing the speeches there was nothing to do, no strategy one could follow, no plan of action. It was the best and worst of the year.

In the school debate that preceded that year's mock presidential election, I represented the Peace and Freedom Party. Donning Panther-style black jacket and beret, I did my best to preach the revolutionary message. We got about ten per cent of the vote, a much better showing than Cleaver managed in the real elections.

In '68 we were a small minority, but two years later I was elected student body president on a platform of draft counselling (a euphemism for draft evasion), a softer approach on drugs, student participation in the curriculum and, believe it or not, an end to mandatory attendance of classes. Within weeks of my election, Nixon invaded Cambodia. In our school, as in many others, some 90 per cent took part in the ensuing strike. At one point I was called in by the principal and asked to deal with a complaint: a group of die-hard, pro-war jocks had claimed they were being intimidated by hippie girls half their size.

The events of 1968 stamped me for life. The frustrations and failures of the year left me with a distrust of revolutionary demagoguery and of unaccountable leaders manufactured by the media, and a wariness over the ease with which politics could be blunted by 'lifestyle' choices. I drew the lesson that spasms of activism were no substitute for building enduring and democratic institutions. The resulting desire for some organisational and ideological stability probably accounts for the 20 years I spent in the Labour Party.

But I also drew from 1968 an absolutely priceless lesson in the mysterious chemistry of social change. I learned that resistance comes in unexpected forms and from unexpected sources. I learned that in the right circumstances large masses of people can move quickly from apathy to radicalism. I learned that what seems permanent and unchangeable can be consigned, in the blink of an eye, to the dustbin of history. I consider myself lucky to have witnessed the dimensions of the possible transformed in a few short years.

2

STREETS OF THE IMAGINATION – THOREAU, PAINE, BLAKE AND SHELLEY

THE VOICE WITHIN: A PILGRIMAGE TO WALDEN POND

First published in 2006.

On a recent visit to the United States, I made a pilgrimage to Walden Pond, a glistening body of water prized for its depth and clarity (only 20 miles from Boston) as well as for its association with the visionary writer, Henry David Thoreau. From July 1845 to September 1847, Thoreau made his home here, living simply in a small self-built cabin, tending his garden, studying the changing seasons, recording the details of the natural life surrounding him, trying to ascertain, by experiment, how much of modern life is given over to the superfluous, how much we could really do without.

The result was his book *Walden; or, Life in the Woods*, a masterpiece of flinty English prose. 'The mass of men lead lives of quiet desperation,' he declared. The only escape was in heeding the voice within: 'Why should we be in such desperate haste to succeed and in such desperate enterprises? If a man does not keep pace with his companions, perhaps it is because he hears a different drummer. Let him step to the music which he hears, however measured or far away.' By the shore of Walden Pond, Thoreau embarked on a voyage which he insisted was of more profit than the celebrated overseas adventures of the day. 'Every man is the lord of a realm beside which the earthly empire of the Czar is but a petty state, a hummock left by the ice.'

Today Thoreau is recognised as a prophet of the environmental movement and an early, trenchant critic of consumerism. His impatience with the wasteful public babble of modern civilisation feels more pertinent than ever. We are inundated with words and images, yet seem increasingly incapable of responding to them meaningfully.

Walden Pond is now conscientiously preserved by the State of Massachusetts (an entity Thoreau regarded as little more than a criminal conspiracy). The foundations of his refuge are marked, and next to them a pile of small stones has risen over the years, as generations of visitors pay an anonymous, appropriately geological homage to the man and the book. Nearby, there's a shop run by the admirable Thoreau Society, stocked with memorabilia, books, CDs, postcards and tee shirts emblazoned with Thoreau's words, my favourite being, 'Beware all enterprises that require new clothes.'

Thoreau is sometimes presented as an American *sannyasin*, but even in retreat, he was an active participant in his society. In July 1846, he was arrested and jailed for a night for refusing to pay his poll tax. In a lecture later published under the title *Civil Disobedience*, he explained why, in certain circumstances, the only place for a just individual in an unjust society was prison. Thoreau was a militant opponent of slavery and of the Mexican-American war of 1846-48 – through which the US seized from Mexico the area now occupied by the states of California, New Mexico, Arizona, Utah and Colorado. 'When a sixth of the population of a nation which has undertaken to be the refuge of liberty are slaves, and a whole country is unjustly overrun and conquered by a foreign army, and subjected to military law, I think that it is not too soon for honest men to rebel and revolutionise,' he wrote, and added, in words that ought to be broadcast today across the US and Britain,

'What makes this duty the more urgent is the fact that the country so overrun is not our own, but ours is the invading army.'

Those who derided his act of 'civil resistance' as a meaningless gesture 'do not know by how much truth is stronger than error, nor how much more eloquently and effectively he can combat injustice who has experienced a little in his own person. Cast your whole vote, not a strip of paper merely, but your whole influence.' Gandhi encountered this essay in 1906, in the midst of his South Africa campaign, as he was formulating his doctrine of Satyagraha. 'It left a deep impression on me,' he later recalled, describing it as 'scientific confirmation of what I was doing.'

Gandhi's US disciple, Martin Luther King, found comfort in Thoreau's arguments on the eve of the Montgomery bus boycott of 1955-56: 'I remembered how, as a college student, I had been moved when I first read this work. I became convinced that what we were preparing to do in Montgomery was related to what Thoreau had expressed. We were simply saying to the white community, "We can no longer lend our cooperation to an evil system".'

Unlike Gandhi and King, Thoreau was not a pacifist. When, in 1859, John Brown led an attack on an armoury in Harper's Ferry (now in West Virginia) in hopes of sparking a slave uprising, he was denounced by the moderate wing of the abolitionist movement, but defended by Thoreau, who saw Brown's audacious raid 'as a touchstone designed to bring out, with glaring distinctness, the character of this government. We needed to be thus assisted to see it by the light of history.' He praised Brown as a true hero, to be elevated above those who merely fought their country's foes, because 'he had the courage to face his country herself, when she was in the wrong.'

Thoreau was contemptuous of those who excoriated Brown's resort to violence while passively endorsing the more sustained violence sponsored by their own government, and not only against slaves. 'We preserve the so-called peace of our community by deeds of petty violence every day. Look at the policeman's billy and handcuffs! Look at the jail! Look at the gallows!'

Referring to the weapons Brown and his band used at Harper's Ferry, Thoreau observed: 'I know that the mass of my countrymen think that the only righteous use that can be made of Sharp's rifles and revolvers is to fight duels with them, when we are insulted by other nations, or to hunt Indians, or shoot fugitive slaves with them, or the like. I think that for once the Sharp's rifles and the revolvers were employed in a righteous cause.'

Fourteen months after John Brown was hanged, the US plunged into civil war. Another fourteen months after that, the 44-year-old Thoreau died of tuberculosis, his repute as a writer restricted to small literary circles in the Boston area. Like Brown, Thoreau was derided in his day as 'crazy' and 'impractical'. Yet, still, today, the stones pile up by Walden Pond, and his words rise above the ubiquitous din, making us look again at the overlooked, in our world and in ourselves.

THOMAS PAINE: RESTLESS DEMOCRAT

First published in 2009.

This interment was a scene to affect and to wound any sensible heart. Contemplating who it was, what man it was, that we were committing to an obscure grave on an open and disregarded bit of land, I could not help but feel most acutely.

The occasion for this lament was the sparsely attended funeral of Thomas Paine, who died, 200 years ago, in June 1809, at the age of 72, and was buried in the small farm he owned in what was then the rural hamlet of New Rochelle, 20 miles north of New York City.

Not long before, New Rochelle's bigwigs had barred Paine from voting, claiming he was not a US citizen. Paine, who had virtually invented the idea of US citizenship, was furious. But this was not the end of his indignities. When he sought a place to be buried, even the Quakers would not oblige him. Hence the muted funeral of the man who had inspired and guided revolutions in North America and France, and equally important, the revolution that did not happen in Britain.

Despite his extraordinary career, Paine was a late starter. When he left England in 1774, at the age of 37, he could boast six years of formal education, teenage service in a sea-going privateer, stints as a corset-maker, excise (tax) officer, tobacconist and school teacher. Having been sacked, for a second time, from a post in the excise, Paine separated from his second wife, sold up and sailed for North America.

There he found a cause, a constituency and the talent to link one with the other. Fourteen months after his arrival in the New World he published *Common Sense*, the pamphlet which galvanised opposition to British rule in North America. Here he called for immediate separation from Britain and, crucially, the establishment of a democratic republic in the former colonies. During the ensuing war, he shuffled between battlefields and Congressional committees, becoming the foremost propagandist of the colonial cause, both at home and abroad.

He had hoped, after the victory of the North Americans, to devote himself to his mechanical interests, notably the design of a single arch bridge. But political controversy waylaid him. When Edmund Burke published his conservative classic, *Reflections on the Revolution in France*, in which he upheld the divine right of kings and decried dangerous tampering with the established order, Paine responded with the First Part of *Rights of Man*, published in March 1791. Declaring 'my country is the world and my religion is to do good,' he mounted a comprehensive defence of the French Revolution ('the tremendous breaking forth of a whole people') and its founding ideas: 'The downfall of [the Bastille] included the idea of the downfall of despotism.' Against Burke's devotion to precedent, Paine offered a central statement of purpose: 'I am contending for the rights of the living, and against their being willed away, and controlled and contracted for, by the manuscript-assumed authority of the dead.'

Paine was to commit even greater offence with the publication of Part Two of *Rights of Man* six months later. Arguing that 'only partial advantages can flow from partial reforms,' he laid out the case for dismantling the British state and replacing it with a democratic republic. In the final chapter, he broached new and even more dangerous territory: the intrusion of democracy into the economic realm. He set forth proposals for what we would now call old-age pensions, child and maternity benefits, state-funded primary education, employment for the casual poor – all funded by redistributive, steeply progressive taxation.

Rights of Man was an immediate best-seller, reaching in its first two years perhaps ten-to-20 per cent of the English reading public and becoming the most widely and hotly debated text of the age. Paine himself became the pre-eminent embodiment of radicalism in Britain. His bold championship of the rights of the excluded majority inspired the plebeian London Corresponding Society, whose story E P Thompson saw as central to *The Making of the English Working Class*, the non-sectarian republicanism of the United Irishmen and the pioneering feminism of Mary Wollstonecraft.

Conversely, for the British establishment Paine became prime menace and demon, the carrier of the dreaded French disease. His writings were banned; those who distributed them were prosecuted. A government-subsidised smear campaign branded him a drunkard and libertine. The burning of Paine's effigy became the central rite of the 'Church and King' mobs that harassed dissidents. Paine himself fled to France. In his absence he was convicted of seditious libel, which barred his return to his native land for the rest of his life.

In France, Paine was hailed as a champion of the revolution and elected a deputy to the National Convention. His biographers tend to see his ensuing French decade as a tragic tale, but for me Paine emerges from this maelstrom with astonishing credit.

Upon his arrival, and before it was popular, Paine advocated the prompt abolition of the monarchy and its replacement by a constitutional republic based on representational democracy. When the King was finally removed, Paine supported his public trial and subsequent conviction but opposed the sentence of execution, for reasons both tactical (the alliance with the USA) and principled: his opposition to the death penalty, which he viewed as a legacy of 'monarchical' cruelty. 'As France has been the first of European nations to abolish royalty, let her also be the first to abolish the punishment of death, and to find out a milder and more effectual substitute.'

A few months later he was writing to Danton, despairing of the revolution, the intimidation of legislators by the Paris crowd and the widespread 'spirit of denunciation'. Under the Jacobin 'Terror', Paine was imprisoned for eight months. He narrowly escaped execution, but his health was permanently impaired. On his release, he again bit the hand that fed him, opposing the Directory's restriction of the franchise. Later, he was ambivalent towards Napoleon but happy to give him advice on making war against the English enemy. Paine remained viscerally hostile to the British empire, its institutions and agents, and consistent in his belief that the American and French revolutions, whatever their disfigurements, had to be defended.

As if he hadn't already alienated enough people, in 1795 Paine published *The Age of Reason*, an assault on state religions ('set up to terrify and enslave mankind, and monopolize power and profit'), on the Bible ('a history of wickedness that has served to corrupt and brutalize mankind') and on Christianity. While praising Jesus as a 'virtuous reformer and revolutionist', Paine damns the religion practised in his name:

> A man is preached instead of God; an execution is an object for gratitude; the preachers daub themselves with the blood, like a troop of assassins, and pretend to admire the brilliancy it gives them; they preach a humdrum sermon on the merits of the execution; then praise Jesus Christ for being executed, and condemn the Jews for doing it.

Paine's writings circulated to a large public, thanks not least to the energy and clarity of his prose. Accessible but never condescending, rigorous in argument but rooted in the spoken language, Paine's style was nearly as threatening as his ideas. It had immediacy, humour, compassion, sardonic irony and a dollop of ad hominem spice (despite the author's disavowals).

When Paine returned to the US in 1802, he received a cool welcome. He was now the infamous author of *The Age of Reason*, an infidel with whom even old allies like his friend in the White House, Thomas Jefferson, were reluctant to associate. Meddlesome Christians urged the sick and dying man to embrace their faith but were brusquely dismissed. One of his friends facetiously suggested that Paine could resolve his financial worries by publishing a 'recantation'. The author of *The Age of Reason* replied, 'Tom Paine never told a lie'.

In the two centuries since his obscure burial, Paine has been claimed by as many as once disclaimed him. Liberals, Marxists, social democrats, anarchists, right wing libertarians, American exceptionalists, neo-liberals (a passage in *Rights of Man* reads like a hymn to globalisation). Even New Rochelle finally got around to awarding Paine posthumous citizenship – in 1945.

Recently 'New Atheists' such as Christopher Hitchens and Richard Dawkins have staked a claim. Dawkins simply omits the fact that Paine was not an atheist but a deist. Hitchens takes a different route, dismissing Paine's deism as a halfway house to atheism. What both miss is that Paine's deism was part and parcel of a sustained challenge to the hierarchies and powers of his day – which cannot be said of their atheism.

Paine's ideas were not static. He was, above all, a participant. His writings were interventions. He changed his mind. He contradicted himself.

Leninists and liberals alike have squeezed Paine into the dubious category of 'bourgeois democrat'. But the democratic thrust that he embodied, that drove him forward, that fuelled his writing, cannot be so easily delimited.

Whatever else he may have been, Paine was and remained a committed 'revolutionary', in theory and practise. He sought not just to ameliorate but to overturn the existing order. His restless egalitarian spirit could not be contained. It flowed from the political into the religious and economic realms.

> Change of ministers amounts to nothing. One goes out, another comes in, and still the same measures, vices, and extravagance are pursued. It signifies not who is minister. The defect lies in the system. The foundation and the superstructure of the government is bad.

Words to remember as we consider current upheavals in British parliamentary politics.

STREETS OF THE IMAGINATION

*First published in October 2011 following the
London riots of August of that year.*

Events over the summer brought to mind William Blake's uncompromisingly angry poem 'London', written in the early 1790s under the impact of revolution in France and repression at home. The poet wanders 'through the charter'd streets / near where the charter'd Thames does flow' where he encounters signs of widespread distress. He hears the sound of 'the mind-forg'd manacles', the fears and prejudices that keep people in thrall to an unjust social system. Above all he sees the exploitation of youth: chimney sweeps, soldiers, prostitutes – victims of state, church and commerce, Blake's tyrannical trinity.

Blake called London's streets 'charter'd' because so much of the city's economic life was subject to 'charters' granting exclusive privileges to private corporations. In 1791, they had been denounced by Thomas Paine as 'aristocratical monopolies' because of which 'an Englishman is not free of his own country; every one of those places presents a barrier in his way, and tells him he is not a freeman – that he has no rights.'

In 'London' Blake confronts what we would call today a *privatised* London (even the river), whose ultimate manifestation is prostitution. 'But most through midnite streets I hear / The youthful harlot's curse' – the contractual commodification of desire, which serves, ironically, to spread sexually transmitted disease. Marriage and prostitution are daringly linked as the twin sides of a pervasive social hypocrisy. The poem ends with the chilling, terrifically compressed image of 'the marriage hearse', society's primary institution of social reproduction damned as a carrier of death.

All this from a walk around London, at that time the world's largest and fastest-growing city. Nowhere else was there such a convergence of wealth and poverty; nowhere else was the market so ruthlessly dominant.

Blake was a lifelong Londoner. Along with Shakespeare, an adoptive Londoner, he is the least well travelled of all major English poets – venturing no further than the Thames estuary and the Sussex coast. As a journeyman engraver, he was one of many London artisans drawn to radical ideas in religion and politics, and from whose ranks the London Corresponding Society, Britain's first plebeian political organisation, was formed in 1792.

Blake grew up in the London of 'Wilkes and Liberty' and always avowed himself 'a Liberty Boy'. Like most London artisans he supported the American Revolution. And when London exploded in five days of riots, the most extensive in the city's history, in June 1780, he was there – at the front of the crowd, whether by accident or design.

The 'Gordon Riots' began in anti-Catholic demonstrations whipped up by the maverick MP George Gordon; in their initial phase, Catholic places of worship and businesses (mostly foreign merchants) were attacked, though no Catholics were killed. Soon the crowd, having mastered the streets, changed tack and targets, turning its ire on the Bank of England, the homes of judges (ransacking the mansion of the Lord Chief Justice) and above all the jails. They broke open crimping houses (where impressed sailors were confined), debtors' hostels, and one after another all the city's prisons, culminating in Newgate – the biggest and most notorious of them all, London's Bastille. Hundreds of prisoners were released and the building was burnt to the ground.

According to Blake's first biographer, Alexander Gilchrist, writing in the 1860s, Blake was minding his own business at his home in Soho when: 'Suddenly he encountered the advancing wave of triumphant blackguardism, and was forced (for from such a great surging mob there is no disentanglement) to go along in the very front rank and witness the storm and burning of the fortress-like prison.' To which a London magistrate in 2011 would mutter 'a likely story!' before imposing a maximum sentence.

It took 10,000 troops to suppress the riots. Betwewen three and four thousand rioters were killed. 450 were arrested. 25 hanged. How 'political' were these events? Who were the rioters and what did they seek? In *The London Hanged*, Peter Linebaugh identifies diverse participants: apprentices, artisans, domestic servants, tripe-sellers, coffee house waiters, laundresses, seamstresses, as well as a number of African-Americans, ex-slaves who made up six to seven percent of London's population. When Thomas Haycock, a waiter, was asked by a judge why he had rioted, he replied simply: 'The cause'. Which cause? Haycock explained: 'There should not be a prison standing on the morrow in London.'

Blake was 23, had just completed his apprenticeship and commenced what would prove to be a deeply frustrating career as an under-employed engraver. In every respect he fit the profile of the rioter and if he later recast his participation as involuntary, there's no doubt of the event's impact on him. That year he first conceived the image later titled 'Glad Day' or 'Albion Rose' – in which a classically proportioned male youth springs majestically from the earth, embodying the exaltation and energy of liberation. Some time later he gave it the caption:

Albion rose from where he labour'd at the mill with slaves
Giving himself for the Nations he danc'd the dance of Eternal Death.

Blake was to live through decades of war and reaction. His hopes for public recognition and an escape from penury were repeatedly dashed. But he pursued his lonely prophetic vocation and continued to produce stunningly original poems and images. He spent his last years in a two room flat in an insalubrious tenement adjacent to where the Savoy Hotel now stands. The one redeeming feature was the small window that afforded a view of the ever-busy Thames.

To the end Blake remained responsive to London's confused, generous, mean-minded, moody, all-powerful and impotent crowd, and to the hypocrisies of its rulers. 'I behold London,' he exclaimed, 'a Human awful wonder of God!' In his final masterpiece, *Jerusalem*, completed in 1820, Blake remembered London's unwilling warriors, the sailors in the crimping houses:

> We were carried away in thousands from London; & in tens
> Of thousands from Westminster & Marybone in ships closd up:
> Chaind hand & foot, compelld to fight under the iron whips
> Of our captains; fearing our officers more than the enemy.

For Blake, London is a psyche, a city of the mind. 'My Streets are my Ideas of Imagination,' he has it declare, 'My Houses are Thoughts; my Inhabitants, Affections.' It is both microcosm (of human civilisation) and macrocosm (containing many worlds). It exists everywhere and nowhere, always and never, like 'Lambeth's Vale / Where Jerusalem's foundations began; where they were laid in ruins.'

In the rhythmic litanies of London place-names found in Blake's later works, the poet traces the course of his giant visionary forms: from 'Highgate's heights & Hampstead's, to Poplar Hackney & Bow: / To Islington & Paddington & the Brook of Albions River / We built Jerusalem...' Out of familiar workaday London, Blake conjures a sanctified geography, treating the modern city and its neighbourhoods the way the Bible treats ancient Palestine. He sees the metropolis as a decisive battleground in an epic spiritual-political struggle through which 'intellectual war' must overcome 'corporeal war'. Here Los, the poet-prophet-blacksmith, labours at his forge. 'On the banks of the Thames, Los builded Golgonooza' – a multifaceted, jewel-like city of applied imagination, Blake's capital of artisans. 'In fears he builded it, in rage & in fury. It is the Spiritual Fourfold London: continually building & continually decaying desolate!'

Finally, Blake sees liberated London as a meeting-place for all that is human: 'In the Exchanges of London every Nation walk'd, / And London walk'd in every Nation, mutual in love & harmony.'

This is a defiantly Republican London. A London without Kings or Priests or financiers or their 'hirelings', the publicists and apologists whom Blake reviled. A London of free labourers, in which individual and collective creativity flourish together, a city thriving off the dialectic of the one and the many.

TIME TO TALK UTOPIA

First published in 2011.

In 1818, Shelley visited his friend Byron in Venice, where his Lordship was camped out in a decaying palazzo, ruminating on the city's faded glories. Their conversations – on human freedom and the prospects for social change – formed the basis for Shelley's poem *Julian and Maddalo*, in which the mild-mannered English rationalist Julian (Shelley) puts the case for hope while the brooding Italian aristocrat Maddalo (Byron) argues for despair. 'We might be otherwise,' Julian insists, 'we might be all / we dream of: happy, high, majestical' were it not for our own 'enchained' wills. To which Maddalo replies bitterly: 'You talk utopia!'

That snap dismissal echoes down to our own day. We've been taught to fear utopian thinking, which is denounced as not only impractical but positively dangerous: the province of fanatics. In ignoring the lessons of history and the realities of human nature, utopian idealism results, inevitably we are told, in dystopian outcomes. It's a modern version of the myth of Pandora's box: a warning against being too enquiring, too ambitious.

Fear of utopia, a mighty weapon in the arsenal of the ruling powers, has a long pedigree. Since Burke, at least, conservatives have warned that tampering with established institutions, encouraging people to expect too much, leads to disaster. The 'failure' of every social experiment, from the French Revolution onward, is seized on as evidence of the perils of utopian thinking. Anti-utopianism was a staple of Cold War liberalism and was resuscitated as the 'end of history' thesis following the collapse of the Soviet Union.

Increasingly we have been told that a utopian denial of realities lurks in even the most modest demands for regulation and redistribution. When it comes to the apparent dearth of alternatives, I'd argue that social democracy's long retreat into the arms of neo-liberalism is as great a factor as the demise of the Communist bloc.

While there are dangers in utopian thinking, the much greater danger is its absence. The reality is that we on the left don't 'talk utopia' nearly enough.

We need the attraction of a possible future as well as a revulsion at the actual present. If people are to make the sacrifices required by any struggle for social justice, then they need a bold and compelling idea of the world they're fighting for.

Utopian thinking is more than just model building: it is a critical tool, a means of interrogating present conditions. We have to exercise that supremely political faculty, the imagination, if we are not to be prisoners of a prevailing consensus.

Utopias provide a perspective from which the assumed limitations of the present can be scrutinised, from which familiar social arrangements are exposed as unjust, irrational or superfluous. You can't chart the surface of the earth, compute distances or even locate where you are without reference to a point of elevation – a mountain top, a star or satellite. Without utopias we enjoy only a restricted view of our own nature and capacities. We cannot know who we are.

We need utopian thinking if we are to engage successfully in the critical battle over what is or is not possible, if we are to challenge what are presented as immutable 'economic realities'. Without a clear alternative – the outlines of a just and sustainable society – we are forced to accept our opponent's parameters. We cede the definition of the possible to those with a vested interest in closing the aperture into a better future. The neo-liberal slogan There Is No Alternative had to be answered by Another World Is Possible, but we need to know and say much more about this other world.

In our utopian activity, let's learn from past errors. It's important to remember that a significant strand of utopianism, including Thomas More's book, is linked to Western colonialism. This took many forms, from dreams of imposing a new order on ancient or (allegedly) empty lands (of which Zionism is a modern case) to Romantic and Orientalist fantasies.

In their critique of utopian socialism, Marx and Engels made two charges. First, that the method was wrong: a socialism imposed from above, reliant on altruistic benefactors. Second, that it was not sweeping enough, that it failed to recognise the need to replace the system as a whole.

Marx described communism as 'the negation of the negation' – and our utopianism must remain at least in part a giant negation: of exploitation, inequality, greed, prejudice. Marx is criticised for not telling us more about what comes after the negation, but he did leave us with a still vital guideline: From each according to his/her ability to each according to his/her need.

Utopia is the good society, not the perfect society. A perfect society would be a static entity. Our utopia is one that is evolving, revising its goals and policies as circumstances change. It's an open not a closed system. Which means identifying its governing principles, its driving processes, may be more important than postulating fixed structures.

A utopia without dissent and argument is a nightmare. I don't want to belong to a community of interminable sweetness and harmony. In fact, argument will flower on a higher plane, grounded in a shared public domain to which all have real and equal access – politics in the best sense, with no professional politicians.

In our utopia the meaning of work will transformed. There will be no more precious commodity than a person's time. 'Choice' too will be redefined, salvaged from consumerism. There will be a deeper sense of ownership than the individualist version touted by the current system.

We cannot leave our utopian activity to think tanks. Nor should it be about some artificial 'pre-figuration', an exercise in isolated purity. It has to involve getting your hands dirty: finding places for the utopian in the everyday and learning from the everyday the meaning of utopia.

We need to draw on the utopian elements in our midst. The NHS is far from perfect, but it operates under egalitarian principles deemed 'utopian' in other fields and enjoys a significant degree of autonomy from the market, which makes it a kind of mini-utopia within British daily life – one reason the government is determined to destroy it.

We need to find ways to connect to the utopian yearnings that move millions of people, and which both the right wing and the advertising industry know too well how to exploit. We have to offer something more participatory, concrete and at the same time dynamic, more of a process, a journey, than an end product polished by the intelligentsia. In doing that, we can draw on a rich tradition going back to the Biblical prophets and found in almost every human society. In England alone, we can look to Langland, Winstanley, Thomas Spence, Ruskin, Morris and John Lennon – not forgetting More himself, in whose *Utopia* 'gold is a badge of infamy'.

Our utopia must imagine a new, humbler relationship between humans and their environment. The techno-utopias of the past with their dreams of total human mastery over nature now feel distinctly dystopic. On the other hand, the idea of an endlessly renewable energy source, a staple of science fiction, has moved from idle fantasy to urgent necessity. The climate change crisis is a good example of utopian thinking proving more realistic than its ostensibly pragmatic opponents. In the light of imminent catastrophe, utopia becomes common sense.

It is the anti-utopians who are guilty of arrogance and presumption in dismissing systematic alternatives as contrary to human nature (or economic 'laws'). The utopians are more historically grounded. They know that capitalism had a beginning and will have an end. In contrast, neo-liberals practise the perjorative form of utopianism: imposing an abstract blueprint on the human species (and the planet), subordinating diverse human needs to the single compulsion of private profit. We are encouraged to entertain limitless, if narrowly defined, aspirations for ourselves as individuals, but our aspirations for our society are strictly ring-fenced. While it is held to be fatal to ignore economic realities, ecological realities can be indefinitely deferred. The anti-utopians who insist There Is No Alternative end up denying the rest of us workable solutions to urgent problems.

The poets and prophets of the past gave us visions of a golden age of abundance, where the curse of labour had been lifted, where the vines were laden with lustrous grapes, the figs were like emeralds and the streams gushed fresh water. Somehow, we need to find our own symbols of shared, sustainable abundance in a world starkly divided into rich to poor.

For William Blake, the work of utopia was a daily duty of the citizen. At the end of his *Vala, or the Four Zoas*, he envisioned a world in which 'the dark religions are departed and sweet science reigns'. It's now up to us to imagine a world free of the dark religion of neo-liberalism, in which the sweet science of human solidarity prevails.

1792: THIS IS WHAT REVOLUTION LOOKS LIKE

First published in 2012.

In France, 1792 was the year of 'the second revolution'. On 10 August, the King was overthrown, bringing to an end three years of uneasy 'constitutional monarchy'. For months the Legislative Assembly had been locked in conflict with Louis XVI, while at the same time fighting a war against invading Austrians and Prussians. The Parisian masses resolved that conflict by direct action, invading the Tuileries palace and arresting the King. In response, the Assembly called a general election – the first ever election in Europe conducted under universal adult male suffrage. Eighty years would pass before the exercise was repeated.

The elections, held in the first two weeks of September, were festive, proudly democratic occasions marked by wide-ranging debates, and the results were a resounding confirmation of the action of the Paris masses. The 750 deputies elected to the 'Convention' were overwhelmingly committed to the formation of a new Republic, though they would soon fall out violently over its direction.

August 10 had ushered in not only a new Republic but a new power: the plebeian Parisians who would come to be known as *sans-culottes*. Organised in the Sections (neighbourhood committees) and Commune of Paris, in the coming year they would mobilise repeatedly to force their 'popular programme' on an often reluctant Convention. That programme included not only stiff measures against 'counter-revolutionaries' but also price controls and action against hoarders and speculators. If this was a 'bourgeois revolution', someone forgot to tell the *sans-culottes*.

In the year of the second revolution, the revolutionary impulse overflowed established categories and surged through ancient barriers.

In the British Isles, the best-seller was Thomas Paine's *Rights of Man*, which thanks to its plain but vibrant style, its cheap price and Paine's disclaiming of what would today be called 'intellectual property rights', reached hundreds of thousands, including London artisans, rural labourers and workers in the new industrial enclaves. In Part I, published in early 1791, Paine defended the French Revolution and debunked what passed for the British constitution. 'The portion of liberty enjoyed in England,' he observed, 'is just enough to enslave a country more productively than by despotism.'

In Part II, published in February 1792, Paine amplified his republican arguments. Insisting that 'only partial advantages can flow from partial reforms', he warned: 'Change of ministers amounts to nothing. One goes out, another comes in, and still the same measures, vices, and extravagance are pursued. It signifies not who is minister. The defect lies in the system.'

Most remarkably in Part II, Paine pushed the democratic revolution into the economic realm. He identified the central contradiction of European progress: 'a great portion of mankind, in what are called civilised countries, are in a state of poverty and wretchedness, far below the condition of an [American] Indian.' He concluded that 'when in countries that are called civilised, we see age going to the workhouse and youth to the gallows, something must be wrong in the system of government.' And went on to propose, in some detail, what would later be known as a welfare state: payments to the elderly, the disabled and parents of young children; universal primary eduction and public works to provide gainful employment. All this 'Not as a matter of grace and favour, but of right'. And all to be funded by a new system of steeply progressive taxation and cuts in military spending. The search for democracy had led Paine to social democracy.

That there was a ready audience for Paine's ideas was shown by the rapid growth of the London Corresponding Society, along with similar bodies in Sheffield, Manchester and elsewhere. Dedicated to parliamentary reform and universal male suffrage, the Corresponding Societies were Britain's first plebeian political associations, charging dues of only a penny a week. The LCS's founding secretary, the shoemaker Thomas Hardy, explained that its members represented 'a class of men who deserve better treatment than they generally meet with from those who are fed, and clothed, and enriched by their labour, industry or ingenuity.'

Paine and the Corresponding Societies created a new radical democratic pole in British politics, squarely opposed to and by Pitt's Tory government. Caught between the two, the liberal Whigs vacillated. Fox and a small band stood out against the attacks on civil liberties and the drift to war with France, but were gradually isolated. Within a year the Whig leaders, driven by their fear of revolution, had joined Pitt's ministry – not the last time Liberals would respond to a national crisis by lining up with Tory reaction.

Paris was the epicentre, but the repercussions were global. The revolutionary contagion spread to Ireland, where the United Irishmen had been formed a year earlier, and to Scotland where in December 1792, the Edinburgh Friends of the People organised a 'general convention' for parliamentary reform, attended by 160 delegates from 35 Scottish towns and villages.

In the Carribbean, the hugely profitable French colony of San Domingue was convulsed by a slave revolt of unprecedented dimensions. On 19 August, the man who was to become its greatest general issued an appeal: 'Brothers and friends, I am Toussaint L'Ouverture, my name is perhaps known to you. I have undertaken vengeance. I want liberty and equality to reign in San Domingo. I work to bring them into existence. Unite yourselves to us brothers, and fight with us...' For the first time, the ideas of the European Enlightenment were turned against European power.

Under the extraordinary conditions of 1792, the question of the 'rights of man' also became, briefly, a question of the 'rights of women'. On 6 March, Pauline Leon, a 23-year-old Parisian chocolate-maker, read a petition to the Legislative Assembly demanding the formation of a women's national guard. The petition was signed by 319 Parisian women, including cooks, seamstresses, market-sellers, wives and daughters of shoemakers, butchers, lawyers and doctors. On 26 March, the 30-year-old Theroigne de Merincourt, a figure romanticised and demonised by historians and novelists, in a speech to one of the Paris sections, took the call for a woman's right to bear arms into broader territory. 'Compare what we are with what we should be in the social order... Break our chains. It is finally time that women emerge from their shameful nullity, where the ignorance, pride and injustice of men have kept them enslaved for such a long time.'

Across the channel, at the same time, Mary Wollstonecraft was completing her *Vindication of the Rights of Women*, extending Paine's radical democratic analysis into gender relations. Cautiously as Wollstonecraft proceeded, focussing mainly on women's rights to education and barely hinting at political equality, her work was greeted with horror by the polite classes and consigned to oblivion for the best part of a century.

She shared that fate with many of the revolutionary agents of 1792, which was also a year of reaction. The Royal Proclamation of May, aimed at Paine and the Corresponding Societies, marked the beginning of a decade of repression ('Pitt's Terror' in popular legend) as severe as anything in British history. The upshot was the silencing of radical dissent and the crushing of popular aspirations, in the course of which a modern elite-driven British nationalism was fashioned, a development whose consequences are still very much with us.

Paine himself barely escaped arrest when in September he crossed the channel to take his seat as an elected deputy in the Convention. The world's first international revolutionary addressed a challenge to his fellow representatives: 'In seeing Royalty abolished and the Republic established, all France has resounded with unanimous plaudits. Yet some who clap their hands do not sufficiently understand the condition they are leaving or that which they are assuming... it is little to throw down an idol; it is the pedestal that above all must be broken down.'

Within little more than a year, Paine would be imprisoned by the revolution he celebrated. On his release after eleven months, he returned to the Convention to restate his commitment to that revolution, and to warn the deputies, unsuccessfully, against limiting the franchise by a property qualification.

In the short-term, the democratic radicals of 1792 suffered defeat, isolation, imprisonment or death. Women's political clubs were banned in November 1793 and nearly all the women militants fell victim to the purges and pendulum swings of 1793-95. Toussaint died in a French prison. Leaders of the LCS and the Edinburgh Convention were jailed and some transported to Botany Bay. In 1798, the United Irishmen were crushed by British military might, at a cost of 30,000 Irish lives.

It would take another 120 years for Ireland to achieve (partial) freedom and for women to win the vote. The anti-colonial struggle, the struggle of the global south, launched in Haiti, remains incomplete in our own day. The social democracy envisioned by Paine only came into existence after 1945, and its vestiges are now being stripped away.

So were all these struggles 'premature', doomed to failure, a waste of passion and effort? Readers can make up their own minds about that.

3

PATHWAYS OF MEMORY – NATIONALISM, CAPITALISM AND THE LOVE OF A GAME

FOR LOVE OF THE GAME

First published during the 1996 Cricket World Cup, hosted by India, Pakistan and Sri Lanka.

For many in the Indian subcontinent, the real World Cup final took place in Bangalore last Saturday, when Pakistan played in India for the first time since 1987. In a tightly contested seesaw match, India knocked out the cup holders (sorely missing their injured captain and ace all-rounder, Wasim Akram) under floodlights before a capacity crowd that celebrated the victory with firecrackers, flaming newspaper torches, mass flag-waving and dancing on the terraces.

By subcontinental standards, the display of chauvinism was subdued. The anti-Pakistan chanting that is a regular feature of cricket matches in India (no matter who is actually playing) was confined to a small minority. There were even banners reading 'Cricket for peace – not violence' and 'World Cup for secularism'. Players and officials from both countries expressed hopes that the match would presage a normalisation of India-Pakistan cricket relations, which have been repeatedly interrupted by military and diplomatic conflicts and the opportunist rantings of religious and nationalist demagogues. The fierce Indian-Pakistani cricket rivalry, which makes the Anglo-Australian Ashes look like an exercise in international hand-holding has for many years been the outstanding exemplar of George Orwell's definition of international sporting contests as 'war minus the shooting'.

India's Hindu right is opposed to any cricket contact with the arch-enemy and took direct action to sabotage Pakistan's last scheduled visit to India, when activists from the semi-fascist Shiv Sena dug up the pitch by Bombay's Wankhede Stadium. Sena leader Bal Thackeray, mercilessly pilloried in Salman Rushdie's *The Moor's Last Sigh,* even has his own version of the Tebbit test. When India lose to Pakistan at cricket, says Thackeray, he wants to see tears in the eyes of Indian Muslims – as proof of their loyalty to India, which he questions. The negative formulation (why not test Muslim loyalty when India wins?) is revealing. As in England, cricket nationalism in India is often an expression of national insecurity – not an assertion of one's place as an equal in what C L R James called 'the community of nations'.

The Sena is now the governing party in the giant western state of Maharashtra, whose capital, Bombay, is the cradle of Indian cricket. The Maharashtra chief minister, Thackeray-henchman Manohar Joshi, who happens also to be the president of the Bombay Cricket Association and a vice-president of the Indian cricket board, declared that Pakistan should not be allowed to play in Bangalore. Members of his party were detained by police in the city on the eve of the match.

The good news is that cricket mania appears to have triumphed, for the time being, over communalist politics. The India-Pakistan meeting was the match the whole subcontinent wanted to see, and the World Cup would have been a lesser event without it. Cricket is unrivalled as the national sport in India, Pakistan and Sri Lanka, and big-time international cricket is followed with passionate intensity by people of all communities and classes. The media are saturated with World Cup coverage, and from elite dinner parties to roadside *dhabas,* the Cup is the number one topic of discussion. In large tracts of England the game is virtually invisible, but in the subcontinent, wherever there is a relatively flat patch of ground and any modicum of open space, from the narrow alleyways of urban slums to the most bedraggled rural hamlets, you will see children playing the game with whatever implements come to hand.

The World Cup began on a sour note when Australia and the West Indies refused to play against Sri Lanka in Colombo because of the terrorist threat from the Tamil Tigers. Most observers here believe that the bomb blast was only a handy excuse and that the Australian decision was merely another episode in the prolonged power struggle within the International Cricket Council (ICC) between third- and first-world countries. The West Indies was dragged into the Australian camp because the poverty-stricken West Indies board is heavily reliant on the regular and lucrative exchange of tours with the Australians. The ICC was split down the middle and unable to broker a compromise. Before a ball had been bowled in this World Cup, cricket stood exposed as a global game without a credible global authority.

Seen as a hypocritical snub in all three World Cup host countries, the Australia-West Indies boycott produced a rare display of South Asian solidarity when a joint India-Pakistan team was hastily assembled to play against the Sri Lankans of Colombo. The result of this 'friendly' match may have been of no consequence, but it was nonetheless a historic occasion. Then thousands of Sri Lankans turned up at the Khetterama Stadium with only 24 hours' notice and bedecked the ground with the flags of the three nations and a welter of home-made banners and placards. Many abused the Australians, but many more carried messages of unity and peace: 'India, Pakistan and Sri Lanka – Keep Together for South Asian Dignity'. For once, the clichés about cricket uniting people and bringing nations together seemed more than bogus sentiment, and international sport something better than 'war minus the shooting'.

The Sri Lankans, for so long the also-rans of world cricket, have been one of the hottest teams in the tournaments. Ana Punchihewa, the go-getting president of the Sri Lankan cricket board – and managing director of Coca-Cola Sri Lanka – aims to turn the Sri Lankans into 'the best in the world' by 2000. There is no doubt that, with the success of the national side, the popularity of the game is soaring in the war-torn island. However, a cricket-loving veteran of the freedom struggle against the British sounded a warning note. He told me he could take little pleasure in recent Sri Lankan triumphs on the cricket pitch; they led to indulgence in what he called a 'spurious nationalism, a Coca-Cola nationalism'. National self-assertion through sport, he argued, had become more strident even as genuine national self-determination had become largely an illusion – thanks to the globalisation of the economy.

Because of its vast popular base, cricket on the subcontinent is an ideal vehicle for multinational corporations seeking to penetrate 'emerging markets'. And, thanks to satellite television, subcontinental cricket can also be used to sell goods in Europe, North America, the Middle East and South-East Asia. As a result, this World Cup has become a kind of carnival of globalisation – sponsored by tobacco, soft drink and credit card giants. Never before in the game's long story has the role of money been so flagrantly celebrated. In English cricket, commercialism rules as it does elsewhere in sport, but is veiled by traditional English sanctimony. In South Asia, every new sponsorship deal, media tie-in, cash incentive is trumpeted triumphally.

Strange as it may seem to those only familiar with the English version of the game, cricket in these parts is considered sexy, trendy and ultra-modern. That's why Coca-Cola paid $3.5 million to become the 'official drink' of the World Cup. And that's why Pepsi trumped its arch rival by buying up Indian and Pakistani cricket stars to proclaim their preference for Pepsi with the cheeky slogan 'Nothing official about it!' Adverts on TV show 23-year-old master batsman Sachin Tendulkar, Pepsi in hand, self-consciously turning his baseball cap back to front, like a street urchin from a North American ghetto. What with every team celebrating wickets with high fives and players sprouting goatees overnight, this World Cup could herald the Americanisation of subcontinental cricket. Certainly Indian and Pakistani cricket bosses, keen to break into the US market, would welcome such a development.

Cricket in the subcontinent is big business and big politics and everyone wants a piece of the action. As a result, tickets to World Cup matches have become a kind of currency of patronage; they are tokens of status in societies where old hierarchies are being swept aside and new ones established by the ruthless drive towards economic 'liberalisation'. Thousands queued overnight for tickets to the India-Pakistan match at Bangalore, only to find that 90 per cent of the 50,000 seats had been allocated to sponsors, politicians, bureaucrats, friends and families before a single ticket went on public sale. The Delhi match between India and Sri Lanka nearly degenerated into a riot because the local cricket association had distributed more VIP passes and sold more tickets than it had seats available. In Pakistan, the early Cup matches were nearly empty because the International Management Group, which had been given the ticketing franchise, was so preoccupied with block sales to prestigious multinational corporations that it failed to make tickets available to the general public.

This World Cup has confirmed the subcontinent's status as the new epicentre of global cricket – and England's relegation to the margins of the game it gave the world. So dismal have been England's performances here that the frisson that once accompanied the humiliation of the former colonial power has given way to bored impatience with its inability to cope with the realities of cricket on the eve of the 21st century.

Once again, English players, management and journalists have succeeded in offending whole populations by crass insults (Atherton's reference to an Urdu-language journalist as a 'buffoon' because his English wasn't up to scratch was only one of several incidents) and non-stop whingeing about food, hygiene and transport. Compare the performance of the South Africans, whose own traumatic domestic history has at least taught them the virtues of diplomacy. The team sent 'felicitations' to their hosts, the people of Pakistan, for Eid, the Muslim holiday, while England were grumbling about pitches and test officials. South African cricket boss Ali Bacher, a survivor of the old regime who has transformed himself into a champion of the new South Africa, announced to the peoples of the subcontinent that 'our twelfth man is Nelson Mandela'. Crowd-pleasing PR, perhaps, but no one who has watched the South Africans play in the World Cup can doubt that the team is infused with a sense of mission and of responsibility toward the new democracy in its homeland.

The biggest burden English cricket bears is its attitude towards the rest of the world and its concomitant narrow view of English society itself. Until that is swept away, the Test and County Cricket Board can mount inquiries until Doomsday and nothing will change for the better.

Dramatic as the long-awaited India-Pakistan confrontation in Bangalore was, the defining moment in this World Cup – and the best antidote to the commercial hype and political cynicism surrounding it – remains Kenya's astonishing victory over the West Indies at Pune. The justification for a tournament of this kind is not only that it brings together the best in the world, but that it gives the lowly and unsung a chance to upend the high and mighty. The irony is that this triumph for enthusiastic amateurs over world-weary professionals came at the expense of the West Indies, who have so often in the past used cricket to overturn social and economic hierarchies.

Whatever its moribund state in England, cricket elsewhere, as displayed in this World Cup, is in a state of rapid evolution. The one-day game has become ever more sophisticated, and the crowd drawn to it ever more indifferent to ancient verities associated with the game. Just where all this is leading is anyone's guess, but there is no doubt that cricket's fate is now tied to the fate of the South Asian societies, the place they find in the global economy, and the impact this economy makes on their cricket-obsessed masses.

TRIUMPH AND TRAVAIL: THE SUBCONTINENTAL STORY

First published in 1996 following that year's Cricket World Cup.

George Orwell once defined 'serious sport' between nations as 'war minus the shooting'. In retrospect, the World Cup has both proved and disproved this dictum, and shown that cricket, as ever, bears the impress of the social conditions under which it is played. In keeping with the liberalisation policies of all three host country governments, the tournament was the most flagrantly commercialised event in the long history of the game. The power of cold cash has always guided cricket's fate, but in the old days it was usually veiled by English hypocrisy.

The English bitterly objected to the International Cricket Council (ICC) decision to award the event to the subcontinent and never reconciled themselves to it (a factor which contributed to the England team's dismal performance). What the English cricket establishment failed to grasp was why the decision was made and why they were outbid and outmanoeuvred by the South Asian nations. Quite simply, the scale and intensity of the passion for cricket across the region gave India, Pakistan and Sri Lanka a financial base which the English could not match.

The ever-growing popularity of cricket in the subcontinent enabled Pilcom to sell the tournament to multinational corporations (MNCs) and media conglomerates. As a result, the World Cup became a carnival of globalisation. Like any world sporting event, it brought nations together to compete on a level playing field – the favoured metaphor of the neo-liberal architects of GATT. It became a stage from which the Indian elite projected themselves to the world, displaying the subcontinent as cricket's new global epicentre. Thanks to satellite TV, subcontinental cricket is being exported not only to the game's traditional homelands but also to new markets in West Asia, South-East Asia and North America. It has also become a vehicle for MNCs to sell their products to a global market – and a means to penetrate the hitherto protected markets of South Asia. But for all its go-getting commercial triumphalism, Pilcom was to find that globalisation was by no means as straightforward a process as its champions have claimed.

First came the wrangle between Doordarshan and WorldTel, in which the contingencies of politics (and demands of democracy) clashed with the compulsions of global marketing. With the aid of the courts, a compromise was brokered, but it is unlikely to prove a lasting one. In Britain, Rupert Murdoch's Sky Sports satellite channel has snapped up rights to the bulk of big-time cricket, leaving the BBC – whose audience is ten times Sky's – with live coverage only of home Test matches (and even these are under threat). The likely long-term impact will be to erode further English cricket's already precarious base, making it even more of a minority sport, with inevitable consequences for the national team's ability to compete in events like the World Cup. There is a warning here for the Indian cricket establishment, but I doubt if it will be heeded.

In signing up with Reebok (after having insisted that the Indian sports goods industry was the equal of any on the world), Mohammed Azharuddin also found the path of globalisation strewn with pitfalls, though his subsequent travails have dwarfed the shoe-autographing imbroglio.

The opening ceremony in Calcutta was a flop not merely because of incompetence on the part of the organisers or foreign experts, but because it was, stylistically, an unsatisfactory compromise between global and local popular cultures. The traditional music, dance and dress of the host nations featured only fleetingly, in deference to an international audience, while the American-style, V-TV razzmatazz was muffled by Pilcom's anxiety not to offend.

Even before the opening ceremony, cricket's global harmony had been shattered by the refusal of the Australians (dragging the West Indies in their wake) to play in Colombo following the LTTE bomb blast there. The Sri Lankans are convinced that the real reason for the boycott was the fear of Taylor, Warne and Co. that they would be made to pay for the controversies that surrounded Sri Lanka's recent tour of Australia. The fracas surrounding the no-balling of off-spinner Muttiah Muralitharan revealed that it is all very well to proclaim sagely that the umpire's decision is final – but which umpire, from which country? The inability or perhaps unwillingness of the ICC to negotiate any compromise on the Colombo issue, compounded by its refusal to mete out any serious penalties to the forfeiting countries, showed that cricket is today a global game without a credible global authority, and confirmed that there is no global consensus over what constitutes fair play.

The silver lining was the solidarity match: in which an unprecedented joint Indo-Pakistan XI flew to Colombo for a hastily arranged 40-overs contest against the spurned Sri Lankans. With only 24 hours' notice, 10,000 cricket-lovers turned up at the Khetterama stadium, warmly welcoming the Indo-Pakistani visitors and festooning the ground with symbols of South Asian solidarity. Spectators stitched together the flags of the three host countries and shouted 'India *zindabad*! Pakistan *zindabad*! Sri Lanka *zindabad*!' Hand-scrawled placards declared, 'India, Pakistan, Sri Lanka keep together for South Asian dignity' and 'Three musketeers – Azhar, Akram, Arjuna'. As the first wicket fell, the scoreline – Kaluwitharana, caught Tendulkar, bowled Wasim Akram – seemed to expose the fundamental absurdity of Indo-Pakistan hostility, though it did nothing to curb the exchange of fire along the disputed Kashmir border.

At Colombo, the cliche that cricket unifies nations and promotes peace came briefly and movingly alive. But, in the end, it had little impact on those for whom cricket is mainly a device to whip up national and communal hatred. The rise of the Shiv Sena in Bombay had already persuaded Pilcom to deny the cradle of Indian cricket the honour of staging a quarter or semi-final (in which the Pakistanis might appear). Manohar Joshi, the Maharashtra Chief Minister, President of the Bombay Cricket Association and a vice-president of the Board of Control for Cricket in India (BCCI), had pleaded for one of the prize knock-out fixtures – a plea whose hypocrisy was exposed by his later denunciation of Pakistan's presence in the country for the Bangalore quarter-final. Surely, Indian cricket is profoundly compromised by the presence of communal elements in senior positions in its hierarchy.

Despite the malign influence of the Sena, the Bombay cricket crowd demonstrated at the tightly contested and thoroughly engrossing India-Australia match that it remains one of the most knowledgeable and relaxed in the country, applauding a splendid Australian performance and restraining its grief over an Indian defeat.

The same could not be said of the crowd at Delhi, where a good match was ruined for many by the worst organisation seen at any World Cup tie. The Delhi Police and the Delhi and District Cricket Association (DDCA), long riven by factional warfare, blamed each other for the mess, but both were guilty. The DDCA had handed out VIP passes with indiscriminate abandon and charged exorbitant prices for the most basic facilities; the police abused their authority to let in non-ticket holders while subjecting paying customers to *lathi* charges outside the gates. Inside the ground, the atmosphere was sour. The extraordinary Sri Lankan batting went largely unacknowledged by the spectators, who amused themselves by chanting 'Pakistan *hai*! *hai*!' with a frequency and ferocity found on few other Indian grounds. It says a great deal about the impoverished state of Indian nationalism today that it takes the form of mindless abuse of an absent third party at a cricket match.

There would seem to be few better exemplars of sport as 'war minus the shooting' than the Indo-Pakistan cricket relationship, buffeted over the decades by military and diplomatic conflict, nuclear rivalry, the Kashmir dispute and nationalist and communalist demagogues on both sides of the border. Many advocates of improved Indo-Pakistan relations awaited the quarter-final meeting of the arch-rivals with trepidation.

In Bangalore, when the Pakistan players ran out onto the field and then jogged round the stadium, they were greeted by warm applause from most of those present. Only a minority engaged in booing. Messages on the handmade banners and placards included: 'Cricket for peace not violence', 'World Cup for secularism' and 'Welcome Pakistan cricketers'. The crowd was, of course, fiercely partisan, but, with only a few exceptions, spectators were not antagonistic to the Pakistan players, and their sharp outfielding and quick returns from the deep were applauded.

Sadly, however, Javed Miandad ended his international career without the ovation he richly deserved. And the celebrations on the streets of Bangalore and elsewhere after the match assumed a disturbingly negative character. Walking back from the Chinnaswamy Stadium with an Indian friend, I watched youth on motorscooters waving flags and screaming their love for 'Bharat Mata'. My friend confessed himself sickened by 'the vulgar display of chauvinism'. Of course, there is nothing wrong in celebrating a national sporting victory; but what was being celebrated here was not so much Indian victory as Pakistani defeat. People in India should not be surprised that in Pakistan, the Calcutta result was met with mirror-image jubilation. The behaviour of sections of the crowd at Eden Gardens was reprehensible, and certainly a blemish on Calcutta's reputation as a sporting mecca. But did it really 'shame the nation'? The thuggishness was mild compared to what has been seen at British club football matches in recent years, and not in the same league as the fascist disruption of last year's England vs Ireland match in Dublin. Still, some will say, that is football – this is cricket. Ask Anil Kumble about playing in the 1995 NatWest Trophy semi-final. As drunken fans engaged in apparently random punch-ups in the stands, Kumble was subject to ceaseless racial taunts and at one time pelted with fruit.

Of course, bad behaviour elsewhere is no excuse for it here. And cricket lovers in Calcutta and around the country are right to express anxiety about the game's future direction in the subcontinent. However, moralistic sermons are of little help. What is needed is thoughful analysis.

Nothing could more clearly confirm the deep love of cricket in the subcontinent than the willingness of fans here to endure all kinds of indignities and discomforts to watch it. At Eden Gardens, where even the Sri Lankan Roshan Mahanama suffered dehydration, there was no provision for drinking water for ordinary spectators. No wonder tempers frayed, just as they had in Delhi, where spectators were abused by the police.

It is important to bear in mind that the majority of spectators at Eden Gardens were even more upset by the loutish behaviour of some of their neighbours than they were by India's defeat. The tragedy is that these innocent bystanders received no support or succour from the authorities. The first concern of any investigation into the events at Eden Gardens should be the failure of those in charge to make any announcements on the public address system or to take any action to retrieve the situation.

But it is necessary to probe more deeply. An angry fan in the 400 rupee seats asked a foreigner there how much he had paid for his ticket. Two-thousand rupees was the reply. 'You're lucky,' said the Indian fan, 'I paid 5,000 for this rubbish.' In other words, at that price, he expected nothing less than an Indian victory. Too many, not only in Calcutta but at matches in both Pakistan and India throughout the tournament, bought tickets not in order to attend a cricket match but to celebrate a national triumph. Denied that triumph (in Delhi as well as in Calcutta), some of them turned ugly and vengeful.

After the Eden Gardens debacle, a smartly dressed, middle-aged man calmly guided his little daughter through the melee in the B.C. Roy clubhouse until he stood opposite a shattered-looking Mohammed Azharuddin. He then screamed at the top of his voice (terrifying his little girl): 'Divorce cricket – no good!' Just what standards of morality did he think he was upholding by this performance?

The overreaction in both Pakistan and India to elimination from the World Cup has revealed not only the depth of feeling the game engenders in the subcontinent but also the forces that threaten to disfigure it. The Indian mood-swing, from the elation in Bangalore to enraged despair in Calcutta, would be categorised by psychoanalysts as a symptom of paranoid schizophrenia. And the virulent manner in which the erstwhile gods of Pakistani cricket have been turned upon by their own devotees displays the same syndrome.

Both Azhar and Wasim have come under heavy fire from their home supporters and both have been accused of selling the World Cup to gambling interests. As always, in the absence of hard evidence, the cock-up is to be preferred to the conspiracy theory. Pakistan lost to India and India to Sri Lanka because on that day they were outplayed by first-class opposition. On other days, the reverse result would be just as likely. However, in the era of *hawala*, it is not surprising to find cricket fans in both India and Pakistan ready, almost eager, to believe that their heroes would sell their country for a fistful of rupees. For their own reasons, the media and advertisers had turned these fallible human beings into super-heroes who, unlike the rest of us, could never commit blunders or experience failure. No wonder the backlash was so intense.

The subcontinent is now the commercial hub of world cricket and will inevitably play a dominant role in shaping global cricket in the years to come. That does not necessarily mean that subcontinental teams will win cricket matches more often, just as the old English dominance did not stop them being routinely thrashed by the poverty-stricken West Indies.

Even before the tournament was over, cricket boards in England, the West Indies as well as India and Pakistan had ordered inquiries into their teams' performances. The outcome of all of these exercises in public relations is drearily predictable. The boards will exonerate themselves and make scapegoats of players or team managers. Meanwhile, the press and the public will attribute failure to whatever malaise they believe their nation is suffering from. Those who see the youth of today as spoiled, decadent or 'Westernised' will rant about Wasim's ear-ring and Azhar's love life. Those who see money as the root of all evil will mutter about gambling interests. Those who see the nation's principal problem as a foreign enemy will claim the players lack 'national loyalty'. In all the fuss, what will be forgotten is that this was a knock-out tournament in which giants could stumble at any hurdle. Australia, after all, failed even to qualify for the semi-finals in 1992.

My own feeling is that there is little wrong with Indian cricket except the exaggerated expectations people have placed on it. The decision to insert Sri Lanka on a turning wicket at Eden Gardens was utterly daft, but it had its roots in the traumatic defeat at the Kotla, when the Sri Lankans overhauled a target of 271 without breaking sweat. That defeat was partly the product of juggling the side in a silly overreaction to a perfectly honourable defeat in Bombay. The panic and 'scapegoating' reflected the huge pressure the management was under from the Indian media, but it was also characteristic of an old streak of inward-looking insecurity in Indian cricket. Australia, Sri Lanka and South Africa have been successful because they have stuck with their most talented players and resisted the urge to chop and change after every setback.

In both Pakistan and India, the high command of the cricket boards, aided and abetted by sponsors, advertisers and much of the media, hyped up the prospects of a home-team victory, rather than the honour of staging the tournament itself. The prolonged, over-publicised build-up generated not only unrealistic but the wrong kind of expectations. What came to be anticipated was not a cricket competition but a national triumph.

At Eden Gardens even the most unruly elements in the crowd never turned anti-Sri Lankan. The bottle-throwing was a demonstration of bitter disgust with the Indian team, and especially with its captain, who had been foolish enough to promise victory 'for the nation'. The whole episode was a sad demonstration of the sado-masochistic character which nationalism in both India and Pakistan has acquired in recent years. As economic globalisation makes the rhetoric of national self-determination ever more hollow, the expression of nationalism through cricket becomes ever more strident and ever more focussed on hostility to perceived enemies.

Triumphalist nationalism has been employed by corporations, both multinational and indigenous, to sell products – and indeed to sell the World Cup itself. Unfortunately the unapologetically aggressive imagery of 'Vimal salutes the spirit of winning' seems more in tune with the times than Onida's unconvincing paeans to an altruistic 'spirit of cricket'. The Pepsi ads, endearing as they have been, have emphasised the competitive and individualistic aspects of a game in which no quarter is given. In contrast, Coke's poetic 'Passion has a colour' montage, accompanied by the soaring lyricism of Nusrat Fateh Ali Khan, evoked the diversity of subcontinental popular culture and the unifying place of cricket within it – not big cricket under floodlights but cricket played in *gallis* and *maidans*, the cricket without which Pilcom would never be able to strut the global stage.

Subcontinental cricket's biggest problem is the emerging conflict between two cultures, between those who adore cricket for its own sake and those for whom it is primarily a means to an end – to either personal or national self-aggrandisement. This is much more than a conflict between generations. The insidious VIP culture, exacerbated by liberalisation and the intensified scramble for privileges, has infiltrated cricket and turned the cricket ticket into a currency of patronage, a token of social status. The result, in Delhi, Bangalore and elsewhere, was the disenfranchisement of the ordinary cricket fan.

In Pakistan, many of the early matches were played before near-empty houses, not because Pakistanis had suddenly become indifferent to cricket, but because the PCB had given the ticketing franchise to the International Management Group, which was so preoccupied with block sales to multinationals and government departments that it neglected to make tickets available to members of the public.

Sponsorship and media deals have reduced the financial importance of gate money. Cricket matches in the subcontinent are very much popular festivals, but they are staged under the aegis of – and generate profits for – an elite. How much of the reported $100 million World Cup revenues profit will find its way to the grassroots of the game? If the trickle down theory is questionable when applied to the economy as a whole, how much more so when applied to cricket, where structures of accountability are notable by their absence?

Despite all of this, the World Cup was, I believe, a success – because of the quality of the cricket it showcased. The competition as a whole was a powerful riposte to those who have dismissed the 50-overs games as a slog-and-run. Witness the varied but equally effective and attractive batting styles of Sachin Tendulkar, Mark Waugh and Aravinda de Silva, among others. Field placings and captaincy have become ever more sophisticated, and success goes to those bowlers who out-think their opponents (take note, Waqar Younis). These days the element of mind has come to the fore in limited-overs cricket, a point confirmed not only by the dismal performances of the England team but also by what happened to the West Indies in Pune.

The Kenyan victory was one of the highlights of the World Cup, vindicating not only the presence of the qualifiers on the global stage but also the much-maligned format of the tournament. Not every match can have the crackle of a semi-final and any tournament played over a month needs time to come to the boil.

The early rounds did, in the end, make a difference: they gave the super-powers a chance to probe one another's strengths and weaknesses, to experiment, learn from mistakes and make tactical adjustments. Those of us who were in Pune were lucky enough to witness a triumph for enthusiasm and commitment over world-weary cynicism, a fillip for all those to whom the five-star hotel remains an alien environment. It was a sharp reminder that global cricket need not be merely an occasion for big business and petty politics.

The two finalists were the most consistent, dynamic and unflappable teams in the tournament. Both had looked down and out in the early stage of their semi-finals. Given the controversy with which the event began, the encounter between the Australians and the Sri Lankans in the Lahore final seemed a rare instance of poetic justice in sport.

Over the last few weeks we have seen some engrossing cricket matches, marked by unexpected twists and turns and dramatic reversals of fortune. The lesson of this tournament has been that the balance between victory and defeat is a fine one – and that in World Cup cricket, 50-overs can be a very long time indeed.

PATHWAYS OF MEMORY

First published in 2006 during the England cricket team's tour of India.

In recent weeks I've been dragging myself out of bed at an ungodly hour. Outside it's still dark. I'm like a guilty child on Christmas morning, unable to sleep, sneaking out of the bedroom to peep at the presents spread under the tree. Only nowadays the waiting treasure, the alluring abundance, comes in a different kind of box. It's Test cricket telecast live from India, and as I ensconce myself under a duvet in front of the tube, I feel like one of my British predecessors, in the days before central heating, hunkering down in front of a glowing hearth, a single source of heat and light.

It doesn't matter that on some days Chandighar looked as dank and drizzly as London. The live action from far away makes me feel snug. It's a comfort zone, a window, a link to a world both distant and familiar. Perhaps because I'm still half-asleep, the rhythm of the cricket, the drone of the commentary seem dream-like. The normal laws of time and space are suspended. Only the adverts intrude. The din of an Indian cricket crowd percolates into the room (this is my dawn chorus) and the past percolates into the present. Sometimes cricket acts on me the way the tea-cake called a 'madeleine' acted on Marcel Proust, triggering a hidden chain of association, an entryway to what the French novelist called 'the vast structure of recollection'.

As the current India-England series has unfolded, I've been taken back to my first experience of following an overseas tour, my first brush with cricket in India. It was December 1976, I was living in a cottage in a small village in Devon, and the first Test of England's winter tour was being broadcast ball-by-ball (and blessedly free from adverts) on BBC radio. The commentators were preoccupied with food, toilets, turbans, paranoia about the wickets, the umpires and the raucous crowds. They talked of Bishen Bedi in his *patka*, all flight, loop and bumptious guile, as a rope-trick conjurer, the embodiment of the age-old mysteries of the East. As for Chandrashekhar with his withered arm, he was the sort of improbable cricketer that only India could produce. As I sat in the dark in Devon, my mind filled with garish, enticing imagery.

I didn't know it at the time, but this tour was something of an anomaly. England dominated the five Test series (winning 3, losing 1), its captain, Tony Greig, made himself hugely popular with the Indian crowds, in the whole series there was only a single Indian century (Gavaskar, of course), and for once it was the Indians and not the English who did the whingeing (the 'vaseline affair'). I also had no idea that this series would prove a harbinger of my own future. I'd never even thought of going to India, and my interest in cricket was still in its infancy (I was a ripe old twenty-three years of age but I'd spent the first 18 of them in the USA). But as it turned out, both cricket and India, and especially Indian cricket, were to have an unexpected influence on my life and how I've earned a living. The '76-77 series moved from Delhi to Bombay, Bangalore, Madras and Calcutta. These places were unknown to me then, but in the following decades I was lucky enough to visit, watch cricket and make friends in all of them.

But here in London I'm drifting mentally into a dusty afternoon in Hampi in 1979. It was my first trip to India. I had been sleeping with some other wandering Westerners in a ruined *mandapa* by the Tungabadra river and my passport had gone missing. I made my way to the local police station to report the matter, and ended up whiling away a pleasant afternoon drinking tea and listening to the radio coverage of the India-Pakistan match with the local constabulary. Back in the mandapa, my fellow Westerners – all German or Italian – couldn't understand what had kept me so long at the police station, and my attempts to explain the extraordinary rhythms of Test cricket fell on deaf ears.

These early morning communions with the television have also touched off memories that have nothing to do with cricket or India. Waking in November 1968 to follow the final stage of the election count that resulted in Richard Nixon squeaking into office and being filled with a queasy sense of foreboding (you didn't have to be a soothsayer to predict that Nixon's presidency would be a disgrace). Or a year later, meandering home through a gray excuse for a dawn after an epic nightlong session with a coterie of friends, listening to music, talking about anything our teenage minds stumbled across. At that moment, with the suburbs asleep around me, I felt thoroughly content with myself and my world.

The human memory is not an Internet search engine. Its criteria of association are more indirect, irregular, far-fetched, and at the same time guided by a deeper logic. Famously, Proust spent all day in bed accessing his inner data. For those of us without that kind of leisure, these break of day television-prompted ruminations are a precious interval, though they do play havoc with one's daily routine.

BRANDING THE NATION

First published in 2006 during the FIFA Football World Cup.

In London at the moment you can't get away from it. The red cross flag of St George is fluttering from cars and balconies, plastered on windows and billboards, inscribed on chocolate bars, pizza boxes and soft drink bottles. And in case anyone was not aware that England were off to compete in the World Cup, the message is re-enforced round the clock by every media outlet in the country.

The flag was first deployed as an emblem for England during the Crusades, but since the 18th century has been superceded by the Union Jack, representing the United Kingdom of Great Britain and Northern Ireland, as it's formally known. For many years, the St George's flag was widely seen as the property of the far right, a symbol of backward-looking, xenophobic Englishness. However, in the last decade or so it has regained respectability as a sporting symbol, the only one available for those who want to show their enthusiasm for the England team in cricket, rugby or football.

Of course, there's an obvious logic in supporting one's home team, a logic that makes itself felt everywhere. And England supporters understandably resent being stereotyped as narrow-minded national chauvinists. Nonetheless, the ubiquitousness of the flag and the branding of every product under the sun with 'England' does raise troubling questions.

Only a month ago, in the English local elections, the racist British National Party seized the headlines by electing 33 candidates to council seats. Though this was less than one percent of the number of seats up for grabs, it was a significant symptom of the broader impact of the politics of immigration. Polls indicated that between 18 and 24 per cent of the electorate might consider voting BNP. Disturbing, but not surprising, when the agenda of the BNP echoes and is echoed by the mainstream preoccupation with the alleged threat posed by asylum-seekers.

Manipulation of the national identity is by no means confined to politicians of the extreme right. Having re-branded itself, New Labour has also sought to rebrand both Britain and England, pepping up the old identities with hyper-modern connotations, while at the same time reassuring the public that the boundaries with which they are familiar will remain intact.

The growth of the European Union, coupled with the devolution of some powers to Scotland and Wales in the late 1990s, has spurred a debate about 'Englishness'. While an awareness that this is not a clear-cut entity is to be welcomed, the problem with this debate is that it never gets very far. The question of what constitutes Englishness always carries with it the question of what constitutes non-Englishness. Cataloging common values, customs or culture proves impossible, not least because England, like every other society, is criss-crossed with conflicting values, customs and cultures.

What's more, Englishness carries both national and ethnic meanings. Being English is frequently used as a synonym for being white native-born English. The presence of non-white players in the England team acts as a corrective for this, as does the eminence of England's Swedish manager. But the context in which England is defined is wider than football. A history of empire – in which the English were a globally privileged stratum – flows into contemporary debates surrounding the war on terror, the presence of British troops in Iraq and Afghanistan, the rights of immigrants and the erosion of civil liberties.

The media, sponsors and advertisers have made a huge investment in the World Cup and will do everything possible to maximise their return on it. That includes dedicating enormous resources to persuading people with no interest in football that the England team's Cup fortunes should be important to them, that there is a mystical link between themselves and the young men in England jerseys kicking a ball on the fields of Germany. Here Englishness becomes a content-free but potent attachment, easily exploited by the marketeers of both products and ideologies.

However, even as the red crosses proliferate, a more relaxed and fluid approach to sporting partisanship is also evident. In my neck of the woods, in north London, where our community includes substantial numbers of people with roots in the Caribbean and west Africa, the banners of Trinidad and Ghana can be seen, sometimes displayed alongside the flag of St George. I've also spotted more than a few individuals wearing Ronaldinho or Ronaldo replica shirts, and Portuguese and Spanish cafes sport their own colours.

The cosmopolitan nature of English club football has also given a shake to the kaleidoscope of loyalties. Compared to national sporting identities, club identities are more a matter of choice and personal circumstance. For the individuals involved, they are therefore more expressive and intimate. Arsenal makes its home hereabouts and I know Arsenal fans whose rule of thumb in this World Cup is simply to support any team that has an Arsenal player in it, which enables them to transform themselves, when required, into supporters of France, Holland, Spain, Ivory Cost, Brazil, Germany, Sweden, Togo or Switzerland.

I'll nail my colours to the mast by declaring that the only result that really matters to me in this World Cup is that England do not win. That's not because I dislike the players or the manager; in fact, this side is one of the best and most entertaining England have sent out for many years. But the impact of a World Cup win on the society I live in would be deleterious. It would ignite an orgy of nationalistic celebration, which in present circumstances cannot be dismissed as harmless fun.

Sport is essentially and intoxicatingly trivial, but in the World Cup it's the trivial magnified to mega-drama. One of the event's compelling, sometimes disturbing features is the way it infuses the pointlessly beautiful (beautifully pointless) game with an aura of immense consequence. When the penalty is missed, the world gasps. The amazing thing is that the event somehow survives the vast economic and ideological weight foisted on it, and remains a gripping showcase for human genius and fallibility.

THE PRIVATISATION OF CRICKET

First published in 2008 following the Indian Premier League player auction.

The most remarkable thing about the Indian Premier League player auction was the spectacle it generated. The heady mix of wealth and fame proved intoxicating for many, not least representatives of the media, who celebrated the auction as a triumph of the new India of the free market. For others it was unsettling: cricketers being evaluated like prize bulls, bought up by the super-rich.

That cricket is a business is nothing new, not at least since Thomas Lord put a fence around his ground and stated charging admission. But the significance of the IPL cannot be in doubt. For the first time since the early 19th century cricket teams are to be privately owned. As a result, cricket as a business will further edge out cricket as a public service and popular institution.

The BCCI is a public body holding the rights to cricket in trust. What it has done through the IPL is to privatise a public asset. Like other privatisations, it has been accompanied by hoopla that obscures the real nature of the transaction, and its real cost to the public.

The model is the globally-popular English football Premier League, whose teams are stuffed with international stars. But what made it possible to acquire those stars was the long-term standing of the clubs (Arsenal, Liverpool, Manchester United, Chelsea are all more than a hundred years old), which provided them with a stable fan base, even in years when the teams weren't winning. What's more, in contrast to the Twenty20 IPL, the English league constitutes the true apex and classic form of the game at its most competitive and demanding. That's a major part of what makes its product so attractive. And it does so not only by buying in stars but by nurturing homegrown talent through a network of youth squads, reserve teams and coaching clinics.

Before plunging head first into IPL-mania, cricket fans should consider the down side in the comparison with the English Premier League, which has become widely associated with venality and dishonesty, on and off the field. There have been extensive allegations of bribery and corruption, many highlighting dubious trade-offs between agents and managers. The newspapers are full of the pathetic misbehaviour of over-paid, under-educated 20-year old football stars, and the public is not amused.

The danger is that the IPL will emulate the worst of English football, and not only in its paper thin culture of instant celebrity. As the football clubs have developed into big businesses, dedicated to the maximum exploitation of the product, they have grown more remote from the people supporting the game. Ticket prices have soared, merchandising is relentless, corporate hospitality rules.

Increasingly, the owners treat the teams as disposable assets, one part of a larger portfolio. Liverpool FC was bought last year by two US businessmen, Tom Hicks and George Gillett, both major donors to George Bush's campaign coffers. Now they are at war with each other over an attempt by Gillett to sell the club to Dubai International Capital, the investment arm of the Dubai government.

The English Premier League came into existence in 1992 when the then first division clubs seceded from the Football League. It's not hard to imagine that the IPL franchises might at some point declare their own independence from the BCCI, arguing, as did the English elite clubs, that as they were generating the profits, they should call the shots, not least by cutting their own deals with broadcasters.

At least in Britain the football fans have well-organised supporters associations, rooted in long-term loyalty to their club of choice, and can sometimes make their voices heard and put pressure on owners. The IPL will have nothing like that.

The auction made it clear that commercial values are not the same as cricketing values, and that the franchise owners' calculations reflect priorities other than putting a winning team on the field. The million-plus bids for Mahendra Singh Dhoni and Andrew Symonds, for example, cannot be explained entirely by their cricketing prowess; clearly their celebrity pulling power enhanced their commercial value: Dhoni as Indian captain and fashion icon, and Symonds as pantomime villain. Ishant Sharma, an exciting prospect but as yet without a single Twenty20 international under his belt, was bought for $950,000 by Kolkata, while Umar Gul – the highest wicket taker in last year's inaugural Twenty20 World Cup – was snapped up by the same team for a mere $150,000. Yusuf Pathan, with only one Twenty20 international to his credit, was bought for $450,000, while Matthew Hayden went for $375,000 and Younis Khan for a bargain $225,000. Cricketers are securing rewards according to their perceived enhancement of the value of the franchise, which is not the same as enhancement of the cricket team.

The creation of the IPL, like other privatisations, has meant an instant windfall for the sellers, in this case the BCCI, thanks to franchise sales, broadcast and sponsorship takings. 'To date we have made $1.749 billion,' declared Lalit Modi, Vice President of the BCCI and chairman of the IPL. But that's not quite the case. To date the BCCI have signed agreements worth that amount, all to be paid over a period of years. But 64 per cent of all central rights money (broadcasting, sponsorship, etc.) goes to the franchises. The SET broadcast rights deal has netted each of them some $5.5 million – a revenue stream guaranteed regardless of the quality of the product on offer.

This vaunted triumph of the free market proves, on examination, to be less about what Adam Smith called 'the invisible hand' and more about a sleight-of-hand, a collusion between public authorities and private interests. For a start, the franchises themselves do not operate in a free market, since each one is guaranteed a monopoly in its respective city, which is not at all the case in English football.

'Our clear focus in designing the league has been to maximise the value of the team owners,' explained Balu Nayar of the International Management Group, the sports management firm working with the BCCI on IPL. In addition to guaranteed revenue streams and monopoly control of markets, the private owners enjoy the right to exploit a variety of public assets at little cost. State associations are facilitating the IPL by providing stadia and players, but it's been made clear that the usual rights of members and affiliated associations will not apply to IPL games. The Ranji Trophy will recede even further from public view. And if the IPL franchises do not prove to be the expected money spinners, the owners will cut and run – an option that is not open to the state associations.

The IPL does not really aim to be a people's sport, as it was understood in the past. The target demographic is people in their twenties and thirties with above average disposable incomes, a growing group but still a minority. Franchise profits will depend less on general ticket sales than on in-stadia advertising, local sponsorships, corporate hospitality, merchandising and licensing. Owners will also measure the success of the cricket venture by its contribution to corporate synergy. Reliance and United Breweries (owners of the Mumbai and Bangalore franchises) will certainly aim to integrate the team within their larger strategies and use it whenever possible to enhance sales of other products and boost the corporate image in general.

Modi has claimed that the money IPL brings into the game will help improve infrastructure. This is said whenever the BCCI strikes a new deal, but at the base of the game the results materialise, at best, in a slow trickle of funds. The biggest factor holding back Indian cricket remains the difficulty of access to coaching, quality competition and decent facilities. The IPL franchises are under no obligation to develop the game as a whole, and are more likely to exacerbate the maldistribution of resources by drawing them into the eight metros involved in the league. When the BCCI or the state associations make a profit, in theory at least it is ploughed back into the game. But in the IPL the profits generated will belong to the franchise owners. So money will actually be taken out of the game.

The Twenty20 World Cup was a smash, but reproducing that kind of excitement day after day for 16 weeks may prove difficult. There must be doubt about whether a steady diet of Twenty20 will win the hearts, minds and pocketbooks of cricket fans. So much of what makes cricket distinctive and appealing is missing from it: the simmering duels between batsman and bowler, the architecture of a century, the variations in tempo and the variety of skills. There's no room in Twenty20 for the genius of a Tendulkar to be fully distinguished from the talent of a lesser light.

For most players, the payment for one Twenty20 IPL match will be many times what they could expect to earn from a full five-day Test match. In the long run, the imbalance is bound to force Test cricket to the margins. This is something almost no one actually wants to see, yet we will be told that it is merely bowing to popular demand. Like other forms of dumbing-down, it's actually driven not by the wishes of the consumer but by the convenience of those doing the dumbing-down. Higher standards cost more money.

The IPL development has been described as 'inevitable', even by those who find it unappealing. This is a sad surrender to the myth that commercial forces are ineluctable, like forces of nature, and it's a mistake to try to hold them back. In fact, the IPL, like other privatisations, is the result of policy, and reflects the power of the narrow social strata that benefits from it. There are alternatives, but they haven't been considered. For example, Barcelona, one of the world's most glamorous football franchises, is a co-operative, owned by local members who elect its officials.

Blazed across the headlines, the startling figures paid for the star players were hailed as testimony to the power of the new Indian market. The IPL profile fits snugly with the self-image of India's elite and their middle-class emulators. The big rewards for the cricketers re-enforce the 'aspirational' individualism which the corporate media promotes, and in which the only aspiration apparent is to make more money for oneself. In the millenial hype surrounding the auction, the disparity between the players' exorbitant remuneration and the income of the majority in India was rarely commented upon. What message do these super-salaries send out about what's valued and what's not in Indian society? People are urged to see the triumphs of the Indian elite – such as IPL buying up the cream of world cricket – as the country's triumphs. An Indian businessman makes an acquisition in Britain or the USA and it's as if Tendulkar had scored a century for India. Status by proxy is offered as a substitute for real empowerment.

Indian cricket is a cultural institution created over many decades by cricketers and cricket-lovers. It's only because of their efforts that the BCCI and the new franchise owners have a product and a market to exploit. Like so many other social activities and public spaces, cricket is being commodifed, and ordinary cricket fans should pause before joining the celebrations.

A LEVEL PLAYING FIELD?: GLOBAL SPORT IN THE NEO-LIBERAL AGE

First published in 2014, the year of the FIFA World Cup in Brazil.

One of the hallmarks of the neo-liberal age has been the exponential expansion of commercial spectator sport – in its economic value, political role and cultural presence. All of which will be thrown into high relief during the coming World Cup. In recent years, the industry has grown in all regions above the local GDP rate, and is estimated to have generated $135 billion in direct revenues in 2013. These revenues derive from four elements: gate receipts, corporate sponsorship, media rights and merchandising. Revenues from sponsorship and media rights have grown fastest and together now make up over half of total revenue. But whereas in North America and Europe gate receipts remain the single biggest source of revenue, in the BRIC counties and in Asia as a whole sponsorship is now the biggest money-spinner, accounting in China for 48 per cent of total sports revenues. Meanwhile, though merchandising is marginal in most of the world, it is significant in North America, where it accounts for 25 per cent of revenues.

Despite its growth, the sports industry, narrowly defined, is still dwarfed by the pharmaceutical ($1.1 trillion a year) and automotive ($1.8 trillion) sectors. But direct revenues tell only a part of the story. Sport is interwoven with other industries: footwear, sportswear, soft drinks, advertising, among others. It's a central driver in media industries – print, broadcast and digital. And it's critical to the gambling industry, legal and illegal, with betting on sports estimated to be worth between $700bn and $1tn a year.

Sport has become a fertile zone of capitalist intersection and mutual aggrandisement. It should therefore not be surprising that it has also become a major carrier of neo-liberal ideology, used to promote a competitive individualism in which the pursuit of victory and success is presented as the purest form of personal self-expression. Nike is the obvious example, with its injunctions to 'just do it' and 'risk everything' and its strategic linkage to sports superstars. What is celebrated is a 'triumph of the will' – in which adverse circumstances are made to bow to individual desire. It's a version of what has been described as 'magical voluntarism', identified by Mark Fisher as a key component of today's dominant ideology.

It needs to be said that this ethos of egocentric assertion is by no means inherent in sport, which is not about 'the law of the jungle' or a 'war of all against all'. On the contrary, it's a competitive activity built on a cooperative basis, requiring mutual agreement among competitors and between competitors and spectators. And it is intensely regulated; in fact, without the regulation, the sport vanishes. Team sports, of course, set a premium on interdependence and a willingness to sacrifice individual priorities for the good of the collective. But even the most successful individual competitors are what they are only because they enjoy a network of personal and social support. No one can ever 'just do it' on their own.

One of the favourite metaphors of advocates of capitalist globalisation is borrowed directly from sports. They hunger for a world-wide 'level playing field' in which competition flourishes freely and fairly. However, as in so many spheres, the impact of neo-liberal globalisation on sport itself has been to create an increasingly uneven playing field, marked by widening inequalities.

As the major male sports swallow an ever increasing share of sports revenues and investment, other sports are pushed to the margin. In South Asia, cricket is so dominant that it has rendered hockey, at which India and Pakistan excelled for decades, nearly invisible. While women's sports have enjoyed increased revenues in absolute terms, the growth of male sports means that women still receive only 0.5 per cent of corporate sports sponsorship.

Elite male European football now accounts for more than 35 per cent of global sports revenues; a similar share goes to the Big Four North American team sports (baseball, basketball, ice hockey and American football). Within European football, the five biggest leagues comprise half the total market and the top 20 teams one-quarter of that market.

The English Premier League breakaway in the early '90s has proved to be a watershed. The big clubs' main motive was to maximise their share of broadcasting revenues. Since then, the tendency has been for the rich teams to get richer, while the rest face perpetual insecurity. In effect, the billionaire-backed clubs are now hoarding the best players, making it even harder for others to compete with them. UEFA has introduced its Financial Fair Play rules in an attempt to restrain the growing inequality, but they are unlikely to affect the overall imbalance.

Meanwhile, European football recruits extensively from Latin America and Africa, whose domestic competitions are thereby weakened. Compounding the talent drain, globalised broadcasting has in many regions made Europe's big clubs more famous and more widely followed than local teams.

The general trend towards a concentration of wealth and power is neatly illustrated by recent events in world cricket. Earlier this year, the three richest cricket boards – India, England and Australia – combined forces to impose a new order on the ICC, the game's governing body. From now on the Big Three will take home a larger share of the game's global revenues, dictate unilaterally which other teams they'll play and how often, and wield an effective veto on all ICC decisions. There's also a plan to introduce a two division structure for Test cricket, with a telling wrinkle in the scheme: none of the Big Three are ever to be relegated to the second division. So their standing in the competition will be guaranteed not by the quality of their cricket but by their financial clout.

Unpredictability and spontaneity are at the heart of sports, and they are at odds with the capitalist drive to maximise profits and eliminate variables. An extreme example is bookmakers who seek to fix results, thus guaranteeing the return on their investment. But sponsors too would prefer some WWE-like scripted entertainment: no annoying upsets or injuries or mysterious losses of form to compromise their projections. The problem for them is that their property would forfeit all value should it be seen to be scripted.

So there's a tension between capitalist imperatives and sporting imperatives. In fact, the whole idea of sports competition as a mirror or metaphor for capitalist competition is misconceived. The 'level playing field' in sport is constituted by a rigid scaffolding of rules without which the competition dissolves. Capitalism's version is a deregulated arena of limitless accumulation. The aim of capitalist competition is to eliminate (or acquire) the competitor. In sport, you need the opponent to survive and return for the next match or season, which always begins the contest afresh. And of course, what's at stake in the two types of competition is fundamentally different. The penalties for coming second do not compare.

All the contradictions of commercial spectator sport will be on display, in heightened form, in this year's World Cup. Dave Zirin, in his invaluable new book, *Brazil's Dance with the Devil*, shows how this sporting mega-event has become a carnival of state-sponsored neo-liberalism, characterised by mass evictions, gentrification, increased repression and surveillance, vast expenditure on redundant facilities and corporate plundering of public funds. It's a boon for the construction, property, security and media industries, but a bane for many others, as was demonstrated last year, when huge numbers of Brazilians took to the streets to protest against the World Cup priorities that have skewed the country's development.

World Cup boosters claim that once the competition is underway and 'the ball is rolling' all the discontents will vanish. What's certain is that there will be a concerted effort to convince us that this is so. Those who persist in talking about the social cost underlying the festivities will be condemned as killjoys and nay-sayers. We are cast as consumers and nothing but consumers, expected to imbibe the corporate-branded spectacle without qualms or conscience. In that context, engaging critically with sports, seeing them as part of the broader human current, becomes a necessary subversive act. FIFA and its corporate partners have a vested interest in promoting tunnel vision, but the rest of us do not. Enjoyment of the football and critique of its context can and should go hand in hand. The idea that one excludes the other is a myth we need to shed.

4

WANDERING IN THE SUBCONTINENT — INDIA AND PAKISTAN

INDIA'S TRYST WITH THE DEATH PENALTY

First published in 2006.

[Note: Muhammed Afzal Guru was sentenced to death by hanging for his alleged role in the attack on the Indian Parliament on 13 December 2001. He was due to be executed on 20 October 2006. His execution was stayed, but a subsequent mercy petition was refused and he was hanged on 9 February 2013.]

In 1793, the French Convention was debating the fate of the deposed and imprisoned king, Louis XVI. Thomas Paine, an Englishman who had already played a key role in fomenting the American Revolution, and whose epochal book, *Rights of Man*, had made him a criminal in his native land, rose to address the assembly.

'Citizen President,' he began, 'my hatred of and aversion to monarchy are well known. They are based on reason and on conviction, and you would have to take my life before you could eradicate them.' But, he went on, he would not and could not support the proposal to execute the former king. 'Since France has been the first of all the nations in Europe to abolish royalty, let her be also the first to abolish the penalty of death, and to substitute for it some other punishment.'

Paine spoke as a proud 'citizen of the world', and in this instance, as in many others, as a voice for the fully human civilisation that we have yet to achieve. In contrast, the voices crying themselves hoarse for the hanging of Afzal Guru speak for the residues of inhumanity, and if they are heeded, a primary condition for the existence of civilised society – respect for the sanctity of human life – will have been profoundly undermined. The claim that the execution of Afzal Guru is required by the 'collective conscience' of the nation insults and compromises that conscience. Yes, no doubt, this is a death that many millions in India would welcome and some would celebrate. But the word 'conscience' is here grossly misapplied to a cocktail of bloodlust, bigotry and vindictiveness. It is the duty of the judiciary to act as a check on this mentality; instead, the court has legitimised it, and in doing so, has made the citizens of India less secure and less free.

It is often forgotten that the ancient injunction of an 'eye for an eye' was in its day an attempt to restrict inequitable punishments, to ensure that *no more* than an eye was taken for an eye. Since then, one hopes, our ideas about what constitutes justice have become more refined. In particular, it is generally recognised that the use of punishment to appease public demand is itself a species of injustice and inimical to democracy. To quote Paine again, 'an avidity to punish is always dangerous to liberty'. Or, as The Temptations put it in their soul masterpiece of 1969, 'Ball of Confusion': 'an eye for an eye, a tooth for a tooth...vote for me and I'll set you free.'

The recognition of human fallibility is a fundamental argument for the rule of law. The irremediable nature of the death penalty makes it incompatible with that rule.

In Britain in the mid 1970s, in response to the Irish Republican Army's terrorist campaign, many civil liberties were sacrificed, but the British Parliament did at least resist calls for the reinstatement of the death penalty, which had been abolished a decade earlier. As a result, though they were found guilty of horrific crimes of mass murder, the people known as the Birmingham Six and the Guildford Four were not put to death. They served 14-17 years in prison before their innocence was finally established and accepted by the courts – but at least they were still alive and could be released to enjoy their freedom and their vindication.

There is already far more doubt about Afzal Guru's guilt than there was about the guilt of the Birmingham Six or Guildford Four at the time of their convictions. If Afzal Guru is put to death, and evidence of his innocence subsequently emerges, there will be no way to rectify the error. That is why Moses Maimonides, the 12th century Arab Jewish theologian, argued, 'It is better and more satisfactory to acquit a thousand guilty persons than to put a single innocent man to death.'

India's use of the death penalty is of course far more restrained than the US's (not to speak of China's). But with eagerness to emulate US society currently so widespread in India, it is worth noting that the US experience shows that the death penalty is no deterrent to violent crime, and especially not to terrorist crime.

In the ten years from 1997 to the end of 2006, the US executed 700 convicted criminals (already, since the new year, another seven have been killed). However, not all US states have the death penalty, and in those states which do not, the murder rate is substantially and consistently lower than in those which do. Some research also indicates that executions (or more precisely, the publicity attending them) actually increases the number of murders. Globally, the murder and violent crime rate in the US is on average three times higher than in European countries that have abolished the death penalty.

By commuting the sentence on Afzal Guru and going on to abolish the death penalty altogether, India has the chance to join a growing vanguard of progressive and democratic nations. Eighty-eight countries have now abolished capital punishment; 30 others have not used it for ten years. Since 1990, more than 40 countries have abolished the death penalty, including South Africa, Mexico, the Philippines, Turkey, and nearly all countries in Eastern Europe. Abolition of the death penalty is a precondition for membership of the European Union, and European and other states will not extradite terrorist suspects to the US if they are to face the death penalty there.

Italy has announced that it will use its current term on the Security Council to promote a global ban on the death penalty. In doing so it has the support of a majority of UN member-states as well as all those working worldwide to enhance respect for human rights. In contrast, the execution of Afzal Guru is bound to undermine India's reputation and specifically its campaign for a permanent seat on the Council – unless, of course, it's been decided that this campaign is exclusively dependent on Washington's sponsorship.

Whatever he may be guilty of, Afzal has not been accused of being either a direct participant or a major conspirator in the 2001 attack on Parliament. The murder of 2,000 Indian citizens in Gujarat in 2002 was, by any realistic standards, a more severe and damaging attack on the fabric of Indian democracy. Yet prominent individuals whose complicity in that crime is far more direct and more clearly established than Afzal Guru's complicity in the attack on Parliament remain unpunished, and indeed have yet to be brought before a court of law.

There is no excuse for the premeditated and avoidable physical destruction of a human being. That applies as much to States as to individuals. In fact, the State especially, as the guardian of the right to life, betrays its fundamental trust when it executes one of its own. Here one sees not the majesty of the law, but its opposite: the obscenity of legally sanctioned murder. The upshot is that society is coarsened, reckless authority is emboldened and respect for human life is decreased.

LIFE-CHANGING HAPPENSTANCE: DISCOVERING INDIA

First published in 2009.

2009 will be marked by the usual crop of anniversaries. Twenty years since the fall of the Berlin Wall, 200 years since the death of Tom Paine, 40 years since Woodstock, and on a micro-scale, 30 years since my first visit to India. A life-changing event for me, as it turned out.

Like so many critical turning points, it came about by accident. Or rather accident combined with some long-held yearning for remote places, different people. I was vaguely planning a camping trip in Scotland with my brother. Then a friend returned from a trekking holiday in Nepal and his tales sparked my imagination. Without preparation, without knowledge, (without visas!) my brother and I set off on Afghan Airlines, stopping in Amsterdam, Frankfurt, Ankara, Tehran and Kabul before landing in a hazy late summer heatwave in Delhi.

Trekking in Nepal was joyful, but it was India that overwhelmed and captivated me. I felt compelled to know and understand more – so much was busily opaque – and I began to read, to ask questions, all the while searching out new landscapes. The most memorable was Hampi, in Karnataka, the remnants of the medieval Vijayanagar capital. It was and still is one of world's most haunting archaeological sites, its ruins sleeping majestically by the limpid Tunghabadra. I spent what felt like a timeless fortnight there roaming the temples, watching the sunset cast the great boulders in a rosy glow, and reading Basham's *The Wonder That Was India*.

Unfortunately my passport was stolen in Hampi and I found myself making another unplanned excursion, to Madras, as it then was. This too was to become a significant way-station for me. While waiting around to get the document replaced, I explored the city, which at first seemed to have a curiously old-fashioned air. Mount Road, as I remember it, was much less choked than now and there were still venerable shopfronts on either side. Triplicaine was what drew me in: it was old yet alive. And I began the arduous task of getting to grips with the idiosyncratic politics of Tamil Nadu.

Out of that visit came the germ of my first book, about a cricket tour in India with a climax at Chepauk Stadium, and beyond that, an abiding interest in Tamil history and eventually a love affair with Carnatic music (and a column in *The Hindu*). When I think how many hours of pleasurable wonder that music has given me, it seems incredible that I could so easily have missed out on the whole experience – had my passport not been stolen in Hampi.

Since that eye- and mind-jolting initial journey, I've returned to South Asia as often as possible; more frequently as the years went on and more opportunities presented themselves. I wandered widely, learning as I went, and met people who became among my closest friends. I'd be incomplete without them.

I've seen India in stress. I was in Delhi days after the assassination of Indira Gandhi and in the midst of the anti-Sikh pogrom. I was visiting again in early 1993 when communal thuggery raged in Bombay. And in 1994, when the plague hit Surat, and the streets of Delhi were full of people selling useless surgical masks and fake prophylactic medications.

And of course I've seen the cricket. 30 years ago, I arrived in the wake of Sunil Gavaskar's great double hundred at the Oval, and found that topic an easy entry-point to conversation with Indians. Since then I've witnessed international cricket at the great venues (and was lucky enough to catch Azharuddin's maiden Test century at Eden Gardens) and observed Indian cricket transmogrified. Best of all, I've stared mesmerised at countless games of informal cricket, on maidans and in galis, on industrial waste ground, palmy beaches and once on the verge of a precipice high in Lahaul. It was truly six-and-out.

Amid all the precious memories – the dome of Sanchi in a saffron dusk, the twin Muslim-Hindu shrines to Kabir in Magahar, 'that cursed place' – much of what I've seen in India over the decades has disturbed and angered me. Liberalisation's inequalities and corruptions; environmental degradation on a scale unimagined 30 years ago; the malign impact of Hindutva and the Sangh Parivar; the bellicosity towards Pakistan, now going through another acute and perilous phase. When I first encountered this phenomenon in 1979 I was shocked by its ferocity and cynicism, its vain chauvinism, and I still am.

India proved a jumping off point for Pakistan – walking through a mist across an eerily quiet Wagah border – and my visits there proved eye-opening and hugely rewarding. Among other things, they expanded my understanding of India. If I had one piece of advice for a young Indian with an itch to travel it would be: get yourself to Pakistan, overcoming if you can all the obstacles that will be put in your path.

Travel actually doesn't always broaden the mind, especially not these days, when it can be so easy: the transition from one environment to another is softened, sometimes obliterated in the air-con. I met a wealthy American lady who'd been globe-trotting for years – through Europe, Asia and South America – and all she could talk about was the various but universally unsatisfactory toilet conditions she had encountered.

As for me, I'll be celebrating this 30th anniversary with gratitude and some surprise at my luck. My experiences in South Asia have shaped and (I like to think) widened my understanding of the world. My writing, political activism and personal life would all have been different had I not bumped into that friend on his way back from a holiday trek in Nepal.

Finally, a footnote plea to the Indian tourism industry (which I know will fall on deaf ears). Forget about swelling the ranks of five-star hotels and concentrate on preserving and creating access to the country's cultural patrimony.

For a society in which 'heritage' and debates about it readily acquire acute political resonance, India displays a remarkable indifference to its actual, physically existing heritage. Despite the efforts of the ASI, innumerable sites of historic and cultural interest are neglected or inaccessible. Urban quarters of distinctive character are crushed beneath bulldozers or smothered in pollution. In small towns, statues of freedom fighters stand forlorn, chipped and scuffed, their achievements left unexplained. The heart sinks at what's been lost in Calcutta in recent years. Yes, many old buildings were in severe dilapidation. But demolition wasn't and isn't the only alternative. Other cities with rotting inner areas have shown that restoration and imaginative renewal can work. The problem is that this is not an attractive proposition for greedy developers.

5

BEHIND MANY PIOUS PHRASES – NATIONALISM, IMPERIALISM AND INTERNATIONALISM

FREE SPEECH AND THE WAR ON TERROR

Originally published in 2005, the year of the 7/7 London bombings.

Two pieces of legislation currently wending their way through Britain's Parliament illustrate how the war on terror is being used to dismantle the very freedoms it's supposed to secure. Both criminalise the expression of ideas and neither is likely to deal effectively with the problem it purports to address. They are opportunistic gambits, characteristic of a government whose moralistic bombast is in inverse proportion to the morality of its behaviour.

In the wake of the 7 July London bombings, the Labour government introduced yet another anti-terror bill (its third in five years). So extreme were its provisions that even normally supine backbench Labour MPs rebelled. A proposal to allow police to detain terrorist suspects without charge for up to 90 days was defeated – though the compromise measure allowing 28 days detention still represented a doubling of the existing limit.

Even in its amended form, the bill contains an insidious clause creating a new offence of 'encouragement of terrorism' which will outlaw any statement that 'glorifies' terrorism. Speeches, books, films, DVDs, CDs, websites, 'images' as well as words, will all be subject to the new ban, which will apply to the 'glorification' of either specific terrorrist acts or 'acts of terrorism in general', 'whether in the past, in the future or generally', and whether or not the 'glorification' was intentional or inadvertent. Those who publish or disseminate offensive statements are as liable as those who make them.

Given the government's murky definition of terrorism (the use or threat of violence 'for the purpose of advancing a political, religious or ideological cause', whether in the UK or abroad), the range of statements that could theoretically fall foul of the new law is alarming. Verbal support for the Iraqi resistance or for the Palestinian intifada. Any laudatory account of the Zionist bombing campaign against the British in the 1940s or of Nelson Mandela's courtroom defence of his right to use violence against the apartheid regime in the 1960s. A poster of Malcolm X with his slogan 'by any means necessary'. A Che Guevara tee shirt. Celebrations of Bhagat Singh, whose birth centenary falls in 2007. A film, song or work of fiction that offers a sympathetic portrait of a suicide bomber.

In reality, the most likely targets of the legislation are Muslim extremists, the 'preachers of hate' highlighted by the British media. The rhetoric deployed by these people is loathsome, but it has as much right to protection as other offensive, irresponsible or idiotic discourses. If the law is passed and clerics who praise suicide bombers are arrested, Muslims will rightly ask why it is that those who 'encourage' or 'glorify' the slaughter of their co-religionists in Iraq and Palestine are not likewise charged.

The new clause will add nothing useful to the police's armory. It is already a criminal offence to incite terrorism (incitement, unlike glorification, is an established and relatively well-defined legal concept). In fact, the bill is likely to feed the extremists, who will be able to portray themselves as martyrs to Western double-standards. The government knows all this but couldn't care less. It is desperate to deny or obfuscate the connection between Britain's participation in the Iraq war and the targeting of London. As is clear from the comments made by the bombers and people in their circle, the perpetrators were moved to mass murder not by anything they heard in a mosque but by what they saw on mainstream television.

While the government takes with one hand, it gives with the other, or so it would like the Muslim community to believe. In an attempt to stop the haemorrhage of Muslim voters alienated by war and attacks on civil liberties, New Labour is pushing, concurrently with its anti-terrorism package, a bill to outlaw 'incitement to religious hatred'. Under this proposal, it will be an offence to utter or publish 'threatening, abusive or insulting' statements (in any media) 'likely to stir up religious hatred'. The offence would be committed regardless of the intent of the alleged perpetrator – so long as it could be shown that religious hatred was 'likely in all the circumstances' to be stirred up.

While no one has the right to threaten or abuse individuals because of their religious affiliation, people do have the right to to criticise, even to mock or insult, any and all belief systems. The proposed law fails to make that critical distinction. Under its provisions, it would be possible to make a case for the prosecution of a disturbingly wide array of books or films, from Tom Paine's *Age of Reason* to Monty Python's *Life of Brian* to Salman Rushdie's *Satanic Verses* to the Bible or indeed the Quran, both of which contain denunciations of non-believers. Periyar's attacks on Hinduism would make him a serial violator. Self-appointed guardians of orthodoxy in any number of faiths could use the legislation to harass dissidents within their own communities. And it's easy to see how it could be deployed against critics of Israel, who are routinely accused of fomenting anti-Semitism.

No one should underestimate the hatred, violence and injustice poured on Muslims in the UK. They are subject to verbal and physical assaults. Their mosques are defaced. They are harassed by police. Members of their community are arbitrarily searched, arrested and detained. Their religion is distorted and vilified, not only in the right-wing anti-immigrant press, but also in more liberal organs. Routinely, the entire Muslim population is placed on trial and considered guilty until it proves itself innocent; Muslims are asked again and again to demonstrate their willingness to 'integrate' and their commitment to 'British values'.

It's not surprising therefore that many within the Muslim community have welcomed the government's religious hatred bill. Sadly, however, it will do nothing to relieve their distress. It will not curb the most powerful fomenters of Islamophobia – the state and the mainstream media. It will not increase anyone's security from assault by bigots. There is already sufficient legislation on the books to enable police to act against anyone threatening or harassing people because they are Muslims or attacking Muslims as a group. What's missing in most cases is the will to take action under the law. And what's really needed to establish legal equality among believers and non-believers of every stripe is the abolition of the blasphemy laws – which protect only Christianity – and the disestablishment of the Church of England.

Both these bills use the pretext of real traumas – terrorist attack and religious hatred – to circumscribe the freedom of opinion with which the government is so evidently uncomfortable. They are attempts at managing appearances, ploys through which Blair and his cabinet seek to evade responsibility for the violence and bigotry spawned by their own policies.

IMPERIAL WHITEWASH

First published in 2006.

As of November last year, anyone applying for British citizenship has to pass a test demonstrating both proficiency in English and 'sufficient knowledge of life in the United Kingdom'. In preparation for the test, applicants are asked to study a booklet that begins with a brief history of Britain. Sanctioned and published by the Home Office, this is the closest we have to an 'official' history, though it was written by an individual, Professor Bernard Crick, political commentator and biographer of Orwell.

Crick disclaims any official status for his 9,000-word essay and states clearly:

> Any account of British history, whether long or short, is an interpretation. No one person would agree with another what to put in, what to leave out, and how to say it.

Nonetheless, his text drew fire from historians, who noted a host of embarrassing errors. Crick misquotes Churchill, misrepresents the Magna Carta, and wrongly asserts that the Massacre of Glencoe took place before the Battle of the Boyne and that unemployment 'vanished' after 1945.

Some of the omissions seem indefensible. There are 210 words on the end of the Highland clans in 1745 but not a single one about the Chartists, the rise of the trade union movement or the general strike of 1926; there is a relatively lengthy account of the Thatcher years – more than 300 words – but no mention of the Falklands War, inner-city riots or the miners' strike of 1984-85, surely one of modern Britain's watershed events.

What is most disturbing, however, is the treatment of the British empire. While the Atlantic slave trade is condemned unequivocally as 'evil', the empire is given a positive gloss:

> For many indigenous peoples in Africa, the Indian subcontinent, and elsewhere, the British empire often brought more regular, acceptable and impartial systems of law and order ... The spread of English helped unite disparate tribal areas ... Public health, peace, and access to education can mean more to ordinary people than precisely who are their rulers.

It is noted that the British did not try to impose Christianity on India, which leads to the observation that 'the English tolerance of different national cultures in the United Kingdom itself may have influenced the character of their imperial rule in India.' So, apparently, there was no policy of divide and rule and no racial discrimination against the natives.

There's not a single mention of the empire carrying out acts of repression or exploitation – anywhere, ever; no mention of the famines that killed millions in British-ruled India; and, crucially, not a word about resistance to empire, except for a passing reference to 'liberation or self-government movements that had been growing in India in the 1930s'. In Crick's account, the empire came to a peaceful end after the Second World War simply because the British public was not interested in it and 'the Labour party believed in establishing self-government in the former colonies.'

But the empire did not quietly expire in 1947. British forces waged wars against insurgents in Malaya (from 1948 to 1960), Cyprus (1955 to 1959) and Aden (1963 to 1967). Between 1952 and 1956, the British suppressed the Mau Mau rebellion in Kenya at horrific cost (the minimum estimate is 12,000 dead, but some studies claim more than 100,000). In 1953 and again in 1962, British troops were used to sabotage democracy in Guyana. And in 1956, Britain joined France and Israel in attacking Egypt in an attempt to repossess the Suez Canal. After that, Britain became a subordinate power to the US, and in that capacity is still deeply enmeshed in the military and economic coercion of people in foreign lands.

The great majority of those who will take the new citizenship test come from countries once ruled by the British or other European empires, and their view of empire is likely to be better informed and more critical than Crick's. What is also worrying is that his kid-glove approach is part of a wider trend, in which right-wing commentators like Niall Fergusson and Robert Kaplan have sought to resuscitate the idea of imperial rule, ignoring or minimising its ill effects while exaggerating its beneficence.

Very few Britons are aware that their country occupied Egypt in 1882 and remained its de facto ruler for 72 years, during which time its economy was profoundly distorted; or that between 1899 and 1920 Britain waged a savage campaign against the Dervish uprising in Somalia, wiping out one third of the population, 100,000 souls.

With 8,000 British troops currently fighting insurgents in Iraq and another 4,000 doing the same in Afghanistan, ignorance of imperial history and attempts to whitewash that history are of more than academic concern. This is not about asking people to feel guilt for the sins of the past; it is about ensuring that today's British citizens are equipped to analyse and contextualise their government's policies.

Because of Kipling and the Great Game, there is some awareness that Britain has been in Afghanistan before. But few have more than a fuzzy idea of the three Anglo-Afghan Wars (1839-42, 1878-80 and 1919), in each of which British forces sought to impose Britain's will on a recalcitrant people, exacting and suffering substantial casualties before being forced to retreat.

Fewer still know of Britain's previous adventures in Iraq. Using Indian soldiers, the British occupied Mesopotamia in 1918 and stayed there, effectively, until 1958. A national revolt in 1920 was put down with the utmost brutality, involving the use of poison gas and the relentless terror bombing of mud, stone and reed villages. In a single year, the RAF dropped 97 tonnes of ordnance, killing some 9,000 Iraqis for the loss of only nine soldiers. The rebellion nevertheless continued for a decade, as did the punitive bombing raids, under the command of Arthur Harris, who was to mastermind the 1945 firebombing of Dresden, which took 35,000 lives.

Harris's statue stands today in London's Fleet Street. Alas, nowhere in Britain is there a memorial to Air Commodore Lionel Charlton, who resigned from his post in 1924 after visiting a hospital and facing the armless and legless victims of British air raids.

Commenting in 1934 on the British and French claim that the 'sole aim' of their appropriation of the old Ottoman possessions in the Middle East was the emancipation of its peoples, Jawaharlal Nehru offered a scathing and still pertinent indictment: 'They shoot and kill and destroy only for the good of the people shot down. The novel feature of the modern type of imperialism is its attempt to hide its terrorism and exploitation behind pious phrases.'

If people in Britain, whether native born or naturalised citizens, are to strip away the pious phrases of today's empire builders, they need a much more realistic account of their past than the one being offered by Professor Crick and the Home Office.

MULTI-CULTURALISM AND THE POLITICS OF WHITE IDENTITY

First published in 2006.

For many years, attacks on 'multi-culturalism' in Britain were confined to the far right, which argued, like its counterparts in other countries, that the nation could only survive if it was homogeneous, welded together by a single racial, religious or cultural identity.

However, since 9/11, 'multi-culturalism' has come under increasing criticism from mainstream and even liberal sources. In recent months, it has been noisily blamed for the emergence of homegrown terrorism and the alleged 'self-segregation' of minority groups, damned as a gateway to moral relativism and social disintegration. Ministers have echoed these notions, and the Government has set up a Commission for Integration and Cohesion, whose remit clearly includes a retreat from 'multi-culturalism.'

It's necessary to surround the term with quotation marks because its use, in Britain at least, is permeated by confusion about its history and meaning.

The anti-racist movements of the 1970s and '80s sought justice, equality and recognition for Britain's growing non-white populations. The slogan 'Here to stay, here to fight' summed up both the unequivocal claim on full human rights, and the determination to achieve these through collective struggle. Multi-culturalism emerged as a concession to this movement. While the acceptance of Britain's diversity was a substantial gain – for the victims of racism, as well as for society as a whole – the manner in which multi-cultural policy treated that diversity was always problematic. For that reason it was criticised from the beginning by anti-racist activists.

In time-honoured colonial fashion, this policy conceived ethnic minorities as discreet self-contained entities, neatly demarcated, without inner divisions, and therefore appropriately represented by designated community leaders. The emphasis was on recognition – the visible inclusion of minorities in sports teams, advertising, television dramas, political posters or religious celebrations in schools. In a sense, multi-culturalism has become a victim of its own success. It has made ethnic minorities seem more accepted and more powerful, and racism less prevalent, than they actually are. That's grist to the mills for the racists and a get-out clause for the political establishment.

One of the most depressing features of the current discussion in Britain is that so much of it rests on a false paradigm. 'Multi-culturalism' is counterposed to 'integration', which has replaced the discredited term 'assimilation' but carries similar implications. Behind both terms is a misconception of culture as reified and static, as well as a desire to manage diversity through imposed categories. The choice the paradigm offers is unreal: neither ethnic separatism nor cultural uniformity is either possible or desirable.

Headlines have warned of Britain 'sleep walking' into segregation and 'apartheid', of 'multi-culturalism' breeding ghettos. We are told that the common values necessary for a functioning society are being undermined by an excessive tolerance for cultural diversity.

Even as it grows more strident, the demand for integration becomes hazier. What is it that minorities are being asked to integrate into? When pressed on what they mean by British values, the integrationists are unable to reach beyond platitudes. The question is unanswerable: are British values the values of Sylvia Pankhurst or Winston Churchilll, Tom Paine or the Duke of Wellington, David Bowie or Geoff Boycott?

Meanwhile, the elephant in the sitting room remains unnoticed and unnamed. This is the reality of power, reflected in the assumption of white and Western supremacy and its manifestation in racism.

According to the Home Office, there were more than 40,000 racially- and religiously-aggravated crimes recorded in 2005-06. The vast majority of victims were from ethnic minorities – people with roots in Africa, Asia or the Caribbean. What's more, recorded offences are only a fraction of the total. Research by the charity Victim Support found that most victims of hate crimes suffer in silence. Of the minority who do report offences, only one in five felt supported by police.

Ethnic minorities are more likely than white people both to be victims of crimes (of all types) and to receive harsher punishment when arrested for committing crimes. According to a Prison Reform Trust report, ethnic minority prison staff are more likely to experience racial abuse from their colleagues than from prisoners. An investigation into a racist murder at a young offenders prison has identified 186 official failings and accused authorities of 'institutional religious intolerance'.

Since 9/11, hostility to and discrimination against Muslims and those perceived to be Muslims has multiplied. Under the Terrorism Act 2000, the number of Asians stopped and searched on the streets by police increased from 744 in 2001-02 to 2,989 in 2002-03. In the five weeks following the London bombings in July 2005, the total stopped increased 15-fold; 35 per cent of those stopped in London were Asians, though they make up only 12 per cent of the city's population. Not one of those stopped was charged with a terrorism-related offence. During the same period, London's police reported a six-fold rise in racial attacks – 269 incidents compared to 40 in the same period the year before. In the wake of the alleged air terror plot in August, there's been another spike, including attacks on three mosques.

Despite the statistical reality that ethnic minorities are on the receiving end of abuse and discrimination from their fellow citizens and the state, they are blamed for a failure to integrate. Facts on the ground, however, do not bear out the self-segregation thesis.

According to the latest census, the indices of residential segregation for all ethnic minority groups fell between 1991 and 2001. The index of isolation – measuring how likely people are not to know people from other groups – is highest for white Christians, followed by white people with no religion. According to CRE studies, 95 per cent of white Britons do not have a Black or Asian friend and one in four would not want to live near them; in contrast, 60 per cent of Muslims have non-Muslim friends.

The preoccupation with cultural difference disguises the core problem afflicting race relations in Britain: the reluctance of a significant section of the white majority to 'integrate' into Britain's multi-cultural society, to accept its democracy, and the willingness of newspapers and politicians to pander to that reluctance. While condemning the identity politics of minority groups, the attack on multi-culturalism appeals to and bolsters the most powerful form of identity politics at work in Britain today, the identity politics of the white majority, inextricable from long-nurtured assumptions of Western power.

The same government that lectures minorities about democratic values has sought an opt-out from inconvenient clauses in the European Convention on Human Rights and violated the UN Charter (the invasion of Iraq) and Geneva Conventions (torture and attacks on civilians in Iraq and Afghanistan). And the same ministers who lecture the nation about cohesion and integration have presided over growing economic inequality. Their policies have generated vast gulfs in income, differences in daily life far greater than the ones associated with cultural practices. Yes, the population is becoming more segregated – by wealth, which means, inevitably, by health. To cite but one statistic, individuals who are 50-59 years old from the poorest fifth of the population are ten times more likely to die than their contemporaries from the richest fifth.

The attack on multi-culturalism is unfolding within – and serves to mask – the twin pillars of British government policy: the war on terror and corporate-dominated globalisation. Those policies undermine democratic, civil and secular values far more extensively than any cultural differences.

A LOVELY, WORLDLY QUIRK: MADEIRA'S NORTH COAST

First published in 2009.

In 1420, a genuinely epochal event took place on a small, isolated, previously uninhabited island in the Atlantic, some 360 miles west of Morocco. That year, the Portuguese fleet – the most advanced in the world at the time, thanks to Prince Henry the Navigator – located Madeira. Within two years they had established an agricultural colony there.

It was the first great stride in European imperialism, the first of the West's extra-European, extra-Mediterranean possessions, the first overseas colony to be settled and developed for the benefit of the motherland. From the outset, and through its near 600 year history, Madeira's economy and society have played a part in and been dependent on emergent global systems.

After seizing Madeira, the Portuguese ventured further south, rounding Cape Bojador in 1434, taking the Cape Verde islands in 1455, reaching Sierra Leone in 1460, Sao Tome in 1471 and the mouth of the Congo in 1482. With Madeira as their jumping off point, they 'brought into being a coherent economic zone,' observed historian Fernand Braudel, 'based essentially on trade in ivory, malaguetta (a pepper substitute), gold dust and the slave trade'.

In 1488, Bartolomeo Diaz rounded the Cape of Good Hope. Ten years later, Vasco da Gama landed at Calicut, the long-prized wealth of India lay at Portugal's feet, and the historic development of both South Asia and Europe was transformed. Soon after, sailing westward from Madeira, the Portuguese found and appropriated the coast of Brazil.

Little Madeira, barely 30 miles long by 15 miles wide, was the springboard for all this.

Madeira was from the first and remains intrinsically import-export reliant. Initially wheat was cultivated for the mainland market. But by 1460, wheat had been replaced by sugar, introduced by Genoese merchants who had financed sugar plantations from the eastern Mediterranean through Sicily, Spain and Portugal. Along with the sugar came slaves – Arabs, Berbers, West Africans – to work the fields and refineries. For 70 years, Madeira dominated the Western European sugar market. Brazil, however, soon outstripped Madeira, producing greater quantities at lower costs.

Madeira had to find another export crop. It turned to wine, and in so doing created one of the earliest global brand names. In Act II, Scene i of *Henry IV Part I*, Shakespeare has Poins round on Falstaff: 'Jack! How agrees the devil and thee about thy soul, that thou soldest him on Good-Friday last for a cup of Madeira and a cold capon's leg?' The reference is anachronistic – in Falstaff's day there was no Madeira – but it's an indication of the popularity the drink had acquired in Shakespeare's London.

Henry the Navigator had ordered Malvasia vines transported from Crete to Madeira, where they flourished and became known throughout the English-speaking world as Malmsey. Other noble varieties were imported by the Jesuits, an early transnational institution. But what makes Madeira special is the wine-making process unique to the island, which evolved as a result of the wine having to make long sea voyages. The wine is warmed over a period of months, fortified with grape spirits, exposed to oxidation and aged in cask before being bottled, sometime decades later. All of which gives it an exceptional longevity and (in the not so cheap brands) complex taste.

English merchants came to dominate the Madeira wine trade, establishing a long-lasting connection between Madeira and another world system, the British empire. The island's overseas market was secured in 1665 when King Charles II, who had just received Bombay from Portugal as a result of his marriage to Catherine of Braganza, guaranteed Madeira a virtual monopoly on wine shipments to British territories in the New World. In the 18th century, American colonists consumed a quarter of all wine produced on the island each year. The signing of the Declaration of Independence, breaking with the British system and establishing a new one, was toasted in Madeira.

British troops occupied the island during the Napoleonic Wars; British merchants bought land and became the island's leading wine makers. Soon after came the first tourists. The mid-Victorian steamboats that carried holiday-makers from the south of England were the pioneers of package tourism, another globe-entangling phenomenon.

Much of the 20th century was unkind to Madeira, especially the decades of fascist dictatorship, during which the island was neglected. As a result, from the 1940s onward, Madeira experienced decades of mass emigration, disseminating its population into the global labour market. Today Madeirans can be found in the hotel kitchens of the Channel Islands, in the oil fields of Venezuela, and running shops and small businesses across South Africa, where there are said be more Madeirans or descendants of Madeirans than on Madeira itself.

Due to a convoluted last-minute change of plans, I recently found myself on this remarkable speck on the map. I had never thought of Madeira as a travel destination but it proved as surprising and intriguing as its history. It's a singular place. Compact, yet astonishingly diverse. Most of the island is mountainous, rising to craggy peaks and fissuring into deep ravines. It's said to have more than 30 micro-climates, from the tropical to the alpine, and given the rapidity with which the weather changes, sun-chasing-cloud-chasing sun, I believe it.

But it's the profusion of plantlife, especially the flowers that carpet much of the island, changing by the month, that most astounds. There are said to be more than 120 wild plants unique to Madeira. But that's only part of the story. Madeira's outward-facing connections are reflected in the lush vegetation. Bulbs and seeds imported over the centuries from Europe, the Mediterranean, Brazil, South Africa, Australia and India sprouted easily in the rich volcanic soil and spread beyond the island's innumerable gardens. For those in the know, Madeira is said to be a 'phytogeographical' treasure.

Most ravishing of all, for me at least, were the primeval bay laurel forests that still cover some 20 per cent of the island. Several million years ago, such forests blanketed Southern Europe and Northern Africa. Now they can only be explored here: a majestic, mysterious, upward-soaring, downward-plunging density of dark green leaves and ancient thick tree trunks.

Luckily, they can be explored with relative ease thanks to Madeira's unique 500-year old system of *levadas*, narrow aqueducts cut into steep mountain walls, carrying water from the high wet interior to the coastal farms. These make for ideal walking: you can get deep access into remote wilderness with little effort.

Despite the tourist industry, and too many poorly planned, unsightly new developments, Madeira remains a gently ageing, unpretentious backwater. It's a bit of provincial Portugal plonked down on an exotic island. Untidied villages are adorned with black and white Baroque churches (an international style). Agriculture and fishing remain the biggest employers. In places Madeira looks like a last redoubt of the long vanishing European peasantry. There's hardly a tractor or mechanical device in sight. The land is cultivated in tiny plots on steep terraces, and farmers walk to their fields with hoe in hand. The overwhelming majority are small holders or tenants. One third of all arable land is still under the *latifundia* system, controlled by distant landlords. Apart from wine grapes and bananas, production is for local consumption.

Since the granting of regional autonomy following the revolution of 1974, and Portugal's admission to the EU in the eighties, Madeira has grown more prosperous, if also more unequal. The island is now ringed by a coastal expressway, as a result of which journeys that used to take two days along the old winding mountain roads can be completed in under an hour. A Free Trade Zone has been established and it's hoped the island will become an offshore banking centre, though it may well be too late for Madeira to cash in on that particular world cycle.

Madeira is a quirk, a lovely quirk. But it's a quirk made possible by its integration into a succession of wider horizons. The most famous Madeiran of this or any other era is one Cristiano Ronaldo, currently of Manchester United. Like the wine, he's become a global brand, an icon of a competitive world system.

CONTESTING WHITE SUPREMACY

First published in June 2010.

Back in August, in the wake of BNP success in the Euro-elections, *Red Pepper* ran a debate about anti-fascist strategy. Although a good start to a necessary discussion, too much of it was polarised between an attack on and a defence of existing strategies and structures. While these have to be debated, we won't get far unless we widen and deepen our perspective.

What exactly does the BNP represent and what dangers does it pose? Here our reliance on the model of the thirties has limitations. Thirties fascisms grew and ultimately achieved power in response to a threat from the left, specifically from organised workers. State corporatism and imperial expansion – the hallmarks of those fascisms – have little do do with the ideology, appeal or the likely effect of today's far right. In the current context the BNP's main impact is, first, to intimidate minority communities, and second, to drag the centre of political gravity to the right. As we've seen in the recent election, the major parties seek to pre-empt the BNP by adopting anti-immigrant policies and rhetoric.

All the contributors to the RP debate argue that at least one of the necessary responses to the BNP is to build social alternatives, to mobilise on community issues and thereby bring together the people the far right wish to divide. While that is certainly necessary, it begs some questions.

I think we're kidding ourselves if we believe a BNP vote is merely a misdirected protest against neglect by the major parties. Unemployment, crap housing, poverty are without doubt the critical context: but if that were the whole story, if the BNP was merely an anti-establishment cry of despair, then one would expect BNP voters to convert directly to the far left when given the chance, which by and large they do not. People vote for the BNP not in spite of its racism but because of it. Racism remains the core of its appeal and its raison d'etre. A vote for the BNP is not merely a negation, but a positive endorsement of a racist ideology (or to put the same thing another way, an emotional vent for hatred, resentment and bigotry). And both this ideology and these emotions are shared far beyond the confines of the far right. The BNP draws strength from them, but it is not their source.

It's true that in the absence of other explanations for social problems, racial 'explanations' have freer run. But the left sometimes treats racism as some kind of 'natural' if misguided response to a material situation. It is anything but. As a way of looking at the world, as an ideology and a material force, racism is constantly constructed, nurtured, revised and bolstered (because it serves the pursuit of profit, power and privilege). Therefore it has to be (and can be) contested and criticised. It is not so much that the BNP have to be exposed as 'racists' as that racism has to be exposed in all its irrationality and malignity and in all its guises.

Keiron Farrow seems to believe we can somehow circumvent the problem by building 'working class alternatives' that would fight racism, apparently, by ignoring it. The reality is that the defence of asylum seekers, Muslims or immigrants is divisive in working class areas as elsewhere. To have any hope of healing that division you have first to make it explicit.

I wish I could believe that the BNP, or even the BNP plus UKIP vote, represented the extent of the 'racist vote' in Britain. The reality is that racist ideas, myths, assumptions, stereotypes and 'explanations' are widespread and deep rooted in British society. The far right are part of a nexus which includes the racism of the state (in immigration, policing, criminal justice), the media and educational institutions; it's a racism that has elite, middle and working class variants. One of the weaknesses of the left approach has been to fix on the latter – on working class racism – as if it existed separately from the others. Perhaps that's why we sometimes sidestep the question of UKIP, whose election campaign relied heavily on anti-immigrant and anti-Muslim messages; its xenophobia is no less noxious than the BNP's, though it is deemed more respectable, a fact not unrelated to its different – middle class, Tory-voting – constituency.

In particular, the current virulence of anti-Muslim racism cannot be isolated to the far right, which in this case has taken its cue from the middle class and a significant section of what passes for the intelligentsia. 'Islamophobia,' writes A. Sivanandan, 'in its most sophisticated form, is the province of middle-class opinion formers, erstwhile liberals, defenders of the true liberal faith against the encroachments of illiberal Islam, as defined by them, the "liberati". Anti-Muslim racism is the province of the working class and is no different from past working-class racisms. Except that now it finds its justification in Islamophobia – suitably translated into the vernacular of stereotype and scapegoat by the tabloids, the carriers of racist culture.' Crucially, Islamophobia 'is not just a body of ideas in a vacuum. It is connected to the war in Iraq and the war on terror and tied therefore to the state, its laws and executive decisions.'

We need to see racism as a protean force, varying in its targets and its definitions, though with a shared underlying logic and force. If we're to trace it from its multiple effects to its common source we have to look not only at its objects (the feared and alien others) but also its subject (the collective, privileged Western self). We pay too little attention to the ideology and psychology of white or Western supremacy, to the power and material prerogatives of 'whiteness', though they permeate our foreign and domestic politics.

Critiques of 'identity politics', including some from the left, tend to ignore the most potent form of identity politics in our society: the politics of the white-identified majority. It draws its strength precisely from this unexamined assumption: that the white/Western perspective is normative, 'neutral' or 'colourless', free of 'identity' in a way that the non-white, non-Western cannot be. The right wing know the power of this identity and exploit it shamelessly. In its promotion of 'British values' and 'cohesion' and its treatment of asylum seekers, New Labour sought to appease it. But we on the left tend just to ignore it, hoping to displace it (largely by sentimental abstractions) without confronting it.

This is in no way a call for cultural relativism. On the contrary, it's asking that white, majority identities and the powers they acquire or presume are scrutinised with the same critical regard, the same measurements of human welfare and freedom, we would demand in relation to other social categories.

Historically, racism, and specifically white supremacism, was the consort of Western colonialism, and it continues to act in that capacity. It's effective today in the bizarre assumption that 'we' act in Iraq or Afghanistan without self-interest, that 'we' transcend the ethnic, tribal or religious animosities of the natives; in the imposition of neo-liberal 'development' strategies; in attempts to control the movements of people; in the curbs on (some people's) civil liberties; and quite nakedly in the detention of asylum seekers, including children. The practise is clearly barbaric and condemned internationally, yet during the election there was not the slightest pressure on politicians to distance themselves from it. The victims here are perceived as belonging to a separate category from 'us'. They are not embraced by that Western norm which champions freedom of movement for some while denying it to others.

We won't finish off the far right unless we also overturn the more disparate bigotry of which it is an outgrowth. To do that, we need a clearer understanding of racism and its role in an increasingly unequal world. And we need to do much more than harass the BNP, important as that remains. The agenda has to be as broad as the problem. It might include a positive campaign to build solidarity with hunger strikers in immigration detention camps, a concerted effort to expose the government's 'Prevent' programme (the domestic anti-terrorism initiative, primarily a vehicle for surveillance and control of the Muslim population), and last but not least, action against the likes of the *Daily Mail*, a far more prolific disseminator of racist ideas than the BNP.

SMALL COUNTRY, BIG STRUGGLE

On returning from a 2010 visit with trade unionists and democracy activists in Swaziland.

Swaziland is a small country with a big problem. The 1.3 million inhabitants of the land-locked Southern African kingdom live under the thumb of one of the world's last absolute monarchies, a venal and repressive regime whose plunder of the country is systematic and comprehensive.

Now presiding over the 37th year of the world's longest running state of emergency, King Mswati III controls the parliament, appoints cabinet ministers, judges and senior civil servants and makes and breaks the law at will. Political parties are banned, along with most demonstrations and meetings. Shouting the wrong slogan or wearing the wrong tee shirt can get you locked up as a 'terrorist'. Trades unionists and human rights activists face surveillance, house searches, arbitrary detention and torture. Strikes are illegal. Gatherings of any kind are often broken up by police assaults. The media is subject to constant harassment and intimidation. During the latest wave of repression, in May, democracy activist Sipho Jele, who had been arrested and interrogated, was allegedly 'found' by police hanging from the rafters in a prison toilet.

In July, Mswati (who was educated at the expensive Sherborne school in Dorset, England) ruled out future political dialogue, insisting that state structures in Swaziland were a 'closed book' and rejecting public consultation in favour of a carefully managed 'Smart Partnership' exercise.

Swaziland's autocracy is based on the *tinkhundla* system through which royally-sponsored traditional leaders dispense patronage and exercise control at local level. The system is celebrated by the government as an authentic product of traditional Swazi culture and those who question it are routinely denounced as 'not Swazi enough'. But Swazis themselves reap no benefits from it.

While 70 per cent of the population live on less than a dollar a day and 25 per cent rely on food aid, the royal family make do on some $67,000 a day. According to US-based business magazine *Forbes*, Mswati's personal net worth is an estimated $200 million, making him the 15th richest monarch in the world, not far behind Queen Elizabeth II, ranked 13, whose UK domain alone generates a GDP 365 times larger than Swaziland's.

Six in ten Swazis are engaged in subsistence farming, mostly on communal land owned in trust by the King, whose family also directly own a major share of the remaining 'privately-owned' land. Forced labour is commonplace. Under Swazi Administration Order No. 6 of 1998, it is a duty of Swazis to obey orders from local chiefs to participate in compulsory works (which may include construction and agricultural labour or even weeding the gardens in Mswati's palaces). There are severe penalties for those who refuse.

Mswati is also head of a multi-million pound conglomerate, set up in 1968 by royal charter, which owns a significant slice of nearly every major Swazi business and industry – sugar, mobile phones, mines, media, tourism. Theoretically, Mswati holds the conglomerate's assets in trust for the nation, but the fund, like all royal assets, is shielded from public scrutiny.

Compounding poverty and repression, Swaziland now suffers the world's highest rate of HIV/AIDS infection – perhaps as much as 40 per cent of the adult population and 42 per cent of all expectant mothers. Swaziland has the highest annual rate of death from AIDS, about 10,000 a year or an annual cull of one per cent of the population. Life expectancy has plummeted and is probably now as low as anywhere in the world. Fifteen per cent of households are headed by orphaned children.

The royal family's response to this crisis would be laughable if it weren't so lethally criminal. The government has issued a call for the circumcision of new born males (and also for Members of Parliament), though there is no evidence that circumcision affects HIV spread. Mswati himself declared a ban on teenage girls wearing mini-skirts. Recently a senior member of the Royal Family (and chair of the above-mentioned royal trust fund) Prince Logcogco claimed that the HIV problem was exaggerated and described himself as 'a fearless human being' undeterred by the threat of AIDS. The comments were part of the Prince's response to a custody battle over a child born four years ago to a 13- or 14-year-old girl (the age of consent is 16).

Royal sex scandals are just about the only Swazi stories that make the international news. When I visited the country in mid-August, the Justice Minister had just been dismissed and arrested for having sex with the 12th of the King's 14 wives. Swazi media were prohibited from reporting the story and copies of the South African daily *City Press* were barred at the border. A democracy activist was then arrested for making photocopies of the banned report, which, in any case, seemed to be common knowledge across the country. The King had picked out this wife at the age of 16 when she took part in the annual Reed Dance, a much-hyped 'cultural' rite in which tens of thousands of 'maidens', many displaying bare breasts, dance for the members of the royal family and ogling tourists.

The government defends royal polygamy, like forced labour and the tinkhundla system, on the grounds of 'tradition'. When Mswati's long-reigning father, Sobhuza II, proclaimed the state of emergency back in 1973, he did so on the grounds that open political competition was 'alien to, and incompatible with...the Swazi way of life'. And 'culture' remains the continuing plea of the Swazi elite (and the big appeal of the royally-controlled Swazi tourist industry). But the 'culture' they claim to be defending is an artificial construction, a monopoly on power and wealth that stifles the creativity and independence of the Swazi people.

Over the course of 150 years, the Swazi monarchy has maintained its grip by collaborating with the prevalent regional powers, first with the Boer Republics, then the British empire and in the 1980s with apartheid South Africa. Besides assisting in the arrest and killing of ANC members who had fled to Swaziland, the King denounced sanctions against South Africa, the only Commonwealth leader besides Margaret Thatcher to do so.

Swazi democracy activists are quick to highlight the disparity between the West's strictures on the likes of Mugabe and their indifference when it comes to the Mswati regime. But unlike Mugabe and others on the West's selective hit-list of human rights abusers, Mswati is an enthusiast for neo-liberalism and multi-national corporations. Take, for example, his partnership with Coca-Cola, whose concentrate plant, exporting to much of Africa, is located in Swaziland because of favourable tax arrangements and access to cheap raw sugar. Coke accounts for up to 40 per cent of Swaziland's GDP, and an unknown but sizeable chunk of this goes directly into the King's pocket. Mswati's pilgrimage to Coca-Cola headquarters in Atlanta, Georgia, has become an annual ritual.

On a visit to Britain in August, Mswati attended the graduation of one of his sons from the military academy at Sandhurst. Not long after, the UK government announced it would deport well-known Swazi democracy activist Thobile Gwebu, who had been staging a weekly picket outside the Swazi High Commission in London, as a 'failed asylum seeker'.

Earlier this year, the Swaziland Democracy Campaign was formed by labour unions, political parties, civil society groups and churches. It has called for a global day of action on 7 September, which will include a mass protest and show of 'defiance' in Swaziland itself. Delegates from the international labour movement will join the action in Swaziland and messages of support for the SDC are to be delivered to Swazi embassies worldwide. SDC activists I spoke to are hopeful that the event will alert a hitherto indifferent global media to the Swaziland story. They see the day of action as a key moment in the development of a more united, more focussed democracy movement and believe that their message is spreading rapidly to new areas, inside and outside the country. Though they face an obstinate, ruthless ruling elite, they are now more 'optimistic' about the future of their struggle than for many years. 'The days of the absolute monarchy,' one told me, 'are definitely numbered.'

'THE GREATEST NATION ON EARTH'?: OBAMA'S VICTORY SPEECH VIEWED FROM OVERSEAS

First published in November 2012 following Barack Obama's reelection as US president.

I woke early on Wednesday morning to check the results. First, I was relieved. Romney had failed, and more importantly the bigots and obscurantists who backed him had failed. Then I watched Obama's victory speech, and what I felt was something other than relief. The speech was dubbed 'magnificent' on the *Guardian*'s front page by Jonathan Freedland, who hailed it, as did others, as a return to the bold, inspirational style of 2008 and a harbinger of a more ambitious second term.

I understand why people in the US clutch at straws, but I wonder how many times Freedland and other liberal commentators will clutch at this particular straw before they realise that it is in fact only a straw? What struck me about Obama's 'soaring rhetoric' was just how rhetorical it was, and especially how heavily it leaned on the rhetoric of American exceptionalism. Dodging specifics, mixing sentimental anecdotes with sweeping platitudes, Obama invoked a special American destiny, unique among nations.

He put the theme up front in his opening sentence: 'Tonight, more than 200 years after a former colony won the right to determine its own destiny, the task of perfecting our union moves forward'. He went on to laud 'the spirit' of America 'that has triumphed over war and depression, the spirit that has lifted this country from the depths of despair to the great heights of hope.'

America here becomes not just another country with a history of its own but a kind of charged metaphysical entity, an abstraction as potent as it is amorphous.

The ideology of American exceptionalism has always been about consolidating national unity – not so much against foreign foes as against domestic division, especially class division. Obama's speech followed that well-worn path, moving towards an affirmation of a unique American bond. 'We remain more than a collection of red states and blue states,' he declared, employing a mantra that served him well in the past, 'We are and forever will be the United States of America.' He concluded by vowing that with 'God's grace we will continue our journey forward and remind the world just why it is that we live in the greatest nation on Earth.'

'The greatest nation on earth'? Imagine if the same boast had been made by the leader of any other country. It would be considered tasteless braggadocio at best, and something altogether more menacing at worst. Imagine the reaction to such a claim being made by the leaders of Iran or China, not to mention Germany or Japan. In the mouths of Russian politicians it's considered mindless, dangerous demagoguery. But this ritual yet at the same time stridently combative flattering of the national ego is deemed part and parcel of US politics, so much so that few comment on it.

Let's stop for a moment and examine the claim.

What constitutes national 'greatness' and how is it to be measured? What exactly is it that makes the US 'the greatest nation on earth'? Obama noted that 'this country has more wealth than any nation' and 'the most powerful military in history' as well as a 'culture' that is 'the envy of the world', but none of these, he insisted, were the real sign of America's 'greatness' – though they seemed to be offered as supporting evidence.

No, the President argued, 'what makes America exceptional' – an explicit reference to the exceptionalist doctrine, of which he is a professed adherent – 'are the bonds that hold together the most diverse nation on earth. The belief that our destiny is shared.'

In fact, the US is no more 'diverse' than, for example, India or South Africa, nor is it unique in being knit together despite its diversity. One of the ploys of American exceptionalism is to take a universal trait or abstraction and make it the special property of the US. Obama went beyond the usual ahistorical claims on 'freedom' and 'democracy' to add in 'love and charity and duty and patriotism. That's what makes America great.'

Love, charity, duty and patriotism are all fine qualities, and undoubtedly assets to any society, but can the US really claim a greater store of them than other countries? And are they subject to the comparative measurement implied in Obama's use of the superlative 'greatest'?

A glance at the CIA World Factbook is enlightening. In the maternal mortality rankings the US, with 21 deaths per 100,000 live births, has the 47th best record, behind Europe, South Korea and Turkey and on a par with Iran. In infant mortality the US ranks 49th, inferior to Cuba, the EU and Japan. When it comes to life expectancy at birth, the US ranks 51st. And in education spending as a percentage of GDP, the US comes in at 44th, its 5.5 per cent far behind Cuba's top ranking 13.6 per cent. On the other hand, when it comes to the percentage of the adult population suffering obesity the US ranks above all except a handful of small Pacific Ocean states (and Saudi Arabia).

These rankings, based on national averages, actually make the US performance look better than it is. If the measurements were confined to the 50 per cent of Americans on below median incomes, the rankings would all be decidedly worse. This is because the US is one of the planet's most unequal societies. According to the Gini coefficient, a measure of income distribution, the US lies 91st, considerably less equal than

Turkey or Ghana or Vietnam or the EU countries. Yet Obama insisted, 'We are not as divided as our politics suggests.'

It's true that the US has the largest total GDP and the highest per capita GDP (barring a few enclaves and tax havens). It certainly has by far the largest military: it accounts for 41 per cent of total global military spending, more than the next six biggest spenders combined. Obama's speech included a specific pledge to preserve this particular form of superiority and hand it down to future generations.

To understand that, it's necessary to clock a few other US 'number ones'.

In the total value of shares issued by publicly traded companies, the US is far and away the top act (70 per cent more than the combined EU total and four times China's holdings), as it is in the total value of direct investment in foreign countries. At the same time it's also the world leader in external debt, owing $14.7 trillion to foreigners, only a little less than the combined EU total. Though it may be only number two in total CO2 emissions (after China) it's far ahead of its rivals in emissions per capita, and still imports more crude oil (in total and per capita) than any other country, a quarter of the global total.

But does any of that matter in 'the land of opportunity'? Obama had a curious 21st century take on what he called 'the promise of our founders':

'It doesn't matter whether you're black or white or Hispanic or Asian or Native American or young or old or rich or poor, able, disabled, gay or straight, *you can make it here in America if you're willing to try.*' (emphasis added)

The crowd cheered the diversity of Obama's catalogue, and of course Romney would have omitted the 'gay or straight' category, but it has to be said that nothing like the idea of 'making it' appears in the Declaration of Independence or the Constitution. 'Life, liberty and the pursuit of happiness' are something different, and they are an entitlement, not conditional, as Obama claimed, not available only 'if you work hard'. This is a neo-liberal twist on American exceptionalism, re-cast in the argot of the prevailing cult of individual success. But it is at the same time a reiteration of one of the central beguiling motifs of American excpetionalism: America as a society embodying the very principle of social mobility.

Surveys show that people in the US have a greater faith in their country being a meritocracy than citizens of other countries. In a poll conducted by the Economic Mobility Project, nearly seven in ten Americans said they had already achieved or expected to achieve 'the American Dream' at some point in their lives. Clearly the old myth endures, even though it has come to bear less and less resemblance to reality.

Studies have demonstrated repeatedly that social mobility is in fact more restricted in the US than in many other wealthy countries. For example, a US male's income is nearly twice as reliant on his father's background as a Canadian male's. In the US, 42 per cent of the sons of fathers born in the poorest quintile remain in that quintile, far higher than the 30 per cent in Britain or the 25 per cent in the Scandinavian countries. The statistics also confound the rags-to-riches narratives celebrated by American exceptionalists. The percentage of sons born to fathers in the poorest quintile who ended up in the wealthiest quintile in the US is 7.9 per cent, far lower than in other wealthy countries, where rates ranged from 10.9 per cent to 14.4 per cent. That's partly because – as reflected in its Gini coefficient – in the US the gap between the poorest and richest quintiles is much greater than it is in other countries.

One of the functions of American exceptionalism is to bind the poor and the working class to a system that exploits them. Like other narratives of national unity, it masks divisions and conflicts of interest and obscures real choices.

You could see the insidiousness of its logic in the two examples Obama offered of 'the spirit at work in America': first, 'the family business whose owners would rather cut their own pay than lay off their neighbours' and second, 'the workers who would rather cut back their hours than see a friend lose a job.'

To the extent that they exist, the first group make their 'sacrifice' individually and voluntarily. Obama says nothing about imposing that sacrifice on top corporate executives, who are, far more often than family businesses, the employers of the second group, the workforces who are compelled, collectively, to trade pay for jobs. Apart from anything else, it's a false counter-position, since pay and jobs are interdependent – pay generating the demand that creates jobs. It was notable that Obama in his lengthy list of thank yous omitted any mention of the unions, despite their massive donation of money and volunteers.

Since Obama is so keen on international superiority, let's compare the US presidential election to the recent election in Venezuela, where Chavez won a much more decisive victory on a significantly higher turn out. The election was deemed scrupulously fair and efficient by observers, something few would claim for the US exercise, marred as it was by attempts at voter suppression. It's been noted that Obama triumphed in the face of four years of aggressive, obnoxious and well-funded opposition, but that was nothing compared to what Chavez had to contend with, including the standing threat of a US-backed coup. He was outspent by his rival by three to one and vehemently opposed by the great bulk of the country's media. He didn't have Obama's high-tech campaign machine but unlike Obama he had the advantage of standing for something decisively, tangibly different from his opponent. As a result Venezuelans enjoyed the kind of 'real choice over issues' that

Obama in his speech improbably claimed made Americans the envy of the world.

Globally, Obama's victory will be greeted by a sigh of relief but few expectations. In contrast, Chavez's victory offers hope to hundreds of millions of the poor across the global south. It shows that there is an alternative to the neo-liberalism to which Obama is so firmly wed, and that this alternative can work. Under Chavez, both relative and absolute poverty in Venezuela have been substantially reduced – the former from nearly 50 to 24 per cent and the latter from 25 to seven per cent. In contrast, under Obama, in the 'greatest' and wealthiest nation on earth, the poverty rate has steadily increased, reaching 15.9 percent last year, 48.5 million people.

Taking cognizance of these contrasting records would benefit no one more than Americans themselves. They are at one with much of the rest of the world in being the victims, not the beneficiaries, of American exceptionalism.

WHITE SUPREMACY ALIVE AND WELL IN BRITAIN

First published in 2013.

Only a year ago, the London Olympics were being hailed as 'a defining moment' in the emergence of a proudly multi-cultural Britain. That claim was always inflated but it looks decidedly hollow, indeed dangerously self-indulgent, in light of recent developments: the electoral advance of UKIP, the enhanced menace of the EDL and most of all the barbaric attacks on Muslims and mosques in the aftermath of Lee Rigby's murder.

The far right resurgence, here and across Europe, poses challenges of many kinds for the left. But whatever else we do, we have to recognise that the far right feeds off and re-enforces a more diffuse phenomenon: the racism, national chauvinism and xenophobia that are part and parcel of the mainstream.

The racism of the mainstream isn't hard to find. Just look at the pages of the *Mail* or *Express* (far more efficient deliverers of racist propaganda than the far right) or at entertainments like *Homeland* or *Argo* (where in accordance with hoary stereotypes the Muslim enemies of the West are portrayed as unappeasable, brutally irrational, and at the same time calculating and duplicitous). Then look at how racism has been shown to infect nearly all our major social institutions – from football to police and prisons to Oxford and Cambridge.

Politicians of all three main parties dabble in it. Here the trick is to claim to be saying something 'unsayable' but widely thought. Jack Straw on the *niqab* a few years back was a classic example of the ploy. Now we have Ed Miliband arguing that Labour failed to 'listen' to 'people' on 'immigration' (all three words have to be placed in quotes because none actually means what it's supposed to mean).

Currently the political centre in this country appears to be taking the line that the far right is voicing some kind of genuine complaint to which the rest of us must listen. Thus the perverse rationale of racism is given legitimacy and the real message of the far right goes uncontested. The scariest thing about UKIP's election performance was the speed with which it elicited knee-jerk concessions from Cameron and others. Once again we've seen that the big danger of the far right is the way they drag the political mainstream in their direction.

Far from being repressed by 'political correctness', 'unsayable' thoughts about race are the common currency of all kinds of 'polite' conversation, including in the media and among the intelligentsia. Nothing the EDL says is any cruder than Martin Amis's musings on Muslim culpability. And Tony Blair's malign wooden-headedness was fully on display in his recent declaration that somehow, when all is said and done, 'Islam' is indeed to blame.

As for the BBC, the heart of the 'liberal' establishment, it has conferred legitimacy on both UKIP and the EDL, but more importantly it acts as one of the great propagators of the 'us' vs 'them' world-view. Its standard treatment of ethnicity, at home or abroad, is one in which a supra-ethnic commentary (Western liberal and in fact very 'English') confronts everything outside its privileged purview as 'Other', as all the things which 'we' are not: 'tribal', 'fanatical', 'sectarian', beyond reason and comprehension. Mainstream commentary, liberal and conservative, is permeated by this habitual optic, which assigns to the Other its society's own dark side (hatred, violence, corruption).

Racism is pliable, elastic, shifting its targets, its grounds of complaint. The line between 'us' and 'them' is drawn and re-drawn. In that process, the 'them' is a construction, a phantom, a projection, as is widely recognised. But the same is true of the 'us': the 'us' that is the heart of white and Western supremacism, an 'us' that is also blithely, routinely invoked across mainstream commentary.

Domestic racism has a global context. In the war on terror, Muslims (and others) become representatives of the enemy abroad, living in our midst but always suspect. In the dehumanisation of drone killings and the denial of responsibility for death and destruction on an immense scale in Iraq and elsewhere, the double-standard of racist consciousness is unmistakeable, as it is in the easy acceptance as a future Indian Prime Minister of Narendra Modi, deeply complicit in the Gujerat anti-Muslim pogrom of 2002, and in the casual assumption of prerogatives to ourselves that we deny others, including possession and use of weapons of mass destruction. It's there in every unexamined use of the pronoun 'we' in the discussion of foreign interventions.

Contrary to right-wing myth, Britain's imperial past goes largely unexamined and unacknowledged, and therefore its assumptions remain active in forming our views of the present. We still live in a world shaped materially and imaginatively by the high imperial epoch, during which a small number of European states dominated the economies and polities of the bulk of humanity. This is not the sort of episode that leaves either party unscarred. White supremacism, racism and xenophobic nationalism are as much a part of our Western cultural heritage as what are loosely referred to as 'Enlightenment values'. This is a legacy that has to be systematically unlearned.

The racist response to Lee Rigby's murder was not automatic or 'natural'. Racism is not a default setting. It's an ideology, a construction, a hulking psycho-social edifice, one that has to be demolished plank by plank. It's not a disease that can be 'cured' on a case by case basis. The therapy has to be collective; some trauma of confrontation and contestation that alters what people have in mind when they think of 'we'.

Living under a global capitalism that reproduces all manner of social hierarchies, anti-racist consciousness cannot be a fixed, once-in-a-lifetime conversion; it's an ongoing struggle, a process that has to be engaged in consciously. There's no point of rest because the ideology we're contesting is never at rest.

An example of that is the way that 'multi-culturalism' has been turned into a whipping boy, declared a 'failure' by Merkel, Cameron and an army of pundits. On no basis at all, a variety of unappealing phenomena are blamed on it, from the 'grooming' of girls by 'Asian' men to the alleged self-segregation of minorities. In fact, like other racist bugbears, 'multi-culturalism' is largely a phantom. The bundle of policies herded under that rubric were concessions made in the past in response to mobilisation in black and Asian communities. There were always objections from the left to the 'multi-cultural' framework, which conceived of minorities as homogeneous communities with fixed cultural identities.

The right's campaign is not, however, about the theory but the fact of multi-culturalism, that is, the presence of people seen as belonging to alien cultures. Modern European societies are and will continue to be comprised of numerous 'cultures', in fact, of a wealth of sub- and counter-cultures, overlapping and intersecting. To deny or lament this reality is to deny and lament the presence of those seen as belonging to other cultures. In this context demands for 'integration' are demands for adherence to a cultural norm set by the dominant group. Amazing that some who boast of an 'Enlightenment' heritage see this as anything other than tyrannical.

Under the guise of an attack on the 'relativism' of 'multi-culturalism', what's going on is a reassertion of the historically pre-eminent form of ethical relativism, the assumed superiority of the Western norm. The most strident and powerful form of 'identity politics' in our society remains that of 'white' or 'Western' identity: the dominant, majority identity that likes to conceive of itself as a threatened minority, under siege in its own land.

The answer to the real as opposed to imagined shortcomings of multi-culturalism is not a reversion to Eurocentrism or mono-culture or the creation of a new, all-embracing cultural synthesis. It lies in the political struggle for equality (not mere representation) and the practise of a solidarity that reaches beyond culture. Olympics-style 'multi-culturalism' is of no use. The only antidote to the culture of racism is the cultivation of resistance.

6

THE LONG BATTLE FOR LABOUR'S SOUL

...AND ALL THOSE AGAINST

First published in 1995.

The magazine *Labour Briefing* and my partner Liz Davies stand accused of 'oppositionism', a crime so heinous that anyone found guilty of it must be denied a pew in Labour's broad church. At least, that seems to be the argument made in recent weeks by, among others, Clare Short, Margaret Hodge and Martin Kettle.

But what precisely is 'oppositionism'?

I have combed the dictionaries and can find no pertinent definition. Its current usage seems to have originated in the mid-1980s, when people on the 'soft left' applied it to those on the 'hard left' who questioned their strategy of 'constructive engagement' with Neil Kinnock's leadership. Whatever one thinks of that particular argument, there can be no doubt that the term is now being bandied about in a much looser fashion and with disturbing consequences for the future of democratic debate.

Clearly, everyone who makes any political statement that is at all meaningful is *opposed* to something as well as *in favour* of something else. In one sense, all socialists are 'oppositionists' – they are opposed to the present social order and wish to change it. Tony Blair is formally the leader of 'Her Majesty's Opposition'.

The implication, however, is that some people are somehow *too* 'oppositionist'. We have opposed too many things, or the wrong things. Somehow we have crossed an invisible boundary and thereby forfeited our rights as Labour Party members. But who draws this boundary? Who decides where it shall be placed? And who polices it?

Inevitably, the ideological border patrols are self-appointed, and equally inevitably their rulings are arbitrary, often guided by expediency. Imagine the constitutional absurdities Labour would create for itself if the leadership tried to proscribe 'oppositionism'. Imagine trying to institutionalise the implications of the Liz Davies decision.

'Oppositionism' is, of course, a purely pejorative label. Like 'deviationism' and 'revisionism', it is part of the Stalinist lexicon of heretical ideologies. It sheds no light on the issues under debate and serves only to stigmatise individuals. Like Blair's 'therapy' crack, its unselfconscious usage betrays a glaring insensitivity to the unsavoury history of repressive party regimes.

This kind of broad-brush name calling is not only a means of distorting what your opponents think and say; it is also a means of avoiding having to answer the substance of their arguments. Never mind that there may be good reasons for opposing a particular development, those reasons can be ignored as long as you can dismiss the people making them.

The irony here is that the left critique of Blair is that he has largely confined himself to *opposing* the Tories, on the one hand, and 'old Labour' on the other. What he is *for* remains notoriously unspecified. At the moment, the 'oppositions' are the ones calling for concrete positive commitments – on the minimum wage, public ownership of the utilities, full employment, progressive taxation, and improvements to pensions and benefits.

The 'oppositionism' charge is also an attempt to divide the left into legitimate and illegitimate camps. The losers here are not only those of us cast into the darkness, but those who remain, or think they remain, within the light. They are accepted on sufferance, and walk in constant fear of being ostracised. The 'oppositionist' tag is not meant only to defame current dissenters, it is also meant to scare off potential dissenters in the future.

In the US in the 1940s and 1950s, McCarthyism had a similar impact. To be accepted as legitimate and to claim your democratic rights, you had to conform to the rhetoric of the Cold War. It was never enough simply to deny that you were a member of the Communist Party; you had to repudiate any associations with communists and swear unconditional allegiance to US foreign policy. Nowadays in new Labour, it is not enough to conform to the rules of the party or to boast of a track record of years of service to it; you have to swear allegiance to what Tony Blair in the *Guardian* called 'my policies' and 'the changes I have made to the party'.

Closely linked to the charge of 'oppositionism' is the charge of 'Trotskyism', which has now become a catch-all term of abuse wantonly applied to anyone whose dissent is not to the taste of the new Labour establishment. What is clearly evident is that those who spit it out know as little about Trotskyism as they do about the people they are denouncing as 'Trots'.

Increasingly, the term is applied to anyone who has ever been influenced by Trotsky's thought or had a brush with Trotskyist organisations or even worked with people in Trotskyist groups. Thus we are treated to Martin Kettle using his *Guardian* column to pick over the alleged past Trotskyist associations of various members of the *Labour Briefing* editorial board. Kettle's own former membership of the Communist Party was not mentioned, of course.

This is little short of absurd. At a fringe meeting in Brighton, Arthur Scargill read out a fascinating (and long) list of current Labour frontbenchers with past Trotskyist associations. Undoubtedly, the culprits would all leap up protesting that they had repudiated their past – and in Kettle's eyes that would be enough to absolve them. Clare Short too held it against the non-Trotskyist Liz Davies that 'she has not repudiated the content of what she wrote' in *Labour Briefing*. One has to wonder what Orwell would have made of this latest fashion in required recantation.

As someone who is not a Trotskyist and has never been a member of any far left group, I am proud to have worked with Trotskyists, many of whom have made substantial contributions to the labour movement and to socialist debate. Of course, I have also known Trotskyists who were a total pain in the arse – though when it comes to 'intimidation' and 'manipulation', the Blair babes leave them standing.

Let's face it, can any tradition on the left look back at its own history without some blushes? Can any claim to have all the answers to the awesome questions now confronting the left as a whole? And is it likely that excluding and demonising one section of the left will help us get any closer to those answers?

The guilt by association practised by the new McCarthyites undermines rational, informed debate, It has already fostered a culture of fear and caution among party members, a culture that inhibits the serious discussion the party needs if it is to be prepared for government. In the end, the witch-hunting of 'oppositionists' is not only bad for Labour, it is bad for the country. It should be remembered that McCarthyism (long before it was known by that name) started as a purge of the communist-linked left inside the US trade union movement – and spread outwards from there.

ALL BECAUSE HE LOVES YOU

First published in 1995, Marqusee imagines Christmas 1999 in 10 Downing Street.

*Hark, the herald angels sing
Glory to the new born king...*

The chance to deliver the Christmas address to the nation live on television was a welcome if unexpected boon. Following the royal family's last appearance on the box, during which opposing factions had accused each other of an astonishing array of financial and sexual shenanigans, BBC moguls had decided that in the public interest no repeat performance would be permitted. But who should fill the vacuum? The split in the Church of England made it impossible to choose either of the Archbishops of Canterbury, and Paxman was on an exclusive contract with Sky.

Thus, thanks to luck and some feverish last-minute lobbying, the prime minister had been awarded with what commentators described as his last throw of the dice. If he blew it this time, he had been told in no uncertain terms, he would be forced to make way for someone else.

As the PM sat alone in his study in 10 Downing Street, a spasm of hate rippled through him. The someone else in question would almost certainly be the former chancellor of the exchequer, whose sarcastic backbench attack on the PM had already been likened to Geoffrey Howe's stab-in-the-back job on Margaret Thatcher.

It seemed inconceivable that so much could have gone so wrong in such a short time. The honeymoon following his election victory had been so intensely romantic – practically a love affair between himself and the British people. No one could have predicted it would be so short-lived. Today, on the verge of the new millennium, his popularity ratings stood below John Major's at his nadir. Even now, after months of media attacks, the PM still found it difficult to absorb the pollsters' data. The figures seemed to defy common sense. How could such bright hopes have come to this? How could people not understand that he was doing what he was doing because he *loved his country*?

Of course, he had always known that there would have to be a final reckoning with the fundamentalists. Even so, the birth of the New Britain Party – his party, created in his own image and stamped at every level with his own authority – had proved more painful than expected. He had always known there would be casualties and desertions along the way – but not this many. He had succeeded in keeping policy commitments to a minimum, but cutting back commitments to individuals had been more difficult. Even with an unprecedented expansion of the cabinet and a record influx into the Lords, he had been unable to placate many who were convinced that he owed them.

Recently, some of his old allies had renewed their increasingly shrill appeals to hold the long-delayed referendum on PR. As before, he had brushed the fools aside. Given the recent party realignments, such a move was preposterous. The PM thought, not for the first time, how wise he had been to legislate quickly for state funding of political parties.

For a while it seemed that he had even succeeded in ridding himself of the egregious Mandelson. The position at the BBC was perfect for Peter, and for the PM, because it had forced Peter to resign from the House and kept him at arm's length from the PM's office. This was much the safest distance, the PM had decided, especially in the wake of Peter's cock-ups over the Civil Service Privatisation Bill. But those who had advised him that Peter would never accept being so far from the action were right. Without warning, Mandelson had abandoned the BBC to pop up as the candidate for Portillo's Britain First Block in the by-election caused by deputy PM John Prescott's elevation to EU commissioner.

After that debacle, the PM had cleaned out the party HQ at Millbank (appointing a new media team with an average age of 19) – only to find his former loyal lieutenants pursuing their vendettas against him in newspaper columns and on television chat-shows. Their vitriol made him wonder whether he had failed to extirpate the entryist Briefing tendency after all.

Though he had known from the beginning that the vested interests would squeal, he had stood by his conviction that education vouchers were an idea whose time had come. In his televised speech unveiling the plan, he had dubbed them 'scratchcards towards individual freedom'. Showing the way, he had cashed in his own family's vouchers and claimed the 'Young Britain' top-up funding to send his son to Eton. The angry rants from the oppositionalists had been predictable, but he would have seen them off easily had it not been for the unexpected, embarrassing failure of the state-of-the-art, business-sponsored computer system his government had established to 'liberate education once and for all from the tyranny of politics'. The backlash against his Health 2001 voucher proposals had been fiercer. Of course, there was nothing wrong with the initiative itself. It had just been badly timed.

Likewise, his ill-fated Vision for Growth. How could he allow a naive minimum wage policy to undermine his strategy of transforming the country's urban heartlands by designating them '24-hour cities'? The tourist boom he had prophesied had nearly got off the ground, and would have got off the ground if it hadn't been cut short by the sterling crisis. The wave of redundancies that followed washed away the bold outlines of the Vision, and he had been forced to call in troops to deal with the mushrooming public sector strike.

The PM stiffened in his seat at the thought of his ex-chancellor's treachery. As if the sterling crisis had been at all avoidable. As if they had not both agreed on the policies that led up to it. As if they both did not know that they had been betrayed by their friends in Europe. Even more outrageously, the ex-chancellor, that one-time prophet of 'workfare', had the cheek to denounce the recent proposals made by Frank Field (deputy PM with a special brief to End Welfare As We Know It) to conscript benefit claimants to work as ancillary staff in the health service.

After his election, they had dubbed him the first 'Internet PM', and there was much excitement as he toured the country preaching the laptop revolution. Then came the crumbling of the Microsoft empire and the rise of Internet piracy and plunder, leading to emergency legislation (bitterly opposed by self-serving leader-writers) to restrict and control access to the Net.

Throughout this *annus horribilis*, he had remained determined, come what may, to show strength. The country needed strong leadership, just as the party had in opposition. Every day, after shaving and dressing and checking that the hairweave wasn't showing, he looked in the mirror and imagined himself as made of steel – bright and hard and impermeable. He could not understand why so many people had rebuffed his patently sincere appeals, the very appeals that had proved so successful when addressed to his party in opposition: if he sometimes did or said things that were painful to them, if he sometimes asked them to make sacrifices, it was only because *he loved his party and he loved his country.*

The PM was still not convinced his suggestion to change the name of the country (to 'New Britain') was as risible as his critics made out. But whatever he did now, he seemed to make enemies.

The disintegration of his own family had been the final, nearly crushing blow. His son had been sent down from Eton, following his arrest on a crack-dealing charge and was spending the holidays in one of Jack Straw's new boot-camps for young offenders. At the party conference, the PM had been forced to sit in silence through Clare Short's stern lecture on the War on Drugs, which he had appointed her to spearhead. His daughter was staying in Ealing with his wife, who had left him six months ago, following a theological dispute. Despite the separation, she had retained the Lord Chancellorship he had bestowed upon her, and was now using it to frustrate his Divorce (Restrictions) Bill, the centrepiece of his new Ministry for the Family.

When he had announced the formation of the ministry, he had promised a mould-breaking appointment to head it up, and for days the press was filled with speculation. Everyone, from Suzanne Moore to Oprah Winfrey, had been mentioned, but the PM had known all along that there was only one man for the job. His dignified, almost sombre announcement that he himself would take charge of the portfolio was not welcomed as universally as he had expected. Indeed, television comedians seemed to find it an endless source of vulgar amusement. But he would show them. His Christmas speech would be made explicitly in his capacity as Minister for the Family. And he would use it to show that, far from disqualifying him, his recent domestic travails made him the ideal man to rally the nation to a new moral awareness. Disappointingly, the media seemed unimpressed by the ingenious Christmas morning photo op arranged by his young staff. A dozen children of private security guards (New Britain's growth industry) had been rounded up and ushered in to 10 Downing Street to share mince pies with the PM in the glare of the television lights. Thus the nation's first ever Minister for the Family would be seen caring for little ones whose hard-working fathers were out patrolling the streets and estates. Unfortunately, there was no snow (it made such a comforting backdrop to seasonal sentiment) and the strangely balmy weather had already led to renewed pressure from the lunatic fringe to control CO_2 emissions. The PM's staff had contemplated dusting the kids with spray-on artificial snowflakes but decided against the move after someone pointed out the pretext it would give for yet more jokes about cocaine and a 'White Christmas at Number Ten'.

The PM scrolled through the text of his speech on the VDU. Its content was a complete secret. Not even his closest aides had seen it. Over the past few days he had crafted it with care, fully aware of the high stakes riding on this first ever Prime Minister's Christmas Day Message to the Nation. He had considered his options carefully. The appeal to self-sacrifice, he now realised, had been too abstract, too impersonal. The public had reacted much as his wife had when he last told her he was doing what he was doing because *he loved her*. People needed something more to rouse them. They needed, whether they knew it or not, a glorious crusade.

Yes, he would rally the nation, or at least half of it. He would call a Million Man March – and personally lead the men of New Britain in acts of individual atonement.

'Yes. Men. British men. Together. Marching. Atoning. Taking the blame. Carrying the shame. Taking responsibility. For ourselves. For our families. For our country. For the future. For all our futures. Not blaming others. Not blaming politicians. Not blaming the government. Not blaming the Bundesbank. Owning up to our failures. As men. Yes. As men of New Britain. Atoning. Marching. Together. Into the new millenium. As your Minister for the Family, I pledge...'

As he read, a dark scowl concealed the famous orthodenture. It was that sensation again. A novel, unpleasant sensation. It had crept up on him in recent months. Eventually he had been forced to call it by its true name – though only when utterly and safely alone – and that name was *doubt*. An emotion he could not afford. He mustn't get bogged down in details. Just get in front of the camera and let the charm flow. Surely the old magic would return. He looked again at the last lines of the speech. 'Too many hostages to fortune', he thought, and reached for the delete key.

ALTERNATIVE CAMPAIGN DIARY

During the 1997 general election that brought Tony Blair's New Labour to power, Mike Marqusee campaigned for Jeremy Corbyn in his seat in Islington North. The following is Marqusee's campaign diary.

March 17: Ominous start: the *Sun* backs Blair. No one wants to discuss what Labour has paid for this endorsement, i.e. abandoning objections to cross-media ownership and, by implication, to the expansion of Murdoch's empire.

March 18: Ward organisers meet in Islington North's new HQ: canvassing timetable discussed and election paraphernalia dished out.

March 22: Major's attempt to supress the Downey report backfires. Brown on BBC unable to explain how Labour's refusal to remove the ceiling on national insurance contributions is compatible with the Party's commitment to a fair tax regime.

March 23: *Sunday Mirror* headline: 'Top Tories used me as their sex toy'.

April 1: Canvass cards pasted up. Maps photocopied. Leaflets printed. Members missing. It's going to be a long campaign.

April 4: Canvassing begins in earnest. Two complaints on the doorstep about Blair and New Labour.

April 7: The Hamiltons ambush Martin Bell on Knutsford Heath. I have to laugh. Hamilton is a liar and a cheat and ought to be in jail, but he is small fry. Corruption is a political issue. The real questions are about the power of money and the absence of accountability. Bell's sanctimonious challenge has turned Tatton into a medieval morality play, a contest between an upright neutral from the BBC and a slimy Tory hack. Of course, that suits Blair and Mandelson – anything to keep politics off the agenda.

April 8: The Institute for Fiscal Studies confirms that if taxes do not rise, Labour will have to make massive cuts in public spending. We said exactly the same thing in the last two *Labour Left Briefing* editorials. Will somebody pay attention now?

April 9: *Newsnight* on Europe. Pressed by Paxman, Robin Cook explains his position on Labour's position on a single currency. 'We have decided that we will take the decision when we have decided what is in the British interest and I will be happy with whatever decision is good for British interests'. Thus, the sharpest brain in the Shadow Cabinet.

April 11: The *Mirror* is running a daily 'Blair Babe' photo on page three. Today's scantily clad young female is 'a real red rose' – 'sultry secretary Nicola Cook was just a baby when the Tories took power. Now 20 years on, she's developed into a stunning Blair Babe. Nicola lives in true blue Bexley in Kent, but says: "I really, really do want Labour to win this election. We need a change and Tony Blair is the man to do it."' New Labour, old sexism.

April 12: Inspiring dockers demo. The best antidote to New Labour's vacuous campaign. I only wish Reclaim the Streets had targeted Millbank instead of the National Gallery.

April 14: Call from the BBC. They are preparing a piece to screen after the election, but can't find anyone inside the Labour Party to say anything critical about Blair. Would I plug the gap? Presumably their last resort, I iron a shirt and put on a jacket, hoping to look slightly more like a pundit and slightly less like a scruffy lefty.

April 15: The Islington North campaign is becoming something of a refuge for the disenchanted and dispossessed. Labour lefties spurned by their own constituencies. Human rights and environmental activists. Kurds, Turks, Kashmiris, Cypriots, Somalis, militant pensioners. Today Patrick, a Nigerian who lives in Camberwell, arrived on my doorstep. He had come to help Mr. Corbyn get re-elected 'because of what he has said about the right of asylum.'

April 16: Users of the nearby Turkish Cultural Centre peer suspiciously at my red rosette. I realise they have taken us for emissaries from Blair, of whom they are not fond. We explain we are here on behalf of Jeremy Corbyn, and – through a translator – we discuss the shortcomings of the Labour Party and the necessity to elect a Labour government. They will help leaflet and stuff envelopes.

April 17: Our big night: public meeting with Tony Benn. 350 people turn up at Highbury Grove School (where once upon a time Rhodes Boyson was Headmaster).

Rapturous reception for Benn – who talks about the two flames of socialism, hope and anger – and for Jeremy. The air is full of the best kind of socialist fervour: determined to elect a Labour government, realistic about its likely inadequacies and prepared to challenge them. I watch people's faces as Benn speaks. They drink in every word, like a crowd finding the oasis in the desert, the political desert of this media-mesmerised election.

April 18: IRA bomb threats close motorways, rail stations, airports and effectively slice the country in half – without a single fatality. A weirdly muted response in the media – as if this was a natural disaster to be endured with a show of British stoicism. You wouldn't know from this election campaign that there was a war of secession going on. That's the price of tri-partisanship on Ireland.

April 19: At last a firm, quantifiable commitment from the front bench. Asked if the prison population would rise or fall under New Labour, Jack Straw answered without equivocation: it would rise.

April 21: Islington North hustings sponsored by local newspaper. The Tory tries the 'you never had it so good' line: unemployment down, house prices up, etc. By the time he gets around to insisting that public transport in London is better than ever, he is being heckled and jeered by most of the audience.

April 22: Canvassing at a local estate literally crumbling away as we knocked on doors. Just as a woman was telling me how useless the Council is, a piece of plaster fell from above and landed at our feet. Here, housing is the biggest single issue on the doorstep, but Labour's housing policy is just the phased release of capital receipts: a welcome promise, but one left over from the last election. I'm already dreading next May's council elections.

April 24: Accompany Jeremy to local pensioners club. A rousing introduction by the chairman, a solid old CPer, then Jeremy lays out his position on pensions and restoring the link with earnings. There are plenty of supporters here, but one man stands up and says there's no money for pensioners because all the bloody foreigners are scrounging off the taxpayer. Half the room bursts into fervent applause.

April 26: Blair on ITN. A mother of two on benefits demands to know why people on £100,000 a year cannot pay more tax. Blair blusters impatiently but never actually answers.

April 28: Blair tells the *Sun*: 'Our candidates are not headbanging nut cases. They are ordinary Labour people. Many of them read the *Sun*. Fifteen years ago young people were headbangers, militants and extremists. Today they are the modernisers'. Worse yet, in today's *Mirror*, Blair promises: 'A New Labour government will keep strict controls on immigration. We intend to curb illegal immigration. Under the Tories, thousands of people illegally settle in this country each year and little is done to stop'. Outraged, I try to call HQ to complain. Impossible. Whatever number you dial, all you get is a recording of Blair urging you to volunteer for New Labour's election team.

April 29: 'Blair plans benefit freeze'. The *Guardian* reports: 'The tough stance is designed to make life on benefits less attractive, especially for the young'. But incapacity benefits and pensions, the article reveals, are also to remain at current levels. Does Blair plan to dragoon the infirm and the disabled into work? Had Blair included this election pledge in his 'Road to the Manifesto' ballot, Party members would have told him to get stuffed. To the Red Rose for Islington North's fundraising comedy evening with Mark Steel and Jeremy Hardy. A packed house is treated to non-stop jokes at the expense of Blair, Staw, Blunkett and New Labour. Thank God the media didn't turn up. After one reference to the leader of the Labour Party as a 'fuckwit' I case a glance around the room. Everyone was heaving with laughter. My favourite jibe of the night was Mark Steel on that great and enduring myth of our time, John Prescott's working class radicalism. 'Just because you're fat and you've got a northern accent and your vest shows through your shirt doesn't mean you're a socialist.'

April 30: Panic as Islington Council cocks up delivery of poll cards. Local Party inundated with phone calls from people who fear they have been struck off the register or who do not know where they are supposed to vote. Apparently the Council contracted out the printing to a private company, who failed to produce the cards on time. Meanwhile the Council's electoral registration office has been unreachable by telephone. We may pay the Chief Executive £90,000 a year for this service, but at least s/he won't have to pay more tax under New Labour.

May 1: The sun is shining and getting out the vote is easy. Mayhem as we try to run three polling stations from my kitchen.

May 2: I visit a friend who has been on the dole for several years. A 30-year-old street-smart cynic who has never voted or even registered to vote in his life, he is cock a hoop over the election result. Although he has no time for Blair, he was so excited by Labour's landslide he'd stayed up all night watching television. 'I never saw that before. You actually can change the government. Amazing. I'm going to vote next time'.

THE SLEEP OF REASON BREEDS MONSTERS

First published in October 1997 following the death of Princess Diana in August of that year.

Let's start with two simple propositions. First, the institution of the monarchy and the broader principle of inherited status and privilege are irrational and incompatible with a democratic society. Second, whatever her merits, Diana Spencer's contribution to public life did not justify the reaction to her death, which was disproportionate by any sober critera.

For at least a week, both of these eminently reasonable propositions were banned from public discourse. Diana-sceptics were bullied into silence. It was an alienating and at times frightening spectacle and a lesson in what the media, state and church can achieve when all are on message. I know there is a school of thought on the left which sees redeeming features in Diana-mania. Some point to the hostility to the Windsors and see an anti-monarchist dynamic at work. Others see the large numbers of people on the street, note that Buckingham Palace was forced to yield to popular pressure, and believe the experience could give the masses an all-important taste of power. It is argued that Diana's associations with progressive causes – AIDS, landmines, homelessness – and her willingness to be photographed with black people made the mass mourning an affirmation of inclusive social values. The popular revulsion against tabloid intrusiveness is also cited as a welcome development. No one on the left has to be lectured about the perfidy of the tabloids. I've seen these bastards at work and it's an ugly sight. But the claim that Diana was hounded to death by the press is neither literally nor metaphorically true and is one of the key falsifications on which the Diana cult has been built.

The rich and famous (Bob Geldof, Michael Jackson, Tom Cruise) have bellowed loudly for a 'privacy law' that would protect them from public scrutiny but leave the rest of us as vulnerable as ever to media misrepresentation. Let's face it, there was no more skilful or ruthless manipulator of the media than Diana Spencer. Her relationship with the tabloids was a symbiotic one. They needed her fame and she needed them to sustain her fame. Together they constructed Diana, Queen of Hearts. *The Economist* observed, 'The development of global media and entertainment industries has turned fame into a commodity in its own right... The globalisation of the media creates a special market for universally recognisable faces and stories', and there was no more universally recognisable face than Diana's. She was the acme of the global celebrity culture and in her death she extended the range and power of that culture.

Sales of the tabloids, as well as other publications, soared in the week following Diana's death. Nothing Earl Spencer said seemed to make a dent in the marketplace, in contrast to the effective boycott of the *Sun* in Liverpool following the Hillsborough nightmare. Indeed, the tabloids appointed themselves 'spokespersons for the nation', admonishing the royal family (and by extension the rest of us) on the proper tribute due to Diana. Did they generate or merely reflect the popular mood against the Windsors? In this post-modern hall of mirrors it's impossible to tell. Chris Dunkley in the *Financial Times* observed, 'By the time of the funeral, the crescendo felt like the human equivalent of the electronic phenomenon known as "howl-round", in which a sound system picks up its own output, amplifies it, and feeds it back into the circuit to produce a louder and louder wail.'

What was revealed in the aftermath of that car crash in Paris was the extent of the tabloidisation of the media as a whole, and along with it much of our public culture. In a letter to the *Financial Times*, Marion Bowman, ITV's 'controller of factual programmes' defended the television overkill by arguing that: 'We were witnessing a constitutional crisis and television was midwife to the most important moments in post-war British history.' The breathtaking arrogance, philistinism and sheer empty-headedness of this statement is characteristic of the performance of much of the rest of the media, notably the BBC, whose editorial judgements were wildly awry. By and large our intelligentsia made fools of themselves, substituting psychobabble for social analysis and indulging in the most uncritical waffle about 'the nation' and 'the people'.

The widespread sense of dislocation which followed news of Diana's death, shared even by people who thought they took little interest in her affairs, was testimony to the sheer inescapability of the global celebrity culture, which seems to be colonising an ever larger share of popular consciousness. But the meaning which was quickly assigned to this sense of dislocation – and which no one, for a while, was permitted to question – was an artificial construction.

Among its authors were not only the tabloids but also the BBC (which initially accepted uncritically the Al-Fayed claim that the paparazzi killed Diana and which identified and sanctioned Buckingham Palace and Kensington Palace as shrines to the dead princess) and Tony Blair, who dubbed Diana 'the people's princess' and who, like the tabloids, set himself up as mediator between the people and the palace. William Hague's complaint about Blair's exploitation of Diana's death would be perfectly justified if it wasn't for the fact that he would have done exactly the same if he had been in Blair's shoes.

Diana-sceptics have been accused of 'sneering' at ordinary people, of failing to respect the emotions felt by so many millions. On the contrary, it seems to me that it is those who refuse to treat their fellow citizens as intelligent beings who are really guilty of condescension. Of course, emotions are emotions. None is 'more real' than another. But this does not mean that all are equally justified or equally healthy or equally deserving of approbation and cultivation. Some commentators claimed to see in the response to Diana's death an abandonment of the stiff upper lip, new British expressiveness and emotional maturity. In fact, I found this officially sanctioned keening quite cruel. People's emotions were appropriated, assigned an explanation and an outlet by forces alien to their interest. The man who could not cry for his dead wife but wept for Diana was held up as an emblematic national figure, when he was clearly a deeply disturbed human being, alienated from his most intimate feelings (or perhaps just a wily self-publicist). What happened here was a massive and orchestrated displacement of emotions from immediate and concrete causes and effects to a realm of fantasy. So Britain has entered the world of pre-packaged, Oprah-style, emotionalism! If that's maturity, I'll stick to adolescence.

When the Italian visitor who had pinched some flowers from the Diana shrine left court after being sentenced, he was thumped by an aggrieved member of the public. According to most of the press, this thug 'spoke for the nation'. It was the logical evolution of all that had come before.

This royal death served the purpose of so many royal occasions: it breathed life into the old idea that we are a single nation, a single people, with a particular identity. Much was made of the affection for Diana crossing the boundaries of class, creed and colour. On the evening of the funeral, Gavin Eslar, speaking for the BBC, claimed that the past week we had 'come together as a people and learned who we were'. What a sad comment on Britain at the desperate end of the 20th century that its sense of nationhood has to be constructed on this fragile bauble.

Of course, large numbers of people in this country kept their heads and their sense of proportion. Forty-one per cent of the population did not bother to tune in to the funeral at all. Most people did not lay flowers or sign condolence books or line the funeral route. But somehow we are not representative of that magical confection, 'the nation'.

Populism is not the same as democracy and this distinction is becoming ever more critical in a world shaped by mass communications. Our rulers and managers, including Tony Blair and Peter Mandelson, would much prefer the nebulous bubble of 'popular mood' (not to mention the 'national will') to the rigours of accountability and representation and the public contest of ideas and social options.

Diana was the people's princess in the sense that her friend Richard Branson is a people's capitalist. Both terms are self-contradictory and highly deceptive. In her battle with her former in-laws, Diana mobilised popular sentiment, just as Branson did in his battle with BA, but she no more challenged the prerogatives of the monarchy than Branson challenged the priorities of capitalism. Far from having weakened the monarchy, this whole episode has re-enforced its centrality in the way the nation is defined. Yes, the Windsors are widely regarded as a bunch of mean-minded arrogant tossers. But would the monarchy be any more acceptable if it was 'staffed' by more sensitive and attractive individuals?

The response to Diana Spencer's death is symptomatic of the retreat from reason and democracy which appears to be characteristic of this phase of capitalism. In her life and death the pre-moden met the post-modern, the world of feudal right and blood status entered the media-refracted 'society of the spectacle'. The result should alarm not only socialists but all those who want to live in a community shaped by informed, critical, genuinely pluralist debate.

MISTAKEN PRIORITIES

First published in 2006.

Thanks to a minor but persistent ailment, I recently paid a series of visits to my local doctors' surgery. As always, the waiting room was filled. The patients – mostly working-class, many from the Turkish and Kurdish communities that are prominent in the area – were calm. We all felt the anxieties that anyone waiting to consult a physician feels but we all knew that there was one thing we didn't have to worry about: money.

Those of us with prior experience of this particular surgery also knew that our miseries would be dealt with promptly and efficiently. Over a period of weeks, I was seen by doctors, technicians and clerical staff; all sympathetic and responsive. Diagnosis and treatment were thoughtful and thorough. It was first-class healthcare, and there was no bill to pay. There was not even a form to fill in or a claim to file. For the umpteenth time since I migrated from the US to Britain 35 years ago, I gave thanks to the gods of social democracy for their wonderful bequest, the National Health Service, a jewel in the crown of human civilisation.

The NHS was launched in 1948 in unpropitious circumstances. Post-war austerity still reigned. Food and fuel were rationed. There was a housing crisis. Sterling was fragile. But there was a strong and confident labour movement and a Labour Party with a solid parliamentary majority and a popular mandate for radical change. What that government created was not a safety net for poor people, but a comprehensive service based on the democratic principle that everyone should have access to the best available healthcare, delivered free at the point of need and funded from general taxation.

From the beginning, there were problems. The sheer scale of the organisation – Europe's largest employer – gave rise to bureaucracy and sometimes made it slow in responding to diverse and changing needs. Rapid developments in medical technology as well as new forms of ill-health steadily increased pressure on resources. But through it all, the NHS has remained Britain's most cherished institution, and the exclusive provider of health services for 90 per cent of the population.

To most people in the USA, where access to medical care is a major anxiety, my recent NHS experience will sound like a utopian fantasy. It's not that the US lacks doctors and nurses; it has more than twice as many per head as the UK and ten times as many as India. And it's not that it doesn't spend lavishly, devoting 15 per cent of GDP to healthcare, a higher proportion than any other country. The problem is a profligate and chaotic healthcare system governed by the priorities of private profit. This is a system that excludes 14 per cent of the population – the 45 million Americans without health insurance – and leaves most of the rest with only partial and often expensive coverage. The Institute of Medicine estimates that at least 18,000 Americans die prematurely each year solely because they lack health insurance.

Although the US spends two and a half times as much per capita on health care than Britain, people in the US are likely to live less long and spend more years in ill health than people in Britain. The child mortality rate is 33 per cent higher in the US than in the UK, and the same as in Malaysia, where per capita income is only one tenth the US. And these average rates disguise extreme inequality within the US. Child mortality among African-Americans is twice the national average and higher than in Sri Lanka or Kerala. A baby boy from a family in the wealthiest five per cent will enjoy a life span 25 per cent longer than a child born in the poorest five per cent.

Meanwhile, thanks to the billing and accountancy required by a fragmented, privatised system, a quarter of US spending on health is swallowed up by administration: $400 billion a year, four times the combined health budgets of the 62 lowest-spending countries in the world, including India and China. Other costly chunks go on marketing, on profits for shareholders and on lobbying politicians to ensure those profits remain healthy – whatever the cost to the health of the nation as a whole.

Now Tony Blair wants to import this madness into Britain. Thatcher did her best to undermine the NHS – cutting services, raising charges, squeezing out dentistry and eye-care, imposing an 'internal market' that prioritised balancing the books over clinical need. But she never dared propose the kind of far-reaching changes currently being sought by Blair's cabinet. Just as only Nixon could go to China, only a Labour government could so compromise the NHS's founding principles. For the first time, NHS primary care provision is being franchised out to private sector entities, including US-based health care giants. NHS hospitals are being asked to 'compete' with private counterparts in providing operations on the cheap. Capital investment in new facilities is mortgaged to private finance – which takes no risk but is guaranteed a long-term income stream from the taxpayer. An ever increasing proportion of NHS spending is winding up in corporate coffers.

Despite substantial increases in the health budget in recent years, the NHS finds itself once again, this winter, in crisis. As a result of a £700 million overspend, services around the country are being rationed, curtailed or eliminated. As ever, the biggest losers are the poor, the elderly and the disabled. The government says the overspend just shows the need to bring in the private sector faster. But in light of £1.5 billion the Exchequer managed to find to prosecute the war in Iraq this year, it seems more likely that this is really a monstrous case of mistaken priorities.

POLITICS AND 'THE ART OF THE POSSIBLE'

First published in 2010.

Whenever a commentator declares that 'politics is the art of the possible', I'm on my guard. What I'm being told, I suspect, is to accept apparent present conditions as immutable facts of life, and to trim my goals accordingly. I'm being told to let injustices stand.

Like all banalities, the familiar dictum contains an obvious truth. To be politically effective, you have to be able to distinguish between your desires and realities on the ground, between aspirations and resources.

But like most banalities, it begs more questions than it answers. How is 'the possible' defined? Where are its limits drawn? Who draws them? Theoretically, the possible is an elastic and speculative category. But the dictum draws no distinctions between the immediately unlikely and the ultimately impossible, takes no notice of the infinite and shifting gradations between them, and of the impact of human agency in shifting an outcome from one category to another.

What's usually meant when politics is pronounced the art of the possible is that politics is a calculation of the probable, an exercise in the pragmatic, the expedient or the opportune. The adage implies forcefully that minimal improvements or lesser evils are the only realistic aim – and any demand for more is self-indulgence. It's an injunction not only to compromise, but to get your compromise in first. To placate hostile forces in advance, as Obama tried to do with healthcare reform.

Obama's election was in itself a vivid display of the eruption of the supposedly impossible into the realm of the ordinary. The slogan 'Yes we can' proposed a generalised defiance of assumed limitations. Now Obama's supporters are being lectured for expecting too much from the President, for not understanding that 'politics is the art of the possible'. Here, as in so many instances, the 'possible' is a code word for what vested interests will permit.

When Francis Bacon was told that his plan for 'The Advancement of Learning' could never be realised, he answered: 'Touching impossibility, I take it those things are to be held possible which may be done by some person, though not by every one; and which may be done by many, though not by any one; and which may be done in succession of ages, though not within the hourglass of one man's life; and which may be done by public designation, though not by private endeavour.'

William Blake regarded Bacon as the epitome of rationalist arrogance. But even more than Bacon, he protested against the shrivelled, static nature of the 'possible' of his day. 'Reason, or the ratio of all we have already known', he wrote in 1788, 'is not the same that it shall be when we know more'.

When people speak of politics as the art of the possible, they imply a world of unexamined assumptions about the limits of the possible – a world which embodies only the limits of their own experience or imagination. In its unreflective way, the dictum treats the superficial conditions of the moment as unchangeable realities. In effect, it serves as a denial of possibility, a closing of the aperture into the future.

It also urges us not to feel the urgency of injustice. The dictum is cold comfort to the oppressed, the victims of poverty, discrimination and violence, who are asked to continue suffering while distant arbiters decide what is or is not 'possible' in their case. It sacrifices the poor, the hungry, the desperate on the altar of a self-serving pragmatism. Impatience, in fact, is a necessary political virtue. Without it, even the most gradual change is inconceivable. And a politician who is not impatient with injustice, with needless death and destruction, is worse than useless.

Those who dispute the dictum are accused of utopianism, which is condemned as an intellectual and emotional error, not just a mistake but a danger. Of course utopias are no substitute for the practice of politics, and can serve as an evasion of present responsibilities. But a practical politics stripped of serious ideas about what would constitute a just human society is a greater and more common menace.

Utopias can be powerful motivators, and thus a real influence on human destinies. For evidence one only has to look at the Indian independence movement or the African-American Civil Rights Movement, at Gandhi and King, who defied assumed limitations to build great mass movements. By word and deed, they alerted people to the greater range of possibilities that lay within their grasp.

Utopias provide a perspective from which the assumed limitations of the present can be examined, from which familiar social arrangements can be revealed as unjust, irrational or unnecessary. They are a means of expanding the borders of the possible. You can't chart the surface of the earth or compute distances without a point of elevation – a mountaintop, a star or a satellite. You can't chart the possible in society without an angle of vision, a mental mountaintop that permits the widest sweep. The pundits championing the art of the possible are the flat-earthers of today, afraid to venture too far from shore lest they fall off the face of the earth.

It's striking how often pundits of 'the possible' rest their case on all kinds of gross improbabilities. In insisting that there was no alternative to neo-liberal economics, many assumed, oblivious to obvious objections, that speculation had no limits, that wealth-making could be severed from productive activity, that private interests would magically coagulate into public benefit, that industrial growth could be limitless on a planet with finite resources. Here the art of the possible stands revealed as a dismal pseudo-science, its certainties built on foundations of sand.

This is very much the vice of the centre-left. The right are bolder, more confident, more reckless and strongly driven by their own utopian visions (which would be dystopias for the rest of us). In contrast, liberals advise each other to trim their ambitions, to sacrifice their goals in order to remain politically viable. In the wake of 9/11, liberals in the US largely signed up to the Afghanistan invasion – because to fail to do so would place them outside an apparently immutable pro-war consensus. Those who kept their nerve and set about building an anti-war movement proved the more far-sighted.

Of course, if your politics is about personal aggrandisement, then it will be 'the art of the possible' in the narrowest sense. But for those who seek in politics a means of changing society for the better, it must be the art of *redefining* the possible. The art-science-craft of coaxing from the present, with its complex mix of possibilities and limitations, a just and sustainable human future.

RIOTS, REASON AND RESISTANCE

First published in 2011 following the English riots in August of that year.

'Criminality pure and simple' was Prime Minister David Cameron's initial verdict on the rioting. From the right came the mantra, 'Down with sociology! Up with water cannon!' Don't think but do act – harshly, punitively, peremptorily.

In the wake of the riots, a powerful vested interest has been at work – a vested interest in people not making links, not searching for causes, not weighing contexts. Above all, an interest in derailing the growing resistance to the government's austerity programme.

In the vast realm of human phenomena there are few things as impure or as complex as a riot, with its ever-shifting array of motives and circumstances. It is a social phenomenon and requires a social analysis and response. It's the denial of that duty that's reckless and irresponsible, not the alleged 'socio-economic excuses' reviled by conservatives.

The opening scene was in Tottenham, an impoverished, multi-ethnic community in north London, where a young man had been shot dead by police in circumstances that remain unexplained. A peaceful vigil was held outside the local police station but the mood turned angry when no one from the police would come out to talk to the bereaved family. What ensued was a running battle between local youths – as multi-ethnic as the local population – and police. The arson and looting came in the wake of that.

The next major flashpoint came 48 hours later in Hackney, just south of Tottenham and sharing all its problems. Here groups of young people faced off against the police for several hours, during which time they took control of and barricaded a nearby public housing complex, to a decidedly mixed response from residents. Again, in this episode, looting was secondary to the confrontation with police.

In the hours and days that followed, various forms of disorder spread to other locales in London and eventually to other English cities, notably Liverpool and Birmingham. In Ealing in west London restaurants and cafes were attacked. In Enfield, to the north of Tottenham, a Sony warehouse was ransacked and incinerated. In Clapham, south of the Thames, a Debenhams department store was looted. Most tragically, in Birmingham, three young Muslims were killed as they protected their family shops. In the London suburb of Eltham, a vigilante mob assembled to hunt for 'rioters' – backed by the Muslim-hating English Defence League.

What happened was a concatenation of actions and reactions, with the riotous behaviour taking several forms: confrontation with police, destruction of property (large chain stores but also small shops), sporadic assaults on individuals, looting (theft), sometimes as a secondary overspill and sometimes as primary purpose, plus a lawless reaction to all of the above.

All Londoners have been distressed by the riots, but only a small minority have been directly affected. At no time did London resemble a 'war zone'. The main business of the city went on as usual. There are small scarred patches but no large burnt-out areas. The exaggeration serves a purpose, however, selling papers, stoking mutual fear and licensing the authoritarian responses that go with fear.

Though no one foresaw the course the riots would take, it wasn't hard to predict some kind of social outburst, and indeed such predictions were made by many, not least the police themselves. To anyone walking around certain areas of London with their eyes open, it was clear that patience was ebbing, anger brewing, grievances converging.

And behind that lies the realm of context and causation that we are being warned not to explore.

The killing in Tottenham elicited a response because it was the latest in a series of events which have left the Metropolitan Police (London's police force) deeply compromised. There have been fatal and near-fatal shootings of innocent young men, the death of a middle-aged newspaper vendor as a result of heavy-handed policing at the G20 protest in 2009, and the death earlier this year of reggae musician Smiley Culture during a police raid on his home (a peaceful protest of thousands was ignored). When student demonstrations against the tripling of tuition fees surged through central London this past winter, they were subjected to stringent police tactics, with many thousands 'kettled' – forcibly confined for hours to small areas without facilities of any kind. Tens of thousands of London youth have found themselves subject to demeaning and discriminatory 'stop and search' operations. Finally came the exposure of police complicity in the Rupert Murdoch-sponsored phone-hacking scandal, culminating in the resignations of the Met's two top cops only weeks before the riot.

When historians look back I suspect they will be most immediately struck by the conjuncture of the rioting with the global stock market turmoil sparked off by the Eurozone crisis and the downgrading of the US's credit rating. They'll scratch their heads and wonder just how it was we missed this connection.

Britain as a whole is a wealthy country but the distribution of that wealth has grown increasingly and palpably unequal. In London in particular there's a concentration of glamour and grimness, luxury goods and lifestyles next to poverty and exclusion. Fifteen yeas of GDP growth passed many of those in the riot-affected areas by, and three years of recession have hit them hard. Average male life expectancy in Tottenham is 18 years less than in wealthy Kensington and Chelsea (and youngsters there are five times more likely to be injured in road accidents). Youth unemployment, running at 20 per cent nationally, runs at double that figure in places like Tottenham and Hackney.

Recession is now being compounded by austerity, with the coalition government cutting public support for housing, education, healthcare, pension contributions, the disabled and the unemployed, while privatising state functions and further easing the tax burden on the rich. Young people face an exceptionally bleak future: it will be much harder for them than for their parents to get an education, a decent job, a secure home, or, in the remote future, a dignified retirement. The life chances of millions are being diminished. 150 people have been made homeless as a result of the recent riots, but tens of thousands will be made homeless by the government's cuts to housing benefit.

There is widespread resentment about the way the burden of austerity has fallen much more heavily on some than on others. Tax evasion by the rich will this year cost the public about 100 times what's being spent repairing riot damage. And the anti-social behaviour of the banks and financial institutions has been as brazen as anything seen in the riots. Their reckless avarice triggered a meltdown that destroyed London's property values to a far greater extent than the riots, but they go on rewarding themselves record-breaking bonuses – sharing among the few a pot of money worth twice the combined spending of all London local authorities.

As so often these days, whenever there is resistance to acknowledging a context of inequality, 'culture' is dragged in as the preferred culprit. Or rather in this case a putative youth sub-culture of selfishness and indiscipline, usually held to be the upshot of an over-permissive society (or overgenerous welfare state). This seems to be Cameron's current line and he will use it to push long-standing right wing ambitions, not least the curtailing of European Union human rights requirements.

There is, of course, a cultural context, and it is provided principally by the dominant culture of the day, a competitive consumerism in which self-aggrandisement is celebrated, brand names fetishised (see the clips of looters in footwear shops), and leisure thoroughly commercialised. Looting is shopping without money, a brief dose of retail therapy. In naked acquisitiveness and contempt for the law, the rioters were merely emulating their betters. One elite scandal has followed another – from MPs' expenses through bankers' bonuses to the Murdoch hacking imbroglio. There must be a cumulative impact, an erosion of authority, and it would be naïve to deny it.

Beyond culture, and informing it, there is the phenomenon of powerlessness, which is both a subjective and objective reality, and poverty's constant companion. Watching the rioters, it was easy to see how pumped up and liberated some were by this brief taste of power, of possession. But in the end the only antidote to powerlessness is power, economic and political. The current route to that is through resistance to austerity, in Britain and across Europe. For that resistance, the challenge now, in the wake of the riots, is to expand in scope and diversity.

For the moment, we're being treated to a familiar demonology – 'feral' youths, an amoral underclass of the irresponsible and rude – a phantom menace that is dangerously elastic, easily shaped by racial, generational and class prejudices. Politicians and media want rioters stripped of benefits and evicted from public housing. The *Sunday Express* wants to see them conscripted into the armed forces (and handed guns). Cameron wants to import a super-cop from USA to run the Met. He's even targeted 'the obsession with health and safety' as a riot factor which must be addressed, of course, with deregulation.

More ominously, the riots are being used as an excuse to criminalise protest and clamp down on Internet freedom.

But the demonology has already been undermined by the diverse social profile of those appearing before the courts. Thousands will pass through this mill in the months to come. Politicians and the media are pressing for harsh penalties, and the six months' sentence handed to a first offender for looting four bottles of water bodes ill for the future. Britain's prisons are already overcrowded, costly and dangerous, with more than 300 deaths in custody in the last decade, including scores of children and young people.

The court appearances and jail terms will inevitably involve injustices, disruption of family life and depletion of family resources. And given what we know of the fates of ex-prisoners we have no excuse for not expecting that many of those imprisoned will re-offend or suffer joblessness, poverty, homelessness, mental illness. The scale of the human damage to be done in the coming months, most of which will go unreported, is disheartening in the extreme. Unlike the riots this damage will be done not spontaneously but deliberately, which makes it all the more chilling.

Discussion on the ground in London is more nuanced than the official version, with its prerequisite of mindless condemnation of 'mindless violence'. There is confusion and disagreement and emotion, inevitably and rightly. But the government's one-dimensional response has little credibility. The battle over the meaning(s) of the riots has only just begun.

POLITICS, OUR MISSING LINK

First published in 2012.

The word comes down to us from ancient Greece, where *polis* was used to describe the city-states that emerged in the sixth century BC. This polis was more than a community or concentration of individuals. It was a self-conscious unit of self-administration (independent of empires) and from the start was made up of separate, contending social classes.

As Ellen Meiksins Wood explains in her revelatory studies of classical antiquity, Athenian democracy was itself the product of a class struggle and a class compromise, involving aristocrats, on the one hand, and, on the other, artisans and small-holding peasants, who became 'free citizens', sharply differentiated from slaves. It was in the context of Athenian democracy that politics emerged as a distinct activity, one concerned with the affairs of the polis, considered as an entity separate from (and superior to) family or clan. Crucially, the polis was contrasted with the more limited and subordinate *oikos*, household, the private realm of 'economy'.

Today we're told that the law of the oikos is dominant, and the polis must yield. Only of course the oikos is no longer the individual household – to which it's deceptively likened – but the imperatives of global capital.

In present day Greece, we're witnessing a dramatic clash between polis and oikos, democracy and capital. Here as elsewhere the latter prevails to the extent that it succeeds in making its laws appear implacable, the alternatives mere wishful thinking. Yet the roots of the crisis lie precisely in the non-political autonomy of the economic, in deregulated finance's detachment from production.

Under neo-liberalism, the political realm has been squeezed; globalisation and privatisation have removed much of the life of the polis from democratic control. Since the fundamental choices have already been made elsewhere, and systemic alternatives are excluded, politics itself becomes depoliticised, a matter of management and expertise, not of ideology or mass constituencies. As the neo-liberal consensus was imbibed by the parties of the centre left, politics increasingly became 'politicking': the manipulation of images and the clash of personalities.

This evisceration of the political lies at the root of today's popular anti-politics: the complaint that 'they're all the same' or 'all in it for themselves', the desire to get over or somehow circumvent the 'divisiveness' of politics, the calls for politicians to 'work together'. 'Politics' is seen as an alien realm of duplicity, opportunism and contrived conflict, not a common concern. Ironically, no one is keener to exploit popular anti-politics than professional politicians. See the rise and fall of Nick Clegg.

A cloud of cynicism settles over everything, leaving vested interests and real choices invisible. It's a a superficial, easily manipulated scepticism, a problem for the left and a boon for the right.

In the end, this illusory non-political politics is the property of the dominant powers. A good example is the Olympics, where the hoary old apartheid-era slogan 'Keep politics out of sport' is once again in favour. Of course, what those who say they want 'politics out of sport' really mean is that they want other people's politics out of sport; they want no politics but their own (i.e. corporate- and state-sponsored messages about competition and identity). This is the paradigm we have to reject, the political ideology that masks itself as non-political.

We have to be clear that there is no non-political, non-partisan answer. That politics needs to be 'divisive'. That the anti-politics of today are impotent. That avoiding choices means handing them to others all too willing to exercise the prerogative.

A kind of anti-politics is also widespread on the left. A healthy contempt for mainstream 'politics' is combined with a more ambiguous distrust of political organisation in general. We need to be careful that in our rejection of what passes for 'politics' we do not inadvertently mirror the de-politicised universe of global capital we want to challenge. In Britain (as elsewhere), politics is our weak spot, the missing mediator without which we can never achieve our goals.

Politics in the sense I'm talking about is the linking of principle with practise, ideas with power, processes with goals, movements with institutions (whereas the simulacrum called 'politics' separates all these). Politics means interaction, intervention, agency in relation to the polis – understood (as in ancient Athens) as the arena in which the direction of the commonwealth is set. It means contesting the existing balance of power.

Engaging with the polis (the citizenry, the larger political whole) isn't about placating the majority but addressing it, honestly and in comprehensible and coherent terms. Politics is therefore always and necessarily partisan. It means making enemies. It therefore carries with it demands for organisation, discipline and sacrifice; it can never be a continuous festival.

Don't get me wrong. I'm not asking for a politics stripped of desire, imagination, spontaneity. No politics can succeed without to some extent generating its own expressive culture, but that culture, no matter how subversive, cannot substitute for political action. Nor does politics mean abandoning utopia. On the contrary, utopian ideas are vital levers in the contest for political power in the here and now. Politics does, however, mean working out the links between today's conditions and tomorrow's utopia, the steps from here to there.

The left has no shortage of policy proposals and alternatives. They're bubbling up everywhere, not least in the pages of *Red Pepper*. But politics means coordinating and integrating this welter of ideas, making choices, rejecting some, prioritising others – in other words, creating a programme.

It's a hard and under-appreciated process, with a negative reputation for dogmatism and sectarian competition. Of course, a programme should be fluid and responsive to changing conditions; 'the letter killeth but the spirit giveth life'. However, without a programme (forged and fought for collectively), we'll remain at a hopeless disadvantage. It will always be an uphill climb to make ourselves more convincing, more credible than the prevailing consensus. Sheer negative reaction to the system will not carry us through.

Finally, politics implies the left-right spectrum (which many Greens seek to evade). This spectrum has its origins in revolutionary France, where it accompanied the birth of modern politics, and reflected a division that was not about ethnicity, religion, or region, but about ideas and classes, which is why it became globally recognised. And still, I think, unavoidable and necessary (if not always straightforward). When someone claims to have superseded the left-right spectrum, they're evading the reality of a divided society.

To come now to the hard part. Yes, politics does imply elections and elections imply parties (and programmes). Of course, a party that is merely an electoral machine has actually abandoned politics. But a movement without an electoral intervention is doomed to lose out in the final analysis. Yes, we can hope to influence the mainstream, to push it towards the left, and above all to use our power in the street to change the political context. But being satisfied with that is letting down all those who need more, those who cannot afford to leave the same corporate sponsored caste in power year after year.

Surely this is one of the lessons of Latin America, where social movements found or created effective political vehicles, won elections, formed governments and achieved real social change, however limited or fragile. To varying degrees, the left parties there have been able to break with neo-liberalism, reclaim the polis and politicise the oikos. In contrast, the evolving Arab Spring looks badly hampered by the absence of political formations, leaving the popular movement at the mercies of Western imperialism and conservative Islamism.

Back in Britain, the prospects for building a political alternative are so forbidding that most of us have given up talking about it. It's the hardest task, with the least promise of immediate success, which is why it can't simply be left to 'history' (to someone else). Having said that, I confess I have no road map, no concrete proposals to take us in that direction. First, I suspect, there will have to be a larger number of people agreeing that we do indeed need to redress the political gap and provide the missing link.

SUCCESS, FAILURE AND OTHER POLITICAL MYTHS

First published in 2013.

As we approach the tenth anniversary of the global anti-war protest of 15 February 2003, people are bound to ask what it actually achieved. Certainly it failed to stop the war, a failure for which Iraqis paid and are paying an exorbitant price. So was it a waste of time, an exercise in futility? There are answers to these questions, but to be persuasive they cannot be glib.

Let me flash back to 15 November 1969, Washington DC and the Moratorium for Peace in Vietnam. This was probably the single biggest anti-war demonstration of the era, estimated at half a million by some and twice that by others. I'd come down from the New York suburbs the day before, on a bus chartered by local activists, and spent the night on the floor of a Quaker meeting house. The next day I wandered among the vast, mostly youthful crowd, listening to the speeches, and feeling despondent and confused. I was 16 but already a veteran of three years of anti-war protest, during which time I'd seen the movement mushroom. In the spring of 1966, I'd accompanied my parents to my first Washington DC protest, which was considered a great success because it attracted a crowd of 10,000. Now there were perhaps a hundred times that number and it felt to me like failure.

Pete Seeger, then aged 50 but already a Methuselah of struggle, led chorus after chorus of the recently-released 'Give Peace a Chance'. I was churlish about this because I thought we were or should be saying a lot more than 'give peace a chance'. So I joined a splinter march chanting 'Ho Ho Ho Chi Minh NLF is gonna win' and got tear gassed outside the Justice Department. None of this was very satisfying and on the long drive home I felt depressed. What was the point of it all? For years we'd been protesting in ever increasing numbers, with ever increasing militancy – and yet they kept escalating the war. What difference had all our earnest activity made? What difference would the Moratorium protest make? What difference would anything make? My commonplace teenage malaise had become intertwined with a precocious experience of political frustration.

My scepticism about the demonstration's effect seemed warranted when five months later, at the end of April, 1970, the US extended the war into Cambodia. In the protests that followed six students, four at Kent State in Ohio and two at Jackson State in Mississippi, were shot dead. The upshot was the biggest student strike in US history: more than four million students walking out of classes in universities, colleges and high schools across the country. Yet still the war did not end. Two and a half more years would pass before the peace treaty was signed in Paris in January 1973. By this time there were millions upon millions dead, disabled, bereaved, traumatised. Nonetheless, the movement against the Vietnam War is widely considered the most 'successful' anti-war movement of modern times, against which more recent movements have measured their 'failure'.

Many years later, I learned that the Moratorium demonstration was, in fact, anything but ineffectual. In July 1969, Nixon and Kissinger had delivered an ultimatum to the Vietnamese: if they did not accept US terms for a ceasefire by 1 November, 'we will be compelled – with great reluctance – to take measures of the greatest consequences.' The US government was threatening and indeed actively planning a nuclear strike against North Vietnam. In his *Memoirs*, Nixon admitted that the key factor in the decision not to proceed with the nuclear option was that 'after all the protests and the Moratorium, American public opinion would be seriously divided by any military escalation of the war.' What would have been the world's second nuclear war was averted by our action, though we couldn't have known it at the time.

So it turns out that marching on that day was anything but an exercise in futility. In fact it's hard to think of a day better spent in the course of a lifetime. My teenage despondency was utterly misplaced.

But this kind of retrospective vindication is rare in the extreme. Most days spent in protest will not be rewarded with such a tangible achievement. The point is that *we don't know and we can't know* which protest, leaflet, meeting, occupation, activity will 'make a difference', tip the balance. We are always the underdog, we are always contending against power, and therefore the likelihood is that we will fail. But no success can be achieved unless we risk that failure. Otherwise when possibilities for success arise they pass by unrealised.

I fear we slip too easily into a capitalist paradigm of 'success' and 'failure'. Here the investment is of value only to the extent it yields measurable gains. If it doesn't it's a failure, dead capital. So we look for evidence that our efforts have had an impact, made a difference. Every success is catalogued on the credit side while the much greater number of failures is left un-tabulated. Sometimes in doing this we start to sound a little desperate, clinging to straws. I wonder if this is the best way to persuade people to invest themselves in a cause. After all, there will always be activities offering more reliable and more tangible rewards.

In evaluating our political efforts, we have to jettison neo-liberalism's stark demarcation between 'success' and 'failure', which erases everything in between and, even worse, denies any combination of the two. In the politics of social justice, unmixed success and unmitigated failure are rare. Every successful revolution or major reform has had unintended consequences, created new problems, fallen short of its goals. In politics, failures contain the seeds of successes, just as successes conceal the roots of failure.

Capitalists like to invoke a 'risk / reward ratio' to justify their profits. Sadly, people on the left sometimes emulate their narrow logic. They promise activists a return on their investment, a guarantee: history is on our side.

But for us, there can be no stable 'ratio' between risk and reward. Our risk has to be taken in defiance of the odds, recognising the likelihood that there will be no reward. At the same time, we take the risk only because of the nature of the reward we seek: a precious step towards a just society. We are not at all indifferent to the outcome. We aim and need to succeed because the consequences of failure are real and widely felt.

So we make the investment. We put our time and energy and skills at the disposal of a cause. This is a greater investment than the capitalist knows – and one that makes us vulnerable in a way the capitalist never is.

We're taught to despise and fear 'failure', but to engage in the politics of social change we have to be brave enough to fail. Science advances through failure; every successful experiment is made possible only by a host of failed ones. In human evolution, failure – incapacities, shortcomings – led to compensation and innovation.

There are worse things than failure, and while failure is nothing to glory in, it's also nothing to be ashamed of. You can learn more from a failure than from a success – if you recognise it as such. But if the only lesson you draw from failure is never to risk failure again, you've learned nothing at all.

Needless risks should always be avoided. We don't have resources to squander. But the elimination of risk is impossible if you're contending with power. Without risks all that can be done is to reproduce existing social relations. There is no truth, no beauty without risk, because these things can only be secured in the teeth of resistance, against institutions and habits of thought. To succeed in any way that matters, you have to take your place in the republic of the uncertain, where you risk yourself, not your stake in other people's labour. It's the action taken in the full knowledge of the possibility of failure, and its consequences, that acquires leverage.

THATCHERISM'S RESISTIBLE RISE

First published in 2013 following the death of Margaret Thatcher.

Thatcher's death and, even more, her reincarnation in Britain's coalition government make this a propitious moment to re-examine the history of the 1980s. With severe cuts being imposed on local government, it's especially worth revisiting the rate-capping controversy of 1984-85.

The history of the 1980s was never a simple tale of triumphal neo-liberalism. The Thatcherite project was resisted every step of the way and at several critical junctures was seriously imperilled. During her first term, until the Falklands War, her government was deeply unpopular. That led to the election in the early eighties of Labour councils with strong left-wing contingents. As unemployment rose, these councils raised spending on services, compensating for cuts in government grants by increasing 'the rates' – the long-established local property tax, paid by residents and businesses.

Determined to close this escape valve, the Tories introduced legislation soon after their 1983 victory to 'cap' rate-rises in what they considered to be profligate councils. From the start, the proposal was controversial, even within the Conservative Party, where a significant minority, including Edward Heath, regarded it as an unwarranted centralisation of power. Nonetheless, the government pushed it through Parliament and rate-capping became law in June 1984.

The debate about how Labour should respond unfolded against the background of the year-long miners' strike. For many on the left, this was an opportunity to open a second front against the government. Support for non-compliance was widespread, but there was considerable disagreement over what form it should take. The strategy eventually adopted – in which affected Labour councils would collectively refuse to set a rate – was a lowest common denominator, the one point of action around which most could unite.

It needs to be stressed that the discussion that led to this decision was intensive and extensive, involving large numbers at the base of the Labour Party. The commitment to non-compliance was not due to the influence of conspiratorial 'entryists'; it was the result of a wide-ranging democratic exercise and reflected a determination among Labour members to fight the Tories not only during but between elections.

At the Labour Party Conference in September 1984, local government attracted more resolutions than any other topic. The official statement from the party's National Executive endorsed non-compliance and called for unity; two resolutions went further, pledging support to councils forced to break the law. Both the statement and the resolutions were agreed by a show of hands – not at all the result the Parliamentary leadership wanted.

Their ambivalence was not shared by Thatcher. In a speech in November, a month after the Brighton bombing, she yoked together all her opponents as enemies of the rule of law. 'At one end of the spectrum are the terrorist gangs within our borders, and the terrorist states which finance and arm them. At the other are the Hard Left operating inside our system, conspiring to use union power and the apparatus of local government to break, defy and subvert the law.'

Despite equivocation at the top, the campaign against rate-capping was taken up vigorously at the grass roots. It was inventive, diverse, populist, reaching out to and involving workforces and unions alongside a wide array of community organisations. In November 1984, 100,000 local government workers took a day's strike action; 30,000 marched in London. Through festivals, demonstrations, meetings, publications and events involving youth clubs, nurseries, play and pensioners groups, the campaign succeeded in alerting a broad public to the menace of rate capping and its effects on services, jobs and local democracy.

Prominent in the leadership of the campaign and its central strategy of non-compliance were Margaret Hodge of Islington, David Blunkett of Sheffield and Ken Livingstone of the GLC, all of whom at this stage were insisting on the need for bold defiance and labour movement solidarity.

From the start, it was clear to all that non-compliance might well entail real personal penalties for the councillors involved. If the district auditor found that the council had suffered financial loss as a result of their votes, councillors could be ordered to repay the lost money in a 'surcharge'. If the surcharge amounted to more than £2,000 each, the councillors would be disqualified from office. On top of that, they could be held 'jointly and severally liable' for the total sum lost to the council – not just their individual share of it.

In February 1985 Neil Kinnock issued his famous edict to Labour's local government conference: 'Better a dented shield than no shield at all.' While this was to become (and remains) the prevailing wisdom in the Labour Party, at the time it was deeply dismaying to activists. Kinnock had effectively advised the Tories that councils who resisted their diktat would be left isolated. It was a declaration, from the top table, that there would be no labour movement unity.

Nonetheless, at this stage, 26 Labour councils remained determined to defy the government. They planned to synchronise their budget meetings for 7 and 8 March, coinciding with TUC-sponsored 'Democracy Day' demonstrations. On this issue, the government looked vulnerable. Thatcher's popularity ratings had dipped: 60 per cent now said they were 'dissatisfied' with her. Then on 5 March 1985, the miners retuned to work after a year-long struggle. Their defeat became, in the short run, a pretext for giving up the rate-capping struggle, and in the long run, for a general accommodation with Thatcherism.

On 7 March, the *Times* made a prediction: 'Labour's left-wing councillors value power more than a place of glory in the Socialist Pantheon... they will cling to office and make the shifts required, shifts which in most cases are perfectly manageable.' The cynicism proved sadly prescient. The first to collapse was the GLC, where Livingstone himself led the climb-down, while his deputy John McDonnell and a minority of Labour councillors insisted on upholding the democratically agreed line. When the GLC voted to set a legal rate on 10 March, Tory minister Kenneth Baker jeered: 'The united front of the militant left has crumbled before our eyes. Instead of opening a second front with the miners some of their troops have fled the battlefield!'

The other rate-capped councils appeared for the moment to be standing firm. Initially nearly all voted to refuse to set a rate and in doing so enjoyed voluble local support. In April, Islington council published a poll of local residents showing that in the argument over rate-capping, 57 per cent supported the council and only 20 per cent the Government. Asked what the council should do, 37 per cent said they wanted the council to continue not to set a rate, 27 per cent wanted the council to resign and force an election on the issue, while only 21 per cent wanted the council to back down and set a legal rate.

But as the threats from district auditors grew more urgent, one by one the Labour councils abandoned non-compliance. In Islington, the retreat was marshalled by Margaret Hodge, who denounced her critics for 'posturing' – an accusation surely more applicable to Hodge herself, along with Blunkett and Livingstone, who made promises they did not keep.

By the middle of June, all but Lambeth and Liverpool had yielded to pressure. In September, the district auditors gave notice to

81 councillors (49 from Liverpool, 32 from Lambeth) that the delay in setting the rates amounted to 'wilful misconduct' and that they were therefore required to repay the costs as a personal surcharge. Since in both cases the amount per councillor was more than £2,000, all 81 were disqualified from office and barred from seeking re-election. A series of judicial appeals failed. At the end of July 1986, the Lambeth councillors were given 21 months to pay 'surcharges' amounting to more than £200,000. The following year, Liverpool councillors were held liable for an even larger total, £333,000. In the end, these sums were paid off by donations from the labour movement, though not without personal sacrifices for a number of the councillors concerned.

The councillors of Lambeth and Liverpool paid the price of principle. It was a very un-eighties thing to do. They stood against the current and should be celebrated for that. They kept faith with their electorates and their consciences, even when abandoned by their leaders, vilified in the media and threatened with bankruptcy.

The defeat of the rate-capping campaign was a significant step in the hollowing out of local democracy and in Labour's long-term adaptation to Thatcherism. Those who led the retreat soon shifted their defence. Initially it was posed as a stark choice of lesser evils. But gradually the 'evil' became celebrated as a virtue: the 'reform' of public services through privatisation and attacks on the workforce. Managerialism replaced politics.

And the pay-off for the 'dented shield', which was supposed to be the election of a Labour government, did not materialise in 1987 or 1992, and when it did, finally, in 1997, it did not herald a re-invigoration of local democracy. Instead, the managerial ethos was entrenched via 'cabinet' government and executive mayors. The fiscal autonomy enjoyed prior to rate capping was never restored.

Of course, Thatcherism was only the British version of the neo-liberal wave of the era. But that global context does not mean its triumph was inevitable. It was resistible. Its hegemony was an end product, established piecemeal, unevenly and painfully. And its triumph required a political struggle.

In that struggle, it was immensely to Thatcher's advantage that every time she singled out a target for attack, she could be confident that the target would be left high and dry by the Labour and trade union leaderships. Thatcher was never the leader of principle vaunted by the media; she was ruthlessly opportunistic. But it was that very quality that made her adept at calling the bluff of the spineless centre – whether among the 'wets' in her own party or the leaders of Labour local government.

WHY I AM AN UNREPENTANT BENNITE

First published in 2014 following the death of Tony Benn.

It was inevitable that Tony Benn's death would be met with tributes from the political establishment to the effect that they admired him even if they didn't agree with him. But for those of us who did agree with him, his life and death mean so much more.

There's one phase of Benn's long career that liberal commentators still can't stomach: his leadership of the Labour left in the early 1980s. The Bennite upsurge of that time is blamed for dividing the Party, saddling it with 'extreme' policies, and costing it the general election of 1983 (and in some accounts 1987 as well).

In fact, this was for me one of Benn's most courageous and prophetic moments.

I was one of many in those years inspired by Benn to become active in the Labour Party and to this day I regard myself as an unrepentant Bennite, early-eighties vintage: what we tried to do, under Tony's leadership, was to reshape the Party from the bottom up, to make it an effective instrument of working class representation. And while we failed to do that, we came close enough to scare the hell out of the British ruling class, who put huge resources into destroying Benn and the Bennite movement. His courage in those days, under ceaseless attack from the media and the leaders of his own party, was exemplary, and enabled many others to stand their ground under pressure.

Looking back, we can now see this moment as the dawn of the neo-liberal age. The choice to be made was between resisting that development, insisting that there was an alternative, or accommodating to it and designing policy and strategy accordingly. Most Labour MPs and trade union leaders, not to mention leader writers, columnists and a significant section of the Communist Party, chose accommodation.

Benn chose resistance, and in doing so placed himself at the head and heart of more than 30 years of often bitter struggle for the better world he insisted was possible.

Crucial to Benn's appeal was his revival of the radical democratic agenda in a labour movement long dominated by economistic and bureaucratic habits. This challenge was central to the Bennite movement, and made it a very different prospect from earlier Labour-left formations. Tony invoked the heritage of the Levellers, Tom Paine, the Chartists and the Suffragettes because he saw democracy in Britain as unfinished business.

Again and again, he stressed the importance of accountability, at every level of civic and economic life. He insisted that party leaders should be elected by party members, at a time when that was largely considered the prerogative of MPs, and that constituency members should have the power to remove ineffective MPs. As a whole Bennism was very much about a revival of popular democracy, expressed in particular through the activities of left-wing local councils.

It's interesting to remember how Benn arrived at his brand of radically democratic socialism. Usually it takes only a mere taste of office to turn politicians into servants of the establishment; Benn, in contrast, was radicalised by his experience in government (in the sixties and seventies). Increasingly, he came to see the necessity of far-reaching, systemic change. Defying convention, he became more not less radical as he grew older. And in this he was, again, an example to us all.

Bennism briefly raised the prospect of a genuinely left-wing Labour government and that terrified the powers-that-be (and those who wanted to join them). They hit back with everything at their disposal. Just now the media will not want to recall how they treated Tony in those years: he was derided as a lunatic and cast as a deadly threat to British society, smeared and misrepresented at every turn.

Much of what happened afterwards to the Labour Party can be seen as a prolonged backlash against the Bennite insurgency; the changes in the Party's structures, the centralisation of power, the marginalisation of the membership, were designed to ensure it could never happen again. They aimed to make the Labour Party safe for capital, and in my view, over the long haul, they succeeded.

Benn warned early on that the acceptance of neo-liberalism by all the main parties was creating, in his words, 'a crisis of representation'. Today we live with the consequences of that crisis. That's why, in recent years, Tony's message has come to seem, to large numbers, more pertinent, more forward-looking, than anything on offer from the self-styled modernisers who cast him as a 'dinosaur'.

Benn was one of the great modern communicators of the socialist cause. The tributes to his eloquence only hint at what he did. He aimed always to clarify what seemed obscure or puzzling, to make plain what was hidden. He could delineate an injustice with a single phrase and make an unconventional position appear the epitome of common sense. In making his case he was concrete, concise, and intelligible to all. He appealed to our shared experience and aspirations. And he refused to be deflected by media ruses.

Of course, it was all lit up with Benn's warmth, humour and generosity of spirit. His was a socialism of the heart as well as the head, and no one who listened to him or worked with him could doubt that.

7

THE JOYS OF ART

ROCKING FOR REVOLUTION

On political songwriter Steve Earle and his 2004 album
The Revolution Starts Now. *First published in 2004.*

From movie theatres to music arenas, popular culture is proving a major battleground in the US presidential election. First there was Michael Moore's film *Fahrenheit 9/11*; now Bruce Springsteen, country music trio the Dixie Chicks and grunge band Pearl Jam have been touring the swing states and 'rockin' the vote'. The gigs are packed but there's a debate about just what effect they have: cynics suggest these artists are merely preaching to the converted.

The complaint misses the real drama of what's happening in the US, however. The polarisation provoked by Bush – social and cultural, as well as political – runs much deeper and is more volatile than the question of who you vote for. And it's unlikely to be accommodated within the existing two-party system.

Among the musicians who've been campaigning against Bush none is more acutely aware of these underlying questions than singer-songwriter Steve Earle, whose new album, *The Revolution Starts Now*, goes way beyond Bush-bashing, politically and artistically.

Earle started speaking out against the war on terror when it was still a risky career move. In the aftermath of 9/11 he boldly challenged the prevailing national mood with the album *Jerusalem*, a masterpiece of politically engaged popular art to set beside Dylan's *The Times They Are A-Changin'* and the best of Bob Marley or the Clash.

In the apocalyptic 'Ashes to Ashes', Earle kicked off *Jerusalem* like an Old Testament prophet, reminding his fellow citizens that 'every tower ever built tumbles / no matter how strong, no matter how tall'. In 'Amerika v. 6.0 (The Best We Can Do)' he looked at what passes for healthcare in the US – 'we got accountants playin' God and countin' out the pills', – observing, 'four score and a hundred and 50 years ago / our forefathers made us equal as long as we can pay'.

But nothing disturbed the guardians of the US's self-image more than the song 'John Walker's Blues', in which Earle projected himself into the heart and mind of the young Californian Taleban captured in Afghanistan in November 2001. The US media demonised the confused young man as the embodiment of America's enemies, without and within. In response, Earle relived Walker's strange journey, finding dignity and humanity in his story:

> As death filled the air, we all offered up prayers
> And prepared for our martyrdom
> But Allah had some other plan, some secret not revealed
> Now they're draggin' me back with my head in a sack
> To the land of the infidel.
>
> *A shadu la ilaha illa Allah.*
> *A shadu la ilaha illa Allah*

Earle was lambasted as a psychopathic traitor, a self-hating American. Yet the irony was that the song, like Earle's work as a whole, was deeply rooted in US musical traditions. In addition to being the country's foremost practising political songwriter, Earle is among the most complete masters of what's sometimes called 'Americana': a catch-all term to describe the rich spectrum of North American folk, country, rock and blues: the musical legacy of generations of US working class experience.

Earle was raised in small-town Texas, but at the age of 14 left home (with his guitar) for Houston. Five years later, he turned up in Nashville. Following a string of casual jobs, stints as a back-up musician and some success writing for established performers, he hit the charts with the albums *Guitar Town* in 1986 and *Copperhead Road* in 1988. By then in his early 30s, he was hailed as the voice of a new wave of country music and a rival to Springsteen as a rock balladeer.

Commercial and critical success, however, was accompanied by personal crisis. Heroin addiction and a prison sentence led to a hiatus in his career in the early 1990s. But after a painful process of self-reconstruction, Earle returned in 1997 with a major album, *El Corazon*. Since then, he's made up for lost time, composing song after song, recording, performing, writing and agitating. He's been an active campaigner against the death penalty, supported welfare and union rights and anti-landmine initiatives, and most recently hit the streets to oppose war and support civil liberties.

Now pushing 50, Earle is at the peak of his powers, a patron saint for late bloomers. He's a distinctive stylist with a strong personality, who nonetheless moves easily from genre to genre, mood to mood. As a guitarist he deploys both crunching power chords and delicate, wistful finger-picking. He dips into folk, country, blues, bluegrass, punk, grunge and even reggae, psychedelia and world music. He's wry, righteous and raucous, but also tender and melancholy.

The sheer abundance of Earle's gift for song means he can lavish it on casual as well as considered projects. *The Revolution Starts Now* was compiled in only a few days, and is presented unapologetically as an intervention in the election. It may not be as complete a work as *Jerusalem*, but it's full of riches, including the title track, a riff-heavy anthem with a razor-sharp rhythmic edge, hypnotic vocal and Beatles-like chorus that reminds us how the revolution starts 'in you own hometown, in your own backyard'.

The mordant 'Home to Houston' sounds like a typical country and western hard-driving trucker's tale, except that it's set in Basra:

> Early in the mornin' and I'm rollin' fast
> Haulin' 9,000 gallons of high test gas
> Sergeant on the radio hollerin' at me
> Look out up ahead here comes a RPG.

Perhaps the most devastating song on the album is 'Rich Man's War', comprised of three sharply etched vignettes. In the first, jobless Jimmy who 'joined the army 'cause he had no place to go' finds himself 'rollin' into Baghdad wonderin' how he got this far'. In the second, patriotic Bobby leaves behind a 'stack of overdue bills' and finds himself in Kandahar, 'chasin' ghosts in the thin dry air'. In the third, Ali, who 'grew up in Gaza throwing bottles and rocks' at Israeli tanks, is called on to martyr himself by 'a fat man in a new Mercedes'. Each vignette ends with the refrain, 'just another poor boy off to fight a rich man's war'.

'Rich Man's War' works not just because it's predicated on a class analysis, but also because it makes the analysis concrete. Here, as elsewhere in his work, Earle draws deeply on country music traditions in which the individual is trapped or tormented by remote forces, and the drama of personal survival is played out against a bleak, unforgiving landscape. As Earle himself would insist, he's a faithful son of Hank Williams as well as Woody Guthrie. He locates the left-wing politics in the classic country music territory of loneliness, heartache and loss.

Other tracks on the new album include 'Condi, Condi' – a sexy, funky calypso disconcertingly addressed to US National Security Advisor Condoleezza Rice ('people say you're cold but I think you're hot.'), and 'F the CC' – a foul-mouthed punk-rock blast at the mainstream media ('fuck the FBI, fuck the CIA, livin' in the motherfuckin' USA'). More affectingly, there's 'Comin' Around', a duet with country icon Emmylou Harris evoking a fragile sense of personal renewal, and 'I Thought You Should Know', a bittersweet erotic soul torch-song that Otis Redding would have relished.

Earle's politics are not only to the left of most of the performers currently assailing Bush (he calls himself a socialist and describes Clinton as 'the only Republican I've ever voted for'); they're infused with an internationalism rare even among the US liberal intelligentsia. 'Frankly, I've never worn red, white and blue that well,' he merrily admits. Crucially, he's an internationalist with a Texan accent, working in an accessible idiom, as proud of his US roots as he is angry at his country's rulers.

In the past, undercurrents of dissent found expression in US popular culture long before they were recognised by political parties or mainstream media. Let's hope Earle's music proves to be the harbinger of a more informed and humane global consciousness. In the meantime, if you're looking for inspiration, solace and stimulation, pick up a Steve Earle CD without delay.

A RASIKA'S TRIBUTE

First published in 2006.

Here I am in London and the December season is underway in Chennai. To the unconverted, Carnatic music is staid, forbiddingly technical, repetitive, elitist. And some of its devotees do seem determined to live up to the stereotype, preoccupied with tradition, treating the music like a zone of purity, forever besieged by the forces (the temptations) of impurity.

I've been lucky enough to pass at least a part of the season in Chennai and I think both parties have got it wrong. At the *kucheris* I was swept away by the melodic and rhythmic richness of Carnatic music. I have my CDs but in Carnatic music one never steps in the same stream twice; there's no substitute for the unfolding of the artistry in the present tense, and the December season is like an extended present tense.

Yes, I know the gripes. There's the competitive social scene, the status seeking and patronage; too many *sabhas* putting on too many similar programmes, flogging the big name artistes to exhaustion; the drab auditoria, variable sound systems, the long-winded oratory of sponsors and award-presenters.

But there's no denying the ceaseless flow of virtuosity and invention. Not to mention the stamina, dedication and general graciousness of the artistes. The season is an event that subsumes performers and audience in a larger community. It really is a festival. It's not Woodstock or Glastonbury but there's a family resemblance (the jostling of big names and wannabes, the parade of accomplished accompanists whose names are known only to aficionados). Of course the season in Chennai is more sedate. Still, it's a good deal less restrained than the European classical tradition, where there's no popping out for a *vada*, and where persistently slapping your thigh will result in ejection.

Coming to Carnatic music belatedly, and from a long distance in every respect, I tend to find in it echoes of the music I already know and enjoy. I can hear gospel in the *bhakti* and bluegrass when the violin drives and dives and soars. Most of all, the ensemble, the interplay of individual and collective, the centrality of *manodharma*, improvisation, remind me of jazz: the way the artist roams far from home but always returns, the space for nuanced individual expression, for wit, for playfulness. I would have loved to hear John Coltrane explore the *Pancharatna Kritis*.

There's also an analogy with European chamber music, and the often-made comparison between the Carnatic Trinity and Mozart, Haydn and Beethoven. However antique the music's roots, the Carnatic canon is relatively modern, mostly 19th and 20th century. Its history is a history of innovation and broken taboos – relating to gender and caste, public and private. The kucheri as we know it dates only from Ariyakudi and the 1930s. In a single evening it can include compositions with lyrics in Tamil, Telugu, Sanskrit, Kannada, Marathi and Hindi. I can't think of another musical culture with a comparable spread.

Despite claims to indigenousness, Carnatic music has not been immune to outside influences – *ragas* from the north, and instruments from the west. Two hundred years after Baluswamy Dikshitar mastered it, the violin is ubiquitous and integral in Carnatic music. As it is in Arabic, Celtic folk and American country music. There's a case to be made that the violin is Western Europe's least equivocal gift to the world, a uniquely supple extension of the human hand, brain and heart.

In recent years, the saxophone, mandolin and guitar have all found new homes in the Carnatic world. Kadri Gopalnath, U. Srinivas and R. Prasanna are not playing fusion music; they're playing Carnatic music, as much as anyone playing the *veena*. And to my ears at least they're playing beautifully. Again, it's hard to find a comparison. In other classical music forms, alien instruments exist only as sonic novelties.

But where would vocalists, violinists or saxophonists be without the intricate rhythms of the *mrindangam*? It's a modest instrument; compared to the *tabla*, it speaks *sotto voce*. Or rather, it sings. With its variations of tone and texture, from the leathery to the bell-like, the mrindangam suffuses the daunting mathematics of cross and counter rhythms with a warm, vocal quality.

Finally, one of the special charms of Carnatic music is that, for all its urbanity and sophistication, it finds room for the humble *morsing* and *ghatam*. In other musical cultures, the likes of the Jew's harp and the clay pot are relegated to the nether regions of folk primitivism. In Carnatic music, they're vehicles for the exquisite.

As will be apparent, I'm very much a neophyte *rasika*. I'm intimidated by experts in the field, and it's a field not wanting in experts. No doubt my tastes are vulgar and my appreciation superficial. I do struggle with a *ragam-tanam-pallavi*. But I'm learning.

MATCHLESS FEAST

First published in 2008.

Is there anywhere like Florence? Or any period of human creativity comparable to that which Florence hosted from the end of the 13th to the beginning of the 16th centuries? These 200 years left behind a material residue – paintings, sculpture, buildings, civic vistas – that never ceases to astonish. The sheer accumulation of beauty can overwhelm the visitor, as it overwhelmed the writer Stendhal in 1817 (he complained of palpitations and dizziness, and fled the city). In addition to the treasures hoarded in the city's great museums, there are hundreds of masterpieces to be found in churches, monastic buildings, palaces and way-side tabernacles. And all within a compact, easily walkable area. It's a matchless feast for the eyes, and though much has survived, it's remarkable to think that even more has been lost.

To tour Florence is to encounter many of the greatest names in the history of Western art in their home city: Giotto, Ghiberti, Masaccio, Fra Angelico, Donatello, Brunelleschi, Botticelli, Leonardo, Michelangelo... not to mention Orcagna, Lippo Lippi, Ghirlandaio, the Della Robias, Pontormo and a score of others.

Even more stunning than the quantity of art is its variety: to wander in and out of Florence's sites is to commune with an extraordinary array of individual visions. The famous technical advances of the Renaissance – in the representation of space and the human body – provided a common platform for highly diverse personal signatures. The ethereal Fra Angelico, the sensous Lippo Lippi and the austere Andrea del Castagno were all painting at the same time, often for the same patrons, and usually dealing with the same subject matter (familiar episodes from the lives of Jesus, Mary and the saints) yet it is impossible to mistake the work of one of them for the others.

These days, the Florentine miracle is often ascribed to nascent capitalism. The free market, it's said, promoted competition among patrons and artists and thereby gave birth to the world's first consumer economy. It's true that the material prosperity that enriched Florence during these years was the necessary basis for expenditure on inessential items like paintings. And it's also true that, among their other innovations, the Italian Renaissance city-states created the apparatus of modern finance capital – bills of exchange, holding companies, insurance, double-entry book keeping. In 1252, the commune of Florence minted the first florin, a gold coin which quickly became the monetary standard across much of Europe.

Initially, Florence owed its wealth to the wool industry, but the emphasis soon shifted to banking and speculation. This swelled the coffers of the richest families, famously the Medici, but gradually undermined Florence's Republican institutions. Far from being a halcyon era of prosperous stability, the entire period was characterised by factional conflict among the elite and discontent among the lower orders.

In 1378, a woolworkers' revolt succeeded in installing, for 41 days, a radical popular government. The regime cut taxes on essential items and suspended small debts. The merchants and the craft guilds coalesced to put down the rebellion, but its memory haunted the city. Indeed, the fear of popular revolution was a critical factor in the Medici's gradual monopolisation of state power.

The Medici's century-long progress from bankers to autocrats was stubbornly resisted by the people they sought to rule. Cosimo, the canniest of the dynasty, was exiled in 1433 because, his rivals claimed, he was setting himself above his fellow citizens. After his return the following year, he worked patiently to undermine the Republic's constitution, rigging the secret ballots, bribing officials and keeping Milanese troops on stand-by for emergencies. Despite the power of the merchants and the mercenaries, Florence's popular republican tradition repeatedly resurfaced. And each time the ancient, quasi-democratic mechanisms of government were resuscitated, the rich would find themselves more heavily taxed. No wonder Cosimo's grandson, Lorenzo (*Il Magnifico*) commented: 'In Florence things can go badly for the rich if they don't run the State.'

The republic was restored in 1494, Lorenzo's heirs were chased from the city and the family's palace was sacked. Ten years later, Michelangelo carved his celebrated *David*, an icon of republican resistance to tyranny, which was placed in front of the town hall as a reminder to the citizenry of the values which made Florence great.

Unlike the humanist men of letters, who mostly belonged to the great merchant families, the painters, sculptors and architects hailed from a middle stratum: many were trained as goldsmiths, and their social status was that of skilled artisans. Crucially, their art reached a wide audience. Though nowadays it's seen as 'high art', a specialist preserve of the educated, it was in its own time a popular art: accessible and comprehensible to a still largely illiterate public. For this public, the paintings were part of a spectrum of cultural activity, including comic theatre, sports (especially a rough and tumble version of football), and street preaching.

A favourite theme of the street preachers was the corruption of wealth. In 1206, at the very dawn of the new era of capitalism, the most powerful popular movement of the age was kicked off when a rich man's son stripped himself of his clothes and renounced his family's riches in Assisi's public square. St Francis not only preached a gospel of service to the poor, he practised it; like Gandhi, he made his life an example. In doing so, he unleashed a movement of human-centred Christianity that is as integral to the art of the period as the patronage of the plutocrats.

Today, the vast and eloquent silence of the 14-15th century masterpieces contrasts with the noisy babble of the tourist throngs. (And it does grate to have to pay €8 to enter a church.) But even at the height of the tourist season, the crafty visitor can manage to steal a few moments alone with a work of exceptional beauty. At which point, analysis and contextualisation fade into the background, and the artist's wordless genius dominates all.

NOT POP AS WE KNOW IT: FLAMENCO AND THE QUEST FOR AUTHENTICITY

First published in 2010.

Flamenco is a name widely known but a music little understood, at least beyond its Andalusian heartland. Forget about Hollywood images of flounces and castanets. Even the bravura solo guitarists and dance troupes are peripheral. The heart of flamenco is the *cante*, the art of flamenco song. Its most compelling spectacle is starkly simple: a lone *cantaor* (singer) and a lone guitarist sitting on straight-backed chairs on a bare stage, plumbing the *cante jondo*, the 'deep songs' associated with the gypsies of southern Spain.

Flamenco is abrupt and angular, frequently harrowing, sometimes ecstatic, always spontaneous and at the same time deeply meditative. There are no choruses, refrains or hooks. It's headlong and forceful, marked by dramatic shifts in mood, volume and tempo. Flamenco demands attention and empathy. It casts its own mood and brooks no compromise. It's a popular music utterly alien to 'pop' as we know it. 'Deep song,' said the poet Federico García Lorca, 'is a stammer, a wavering emission of the voice, a marvellous undulation that smashes the resonant cells of our tempered scale, [and] eludes the cold, rigid staves of modern music.'

It's impossible to tell the story of flamenco without talking about Lorca, who found in it a source of inspiration in a lifelong political-cultural-sexual struggle against bourgeois philistinism. The recovery and promotion of deep song was part of the poet-dramatist's larger democratic embrace of popular beauty, an antidote to what he came to see as the inhuman machine of modern capitalism. As a leftist and modernist, he was ahead of his time in embracing cultural diversity and plural identities. For him, the universality of flamenco lay in its peculiarity, in its unique expressive forms, in the access they gave to remote but shared human realms. He championed the music of the gypsies as he did the Muslim and Jewish roots of Spanish culture. All of which made him a prime target for the fascists, who murdered him in the early days of the Civil War.

In flamenco, the major creator is the cantaor, who in each performance invents the song anew, building it extemporaneously from a fixed framework provided by the sub-genres known as the *palos*. Among the more frequently heard of these are the solemn *siguiriyas* and *soleas*, the Moorish-influenced *fandangos*, the dancing *bulerias* and festive *allegrias*. Each palo has its own history, rhythmic pattern (*compas*), melodic scale and associated lyrics. It's not meaningful in flamenco to say someone 'covers' someone else's song; its essence is improvised. In this respect, as well as in its use of modes outside the familiar major and minor scales of Western music, it resembles Arabic and Indian classical music.

The cantaor can dwell at length on a single phrase, probing and elongating it, then complete the rest of the verse in a rush of tumbling syllables. The voice slides into and around the notes, dredging up micro-tones from hidden depths. It's an immensely suspenseful music, building to serial climaxes, hesitating, holding back, plunging forward.

Remarkably, this intensely rhythmic music makes no use of percussion instruments (the castanets are for tourists). Instead, hand clapping, finger snapping, knuckle rapping and foot tapping create a rhythmic brocade, enriched by cross and counter-rhythms and studded with syncopations. It's a sophisticated and highly technical folk music; even the hand clapping requires intensive study and is not to be attempted by amateurs.

Flamenco's roots spread wide. There are Arab, Berber, Jewish, Byzantine, Spanish American and even South Asian influences. All these and more were fused in the forge of the gypsy experience into a singular art form, unlike any of its sources, evoking its own world-view, its own existential stance. It's as silly to say *gachos* (non-gypsies) can't sing the cante as to say that white people can't play the blues (there have been numerous *gacho* masters), but what is true is that it was in the gypsy barrios of Seville, Jerez, Granada, Malaga and Cadiz that flamenco flourished, and it is indelibly marked by that history.

The singers draw from a treasury of colloquial *coplas* (verses), brief, trenchant lyrics that face death, loss, persecution, love, loneliness, injustice and jealousy without trimmings. They are bare and stark, 'a song without landscape,' Lorca said, 'withdrawn into itself and terrible in the dark.'

> Only to the earth
> do I tell my troubles
> for there is no one in the world
> whom I can trust.

In the coplas, love is a wrenching, perilous experience: 'When we walk alone / and your dress rubs against me / a shudder runs deep in my bones'. Or: 'I went to a field to cry / screaming like a madman / and even the wind kept telling me / you loved someone else.' Emotions are presented as facts, without justification: 'I am jealous of the breeze / that touches your face / if the breeze were a man / I would kill him.' The injustices of the world stand unmitigated; the songs are pure indictment. 'You killed my brother / I'll never forgive you / wrapped in a cape you killed him / he did nothing to you.'

It's often said that flamenco is not political because it dwells on the personal fate of the individual. That seems to me to imply a narrow definition of both the political and the personal. The palos and the coplas are, of course, collective creations. In using them as the foundation for a highly personal act of expression, the performer reconnects with that common experience, an experience shaped by poverty and persecution. The songs confront blank, powerful forces with nothing but the singer's own irreducible being. It's a music of clannish outsiders, and much of it certainly feels like a prolonged protest, an act of defiance whose only reward is itself.

The dominant figure in modern flamenco, its chief icon and martyr, was the marvellous Camarón de la Isla ('the shrimp from the island'), a gypsy from an impoverished but musical family who died in 1992, at the age of only 42, from the combined effects of cancer and long-term drug abuse. Small of stature, quietly spoken and affable, Camarón was nonetheless hugely charismatic, a master of the deepest core of flamenco tradition and at the same time a bold innovator. His 1979 album, *La Leyenda del Tiempo*, is often lazily dubbed 'the *Sergeant Pepper's* of flamenco', in that it mixed studio techniques, unorthodox instruments, pop-style choruses and lyrics drawn from Lorca poems. Not all the fusion elements work, but the heartfelt, rhythmically compelling singing is ravishing. Camarón possessed one of the great voices of the 20th century. As a genius of modern popular culture, he stands with the likes of Louis Armstrong, Bob Marley and Bob Dylan.

On his left hand Camarón wore a tattoo of the Jewish Star of David and the Muslim Crescent – a powerful statement from a gypsy in a country only just emerging from the centralist Castillian-Catholic hegemony of the Franco years.

In Camaron's wake, innovation and fusion have become commonplace, but continue to arouse passionate resistance. Though I'm a newcomer to flamenco, I understand the fear that something precious and irreplaceable will be lost if the core of the cante is compromised. However, flamenco does seem alive and well in southern Spain, with hundreds of clubs and schools, numerous festivals, and scores of new as well as old performers making magical music. Despite the dissolution of much of its social base, as gypsy barrios have been decanted into tower block suburbs, flamenco continues to bring a multi-dimensional past into a living present.

As one of the first folk musics to undergo commercialisation (as early as the mid-19th century), flamenco has long been the site of fierce arguments about purity, authenticity, tradition and innovation. For ethnomusicologists, it's a field day. The post-modernists have taught us to be wary of claims to authenticity or purity; nonetheless, flamenco itself remains a quest for authenticity, for the pure expression of those human emotions that are both uniquely, intimately personal, and universally shared. And while authenticity may remain elusive, I suspect the search for it will continue to play a part in any effort to redeem our humanity from an inhuman society.

JOHN FORD: MELANCHOLY DEMOCRAT

First published in 2010.

The fact that *Stagecoach*, a milestone in the development of the Western and the first complete masterpiece of its director, John Ford, begins with the announcement that 'Geronimo has jumped the reservation' and the Apache are 'on the warpath' may be enough to put many off the film, the genre and the director. That would be a pity: Ford was one of the greatest and subtlest artists ever to work in the medium. His films are rich in emotions and ideas; his vision is both compassionate and sceptical.

At the age of 20 in 1915, Ford, the son of Irish immigrants, made his way from Maine to Hollywood, where he entered the fledgling industry at the bottom – as prop and stunt man – but quickly graduated to directing. Over the next 20 years Ford directed scores of films, enjoyed commercial success and occasional critical plaudits. But it was not until he was past 40 that his style reached maturity. In the films he made between 1939, the year of *Stagecoach*, and his departure for service in the Navy two years later, he created a unique blend of German-influenced expressionism, with its carefully lit compositions, and the easy-going, idiomatic naturalism of US popular culture.

A key element in the crystallisation of Ford's cinematic vision was the Popular Front, which in the US took the form of an alliance between leftists and liberals. The cultural wing of this social movement crossed many boundaries. Government-funded painters filled libraries, courthouses, post offices and schools with murals depicting episodes from US history, usually stressing the role of ordinary people. Various styles of American folk music were recovered and recorded, along with the new songs pouring out of Woody Guthrie. In Hollywood, the political moment left its stamp on the works of Frank Capra and Orson Welles as well as Ford, who described himself in a letter to a nephew serving in the International Brigades in Spain as 'a socialistic Democrat – always left'.

In *Stagecoach*, the Native Americans pose an existential threat; they are presented as an intrinsic part of a hostile environment. The real conflict in the film is among the whites crammed into the eponymous vehicle. The heroes are an escaped prisoner (John Wayne, mesmerising in the role that made him a star), a prostitute and a drunken doctor, all up against what the latter dubs 'the disease of social prejudice'. The villain is a banker spouting the Republican ideology of the day ('America for Americans!' 'Keep government out of business!'). In the course of the journey, the other characters reconsider their initial intolerance and a democratic bond is forged, though the film ends with a sour-jocular remark by the doctor about being 'spared the blessings of civilisation'.

In Ford's next film, *Young Mr Lincoln*, Henry Fonda plays the future President as a wisecracking, justice-seeking country lawyer, seeing off a lynch mob, getting an innocent man off a murder charge, discomfiting the pompous with his homespun wit. He's an easy-going populist with a firm moral centre. He's also an introspective man haunted by lost love and future challenges. Ford shows Lincoln responding to the various facets of US democracy: the good-natured rituals of a 4th of July, a hate-driven mob, a canting elite. Though hardly a detail is without significance, the pace of the film is relaxed and many of its most charged moments consist of deceptively simple gestures.

Ford's film of *The Grapes of Wrath*, made in 1940, is better than Steinbeck's book: warmer, less mechanically deterministic. The tale of Dust Bowl refugees facing discrimination and exploitation becomes a political learning curve for the protagonist (Fonda as a taciturn but sensitive Tom Joad), who bids farewell to his beloved Ma with an assertion of his oneness with the struggle for justice everywhere: 'Wherever there's a cop beating a guy, wherever children are hungry.... I'll be there'. Watching it recently, I couldn't help but find the scene in which the big 'Cats' (bulldozers) destroy the farmers' homes at the behest of the bankers all too contemporary. Topical as it was and remains, the film gains immensely from Ford's long-term preoccupations with migration, family breakup, the rituals of community and the solidarity of marginal groups in the face of a hostile world.

After his return from World War II service, Ford made the anti-triumphalist *They Were Expendable*, the story of a bitter US defeat – the loss of the Philippines in the early days of the war – and the fate of those deemed 'expendable'. It is a slow, meditative film, a study of comradeship and sacrifice, a stoic but deeply felt evocation of the futility that marks even a just war.

In the late forties Ford took a brief bold stand against red-baiting in the Directors Guild but thereafter gravitated to the right, ending his days as a champion of Richard Nixon and the Vietnam War. But that political CV hardly does justice to the rich ambivalences in Ford's work, the complexity of his vision of history's gains and losses. He was, from the beginning to the end, both a liberal and a conservative, an idealist and a sceptic, and this duality gives his films tension and depth.

Ford made his greatest films between 1946 and 1956. Because these were mainly Westerns, they received little serious attention in the USA, though critics in France and Britain, notably Lindsay Anderson (later to direct the insurrectionary *If....*) began to make the case for Ford as a great artist. In *My Darling Clementine*, *Wagon Master*, *Fort Apache*, *Rio Grande* and *She Wore a Yellow Ribbon*, Ford created a densely peopled world in which honour and camaraderie are mixed with defeat and melancholy. Native Americans remain a threat but are increasingly seen as victims of white duplicity. In different ways, each film deals with the contradictions of the 'civilising' process of westward expansion.

Ford's career climaxes with *The Searchers* (1956), ignored on release in the USA but now widely recognised as one of the greats. It tells the story of a five year search, ranging across a vast and varied western landscape, for two white girls captured by Comanche. At its core is the figure of Ethan Edwards, an obsessive anti-hero, driven by a combination of loyalty, vengeance and racism (in particular, disgust at miscegenation), and played by Wayne so majestically, with such contained power and suggested depth, that it's amazing anyone could doubt his genius as a screen actor, however deplorable his off-screen politics. In the course of the film, Edwards comes to resemble more and more his 'savage' adversary. A stark scene depicts the aftermath of a massacre of Native civilians by US Cavalry. Categories of savage and civilised, profane and religious, progress and barbarism are subject to an interrogation that is all the more powerful for being implicit.

In its evocations of space and time, *The Searchers* has a special magic. Here as elsewhere, Ford's famous landscapes are not just picture postcards but images saturated with meaning. He was unsurpassable in orchestrating remote figures across vast spaces. In interiors as well as exteriors he made the actors' movements within the frame, foreground and background, richly expressive. (There's always a lot going on in a Ford frame.) Under his lens, gesture and posture became a subtle but revelatory language.

Ford filled his films with humour, sometimes coarse or childlike, but often riotously funny. He segued from the gravest drama to broad comedy with the elan of Shakespeare. This was never just for the sake of 'relief': Ford positively valued informality; stuffiness and self-righteousness were always suspect.

Ford's last masterpiece, *The Man Who Shot Liberty Valance*, revisited the Western genre itself and the contradictory process of history making. It's an austere, elegiac film about memory and myth, dubious about manifest destiny, enriched by a comic-affectionate depiction of frontier democracy.

Ford created his highly personal work within a commercial industry whose constraints he largely accepted, however he chafed at them. As Joseph McBride shows in his authoritative, nuanced biography, he was a multi-layered personality, generous and loyal but also cruel, jealous and insecure. He protected a vulnerable poet's soul within a shell of earthy machismo.

Ford welcomes us into a world that belongs to him alone but is at the same time universally accessible. It's a warm, human world, sad, funny, heroic, tragic. A world of poignant relationships: between culturally diverse communities, between the individual and the collective, between humans and their environment. Anyone with a taste for the dialectics of history should relish it.

MY FANTASY CAREER (OR WHY THERE IS NO SUCH THING AS WORLD MUSIC)

First published in 2011.

In another life, I'd like to have been an ethnomusicologist. It would have been a wonderfully open-ended excuse to discover new music, to travel and imbibe foreign cultures at close range.

As an academic discipline, ethnomusicology began as a Western study of non-Western music, but in recent decades it has come to embrace the study of the musics of the peoples of the world, Western and non-Western, elite and popular, parochial and cosmopolitan. In particular, ethnomusicology studies the musics of the peoples of the world in their social settings. It hears them as part of, and sometimes a key to, a larger culture.

In trying to explain the complex ties between a music and its place and time, ethnomusicology faces a host of thorny questions. This for me is one of its fascinations. Each musical style, each performance casts in a new light the ever-shifting relations between audience and performer, tradition and innovation, individual and collective, art and economics. It's a ticket to explore the glorious, borderless mystery of human creativity.

Songs, scales and rhythms have been described as 'indefatigable tourists'. They cross geographical, linguistic, political and cultural barriers. As they do so, they are modified. The history of music is fluid, with local and global engaged in a perpetual mutual exchange. So, whatever course it takes, ethnomusicology is always a journey, through both space and time.

I come from an entirely unmusical family. But growing up in the sixties and early seventies, I was lucky enough to be introduced to music during an extraordinarily fertile era for Anglo-American rock, soul and pop. There were of course the Beatles and Dylan, and along with them a brilliant array of individual stylists, musical explorers and genre-busters: Van Morrison, Joni Mitchell, Gram Parsons, Aretha Franklin, Marvin Gaye, Captain Beefheart, Randy Newman, Stevie Wonder, to name only a few. Each of these formed part of my musical education. Like many others I followed the contemporary sounds to their sources in blues, folk, jazz and country – the musics of North America's marginalised communities. The sixties/seventies taught me my first lesson in the social context of music: no one could miss, though many misinterpreted, the connection between the era's innovative pop and its political turmoil. A number of those for whom ethnomusiclogy is not merely a fantasy career embarked on their studies from the same starting point, alerted by personal experience to the richness of the subject.

After that my musical journey has been shaped by travel, politics and accidental connections. When I worked in a north London youth club in the early eighties I listened to a lot of reggae. It's amazing that the music of a small, marginalised island community could be so warmly embraced by such a wide global audience. But then perhaps not so amazing, when you reflect that reggae mixed influences from Africa, North and South America, dancehall and church, local patois and internationalist anti-colonial politics. In other words, it was a distinctively Caribbean contribution to global culture.

As a result of much travelling in India, I fell in love with Carnatic music, which, I learned, was not nearly as conservative and hidebound (or as ancient and unchanging) as it was made out to be. I've heard some bravura celebrity recitals during the annual Chennai season, but nothing more quietly moving than modest restraint of the Bombay Sisters at a sparsely attended Christmas morning *kutcheri*.

One of the things I cherish about Carnatic music is that for all its elaboration, the song remains at its heart. But I've also come to enjoy the more expansive Hindustani school, largely because I've been fortunate enough to hear Hari Prausad Chaurasia, Amjad Ali Khan, Shiv Kumar Sharma and Zakir Hussein live. And on record there's nothing sweeter than the sound of Bismillah Khan's *shehnai*. I'm also a fan of fifties and sixties Bollywood music, especially the folk inspired S D Burman and the classically minded Naushad. Bollywood is a delight for the sociologist of music, harnessing folk, classical and Western instruments and influences, Urdu poetry and Goan orchestrators.

Later visits to Morocco, Portugal and Spain triggered excursions into Andalusian (*al ala*, the plangent, ruminative classical music of the Arabic west), *Fado* (not least the heart-shaking voice of Amalia Rodrigues) and especially flamenco, which has become something of an obsession. It's one of the world's least classifiable but most easily recognisable musical genres, technically sophisticated and at the same time daringly emotional.

An intriguing book by Timothy Brennan called *Secular Devotion: Afro-Latin Music and Imperial Jazz* prompted a detour into the lavish melodies and percussive abundance of salsa, which draws on Cuban sources but was forged entirely in the ghettos of North America. Salsa is as authentically and completely 'New York' as the Broadway musical, which was itself an amalgam of African-American, Jewish and Western European influences.

Just now I'm investigating the Arabic music of West Asia and relishing the discovery of two 20th century greats: the majestic Egyptian, Umm Kalthoum, and the supple Lebanese, Fairouz, neither of whose careers can be understood without reference to the tragic politics of the region.

So I'm not even a pretend ethnomusicologist. Just a blundering amateur. These days you don't have to spend years in the field to sample the banquet of the world's many musics. It's all recorded, readily accessible and downloadable. That's a great boon, but there's still no substitute for live performance, for being part of an audience, for contact not only with the music but with its context.

Brennan's book includes a chapter titled 'There is no such thing as world music', which made me want to cheer on sight. He's referring to the marketing category launched in the 1980s to bring artists from the developing world to Western notice. While it did succeed in creating new audiences for the likes of Nusrat Fateh Ali Khan and Youssou N'Dour, 'world music' is an amorphous and deeply patronising catch-all. If you visit the 'world music' racks in a London emporium, you'll find Indian classical alongside Algerian Rai, Afro-Beat, Berber gnawa, klezmer, Qawwalli, Fado, flamenco and all manner of Latin American styles (which in New York would have a rack to themselves), but not jazz or Western classical.

The only music with anything like a global reach today is the one that's never found in the 'world music' racks – mainstream Western pop, whose ubiquity stems from the global distribution of power and wealth. Anyway, what could a truly 'world music' be other than a dismal lowest common denominator? The world muzak of airport lounges and hotel lobbies?

Music is a human universal that exists only in infinitely varied forms. It's in the differences, the variations, that its beauty and meaning resides. And that variety derives from the specifics of historical development. Which is what makes the ethnomusicologist's quest so rewarding – and so endless. It's a reassuringly inexhaustible field.

You encounter a new music. Gradually, your ears adjust, your consciousness makes space. What was alien and forbidding becomes familiar and intimate. It's a small miracle but in it there's a portent of something much greater.

'LIFE IS POSSIBLE ON THIS EARTH': THE POETRY OF MAHMOUD DARWISH

First published in 2011.

On a bright winter morning we made a pilgrimage to the hill of Al Rabweh, on the outskirts of Ramallah, where the poet Mahmoud Darwish is buried. An ambitious memorial garden is planned, but at the moment it's a construction site littered with diggers and cement mixers. The oversize tombstone is crated up in plywood. We were welcomed by cheerful building workers and joined by Palestinian families paying their respects and taking snaps. Sitting amid the pines overlooking the tomb (and a nearby waste ground populated by stray dogs), we spent an hour reading Darwish's *State of Siege*, a sequence of poems he wrote in response to Israel's 2002 assault on the city. Here he called on poetry to 'lay siege to your siege' but observed bitterly that:

> This land might just be cinched too tight
> for a population of humans and gods

Darwish was six in 1948 when his family fled their village in western Galilee. When they returned a year later they found the village destroyed and their land occupied. Since they had missed the census they were denied Israeli citizenship and declared 'present-absentees', an ambiguous status which Darwish was to transform into a metaphor for Palestine and much more.

He was 22 when he read his poem 'Identity Card', with its defiant refrain 'Record: I am an Arab', to a cheering crowd in a Nazareth movie house. Repudiating Golda Meir's assertion 'there are no Palestinians', his poems played a key role in the Palestinian movement that emerged after 1967, fashioning a modern Palestinian identity using traditional poetic forms in a renewed, accessible Arabic.

Repeatedly arrested and imprisoned, Darwish left Israel in 1970 and remained in exile for more than a quarter of a century. His political journey led from the Israeli Communist Party to the PLO, which he joined in 1973 (pennng Arafat's famous 'Don't let the olive branch fall from my hand' speech to the UN). He settled in Beirut, from which he was expelled along with the PLO following the Israeli invasion of 1982, the subject of his inventive and harrowing prose memoir, *Memory for Forgetfulness*.

In the years that followed, Darwish wandered – Tunis, Cyprus, Damascus, Athens, Paris – broadening his poetic scope and deepening his insight. He was elected to the PLO Executive Committee in 1987 but resigned in 1993 in protest at the Oslo Accords. 'There was no clear link between the interim period and the final status, and no clear commitment to withdraw from the occupied territories,' he explained. It's said that when Arafat complained to Darwish that the Palestinian people were 'ungrateful', the poet (remembering Brecht) snapped back, 'Then find yourself another people.'

Oslo did allow Darwish to return to Palestine and in 1996 he settled in Ramallah, only to find himself under siege again six years later. In his last years he wrote more prolifically then ever, responding to the tragedies of Iraq, Lebanon and the violent conflict between Palestinian factions:

> Did we have to fall from a tremendous height so as to see our blood on our hands...to realize that we are no angels...as we thought?
>
> Did we also have to expose our flaws before the world so that our truth would no longer stay virgin? How much we lied when we said: we are the exception!

When Darwish died in 2008, thousands joined the cortège and there were candle-lit vigils in towns across the West Bank and Gaza. The PA declared three days or mourning and issued a series of postage stamps in his honour.

Being the Palestinian national poet was a heavy burden, one which Darwish bore from an early age, and though he chafed under it he never shirked the load. Instead, he succeeded in transforming the Palestinian experience into a universal one. The themes of loss, exile, the search for justice, the dream of a homeland, the conundrum of identity: all became, as his work evolved, human and existential explorations, without ceasing for a moment to be rooted deeply in the vicissitudes of Palestinian life. For decades he mourned Palestine's losses, denounced its tormentors, celebrated its perseverance, and imagined its future.

> And we have a land without borders, like our idea of the unknown, narrow and wide
> ... we shout in its labyrinth: and we still love you, our love is a hereditary illness.

Though preserving Palestinian memory and identity was his life's work, Darwish conceived of this as a creative act of self-renewal. 'Identity is what we bequeath and not what we inherit. What we invent and not what we remember.' Among his last verses was this admonition:

> We will become a people when the morality police protect a prostitute from being beaten up in the streets
> We will become a people when the Palestinian only remembers his flag on the football pitch, at camel races, and on the day of the Nakba

Darwish was a 'national poet' who challenged as well as consoled and inspired his national audience. As he moved away from his earlier declamatory, public style towards a more personal idiom, elliptical and oblique, and at times (unpardonable sin for a 'national' poet) obscure, he met resistance. 'The biggest achievement of my life is winning the audience's trust,' he reflected in 2002, 'We fought before: whenever I changed my style, they were shocked and wanted to hear the old poems. Now they expect me to change; they demand that I give not answers but more questions.'

Even in translation, where we miss so much, Darwish's voice rings clear. In his mature style there's a seductive fluidity: he moves lightly from realm to realm, pronoun to pronoun ('I' to 'we', 'I' to 'you', 'us' to 'them'), from the intimate to the epic, past to future, abstract to concrete. Metaphors topple over each other, abundant and inter-laced. This is poetry that fuses the political and the personal at the deepest level.

Throughout, his evocation of loss and exile, of coming from 'a country with no passport stamps', is poignant, elegiac but open-ended, conjuring resolution from despair:

We travel like everyone else, but we return to nothing', 'There is yet another road in the road, another chance for migration', 'Where should we go after the last border? Where should birds fly after the last sky?', 'In my language there is seasickness. / In my language a mysterious departure from Tyre..:

Guests on the sea. Our visit is short.
And the earth is smaller than our visit
...where are we to go
when we leave? Where are we to go back to when we return?...
What is left us that we may set off once again?

Yet, convinced that 'Out of the earthly / the hidden heavenly commences', Darwish affirmed the richness and beauty of life, especially life in its ordinariness:

> We have on this earth what makes life worth living: April's hesitation, the aroma of bread
> at dawn, a woman's point of view about men, the works of Aeschylus, the beginning
> of love, grass on a stone, mothers living on a flute's sigh and the invaders' fear of memories.

In one of his late poems, Darwish pays tribute to his friend Edward Said, putting this advice in Said's mouth:

> Do not describe what the camera sees of your wounds
> Shout so that you hear yourself, shout so that you know that you are still alive, and you know life is possible on this earth.

1200 BC: THE WORLD'S FIRST INDUSTRIAL ACTION...RESCUING THE PAST FOR THE FUTURE

First published in 2013.

The city of Luxor in southern Egypt made the headlines in Britain at the end of February, when 19 tourists were killed in a hot-air balloon accident. That tragedy will compound the woes of Egypt's tourist industry, once a major source of employment and foreign currency, now languishing as foreign visitors are driven away by (misconceived and exaggerated) fears of instability and violence.

Luxor, the site of ancient Thebes, the principal capital of the Egyptian New Kingdom (1550-1050 BC), is studded with colossal carved temples and richly decorated tombs. But the most revealing and moving of its many ruins may be the least spectacular. Known as Deir el Medinah, these are the low-lying remains of the workers' village, home to the artisans who built the tombs and temples. Their small, sturdy domestic units are laid out on a grid pattern. Here lived stonemasons, tomb painters, carpenters, ropemakers, porters. Scattered among the excavated foundations are mini-pyramids and entrances to underground burial vaults, small in scale but decorated with as much care, as much wealth of colour and detail, as the royal tombs in the nearby Valley of the Kings. These workers had their own visions of an afterlife, a better life. And they had a sense of their own value.

This is the site of history's first recorded strike. The workers were paid in grain, from which they made bread and beer, the staples of the Nile Valley diet. In about 1200 BC, the state treasury, drained by Rameses III's imperial wars, failed to meet its commitments. The workers downed tools and staged a sit-in at the construction site of the Pharaoh's mortuary temple. Perhaps surprisingly, they won the dispute. Their leverage was their masters' fear of dying without the proper funerary arrangements, entering the afterlife under-equipped. The Egyptian cult of the dead, for once, benefited the living.

What are we to make of this episode from remote antiquity? Walter Benjamin, in his prophetic final essay, *Theses on the Philosophy of History*, written in 1940, distinguished between two opposing approaches to the past: 'historicism' and 'historical materialism'. For the former, time is linear, uniform, cumulative. 'Its method is additive: it offers a mass of facts, in order to fill up a homogeneous and empty time.' In contrast, the historical materialist 'records the constellation in which his own epoch comes into contact with that of an earlier one.' The job of the historical materialist is not to reproduce but 'to explode the continuum of history.'

Benjamin asks: 'With whom does the writer of historicism actually empathize?' 'The answer,' he insists, 'is irrefutably with the victor.' History becomes a 'triumphal procession in which today's rulers tread over those who are sprawled underfoot. The spoils are, as was ever the case, carried along in the triumphal procession. They are known as the cultural heritage.' In contrast, for the historical materialist, 'the cultural heritage is part and parcel of a lineage which he cannot contemplate without horror. It owes its existence not only to the toil of the great geniuses, who created it, but also to the nameless drudgery of its contemporaries. There has never been a document of civilisation which is not simultaneously one of barbarism.'

There's no better illustration of that ringing dictum than the art of ancient Egypt, the product of a brutally stratified society governed by a religion of state power, personified in a god-man ruler. Yet long after the system that oppressed them crumbled, the work of the artisans of Deir el Medinah remains vital, colourful, rhythmic and refined; it excels at grand effects but also in delicate naturalistic detail. Whether in the vast vaults of the Valley of the Kings or in the humble tombs of Deir el

Medinah itself, the afterlife is depicted as a better version of this life, furnished in abundance with the good things of this life: food, drink, flowers, birds, song, dance, family. Ancient Egyptian art remains alien, at times weird. But it's also recognisably human; it leaps across chasms to forge a connection.

On the left we see ourselves as makers of the future fully engaged with the present. We look ahead, not behind, and we resent the charge that we are 'wed to out-moded doctrines' and in particular that we have failed to adapt to the changes of the last 30 years. But we should not be ashamed of being 'conservative' in defending rights won in previous generations or communities threatened by 'development'. Capitalism's disregard for the future, its bias in favour of the short-term, is notoriously reckless. But it is equally reckless in its disregard for the past, unless that past can be packaged for consumption or the transmission of propaganda. In either case, the past is not allowed to stand independently, to speak with a voice of its own. And to demand from us some accountability.

Benjamin says our task is 'to brush history against the grain.' An example of this in our own moment is the 23 year campaign for justice for those killed at Hillsborough. Though justice itself has yet to be done, much of the truth has now been established. This was achieved only because the families and their supporters defied the massed chorus telling them their quest was futile, emotion-driven or vindictive. Their sense of duty to the dead was not diverted by appeals to pragmatism and the virtues of adjustment, of 'living in the present'. As a result, they succeeded in recovering a suppressed history which, in turn, becomes an active element in our present and future.

In Spain, the Association for the Recovery of Historical Memory aims to document the fate of Franco's victims and to excavate and identify their bodies, including the tens of thousands dumped in mass graves. To do this, the Association has had to defy the 'pact of oblivion' that smoothed the transition to democracy by shielding members of the old regime from accountability. In this case, a sense of obligation to the dead, to those who were on the losing side, was not a 'backward-looking' indulgence: it was a social necessity. We can't decipher the present without examining its foundations in the battles of the past, acknowledging losses as well as gains.

The Palestinian insistence on recognition of the Nakba – characterised by pro-Israel commentators as a vain desire to recoup a lost battle – is in fact a necessary engagement with the realities of the present: the ongoing impact of the Nakba in the policies of dispossession and ethnic cleansing. At the same time, it's a steadfast insistence on a future of self-determination.

Despite their brief victory, the workers of Deir el Medinah never escaped their state of impoverished servitude. They were on the 'losing side' in the march of history. Nonetheless, in their art and in their action, the workers of Deir el Medinah remind us, in Benjamin's words, that the 'fine and spiritual ... are present in the class struggle as something other than mere booty, which falls to the victor. They are present as confidence, as courage, as humour, as cunning, as steadfastness in this struggle, and they reach far back into the mists of time. They will, ever and anon, call every victory which has ever been won by the rulers into question.'

PAST VISIONS, FUTURE DREAMS

First published in 2014.

Last spring, I made the steep climb to the mountainside entrance to the Cuevas de Covalanas, one of several caves in the Cantabrian region of northern Spain decorated with pre-historic paintings. I had seen reproductions of this type of art in books, but nothing prepared me for the experience of the paintings themselves, on site and in person. Afterwards, I wondered how, not having seen these creations, I could ever have thought I knew anything about art history. I kicked myself for my presumption.

These 20,000-year-old works of art are arrestingly vivid. As the guide's torch throws its beams on the stony walls, the dark interior of the cave comes alive with animate beings: bounding, leaping, rushing, thrusting. Deer, bear and horses and are rendered with fluid, confident, ever-varying lines that demonstrate tremendous powers of visual distillation. These are studies of motion, captured in a moment's vision. The animals are not repeated types; each figure has its own distinct form and energy. But all participate in the larger flow, the moving parade of wild beasts up and down the cave walls, which I think was the artists' central aesthetic concern.

The people who created this art were hunter-gatherers in a hostile environment. Apart from that, we know little about them. Their ideologies and social structures remain a mystery. Significantly, there is no evidence of any other human activity (ritual or social) taking place in the painted caves. No fires, no animal or human remains, just the artists' rudimentary implements. This suggests that for these people the art itself somehow had a primary, autonomous value. It also seems to have been a specialist practice, assigned to individuals with the necessary skills and sensitivities.

Even at this early stage, when humans had barely begun to master their environment and ensure their reproduction, communities set aside labour and resources for the creation of an aesthetic good. However interwoven with religious, social and economic functions, the artistry in the caves seems to have been recognised as having a worth of its own. Otherwise, why go to the trouble of creating such subtle effects?

It's hard not to feel the artists' fascination and awe in relation to the animals they're representing, who at this stage would have been a much more dominant presence in the landscape than humans. Yes, these were creatures they sought to capture, kill and eat, but the joy in the rendering of animal movement is palpable; as is the reverence for an abundant and life-giving if deeply mysterious natural environment.

One of the pleasures of the cave paintings is the way they defy the binary categories favored in much art history: naturalism vs. ideal form, expressionism vs. classicism, spontaneous vs. conventional, sophisticated vs. naïve, individual vs. collective. Above all, they confirm that *there is no progress in art*. There is stylistic and technical development (and regression), but none of it necessarily amounts to qualitative improvement. There are many works of greater complexity than the cave paintings, but they are not more beautiful; they are not 'better' art. Picasso, emerging from a tour of one of the Cantabrian caves, declared, 'After this, everything is decadence' – and from my own experience in the Cuevas de Covalanas, I know what he meant.

On the left, we like to think we look forward, not back. We're engaged with the present in an attempt to shape the future. But the past, and especially, at least for me, the art of the past, is a precious, irreplaceable resource, and one that can be a powerful stimulant in the struggle for that other world we insist is possible. Listening to the voices of the dead is a necessary aspect of 'contending for the living'. What might be called 'present-centrism' is as misguided as Euro-centrism: a myopia that allows the immediate and familiar to crowd out the larger picture. We need a temporal as well as geographic decentering.

Years ago I got hooked on the visual arts (for which I have no talent) and over the decades I've sought out artworks from as many places and eras as I could manage – and rarely been disappointed. I keep re-learning how varied and unexpected aesthetic means and ends can be. Paintings, sculptures, architecture have the capacity to appeal, stimulate and please in so many ways and on so many levels: sensual, psychological, intellectual, political. That's why I've become ever warier of any definition of the aesthetic that narrows down that richly diverse reality. I need something broad enough to embrace the ceramic tiles of Portugal and Pakistan, the sculpture of the medieval temples of south India, Moghul miniatures, Byzantine mosaics, the Gothic, the classical and the Baroque, Fra Angelico as well as Caravaggio, Velázquez as well as Hogarth, Munch as well as Miró, and so on literally without end.

Art is of course an ideological product and a potent carrier of ideology, but it also can and often does subvert and violate ideology. In its concreteness, its direct address to (or through) the senses, it can embody all kinds of impossible contradictions and even transform them into a kind of unified whole. The point is that it's a mistake to reduce art to ideology. Similarly, while art is always the product of a particular social and historical context, it cannot be reduced to that context, not if it is of any lasting value. The artwork, a fusion of manual and mental labour, is at once too particular and too universal for that. It's not a question of transcending its context, its moment of creation, but giving it a body and form that communicates beyond that moment. This is what the cave artists achieved.

Under capitalism, art is treated as a commodity, but there is something in art of any value that resists that status, breaks out of that dimension. There's always a disconnection between its market value and its artistic value – whose very nature resists quantification. Each work of art has a claim of its own that cannot be measured in terms of another and thus cannot be reduced to exchange value. This was what William Blake had in mind when he declared, 'Where any view of Money exists Art cannot be carried on, but War only.'

Crucially, art of value is not something that can be passively consumed. It demands and rewards personal engagement, the active involvement of a variety of faculties, predicated on an openness to the possibilities of art. That's why the labelling of works of art as 'great' or otherwise can be more of a hindrance than a help in appreciating them. The excitement of art is that it challenges us to form our own judgements, not instantly but through patient attention. What makes any 'great' art 'great' is that it reveals unexpected faces, emerges in new lights, in different eras, to different eyes and at different stages of the viewer's life.

The problem isn't having a canon; it's having a canon dictated by convention or institutional authority. That's received wisdom of precisely the type that close engagement with an artwork always challenges. Each of us has to create our own canon and constantly revise it. There's no end point here: every artwork we engage with shifts the array of the whole, a whole that is not structured as a simple hierarchy.

At a certain point, for reasons unknown, these prehistoric people stopped painting the caves. By the time the next surviving major artworks were created, beginning in about 4000 BC, the cave paintings had been forgotten, sealed in obscurity, and never served as a source or an influence. So while these are the earliest examples we have of European art, they are not in any way its 'foundation' or 'origin'. It's a line of development that was truncated, a possibility unpursued. For me that makes it all the more intriguing.

I left the Cuevas de Covalanas invigorated by my encounter with this specimen of the oldest surviving human art, thrillingly new and fresh to me. Much of the joy derived from taking part in an act of communion with people so remote and alien. In reconfirming art's ever-astonishing capacity to cross vast distances of time and culture, the experience also testified to the existence of a shared humanity, a continuing commonality of dreams and desires.

8

REFLECTIONS ON IDENTITY

SOME CRUCIAL DISTINCTIONS

First published in 2005.

The High Holy Days celebrated during the past fortnight are the premiere events in the Jewish calendar. Rosh Hashanah, the Jewish New Year, accompanied by exuberant blowing on the ram's horn, is followed by Yom Kippur, the Day of Atonement, marked by fasting and prayer. These are the two occasions on which Jews worldwide are most likely to attend synagogue.

The globe's 13 million Jews are less than ¼ of one per cent of its total population. But their impact on the wider human community has been disproportionate: as contributors in science, arts, philosophy, socialist politics and capitalist finance; as the victims of the greatest crime of modern European civilisation; and today, in the eyes of many, as perpetrators of another crime.

As a Jew who opposes Israeli policies and rejects Zionism, I'm distressed whenever Jews as a whole are blamed for the crimes of the Israeli state. In this debate, crucial distinctions are too often blurred. Israel is a nation-state; Zionism is a political ideology. Judaism and Jewishness are harder to define but they are clearly entities of a different kind and not reducible to a state or an ideology. To criticise Israel or denounce Zionism is not anti-Semitic. Nor is Israel's treatment of the Palestinians an excuse for attacks on Jews or stereotyping Jewish people.

While hostility to Israel in many parts of the world does take on an anti-Semitic colouring, it is Zionism itself that insists on the identification between Israel and Jews, and it is the advocates of Israel who are keenest to cement that link. Any attack on the rights and lives of Palestinians is jusitified by an appeal to Jewish history and collective Jewish interests. The occupation, the settlements, the targeted assassinations, the shooting of children, the bulldozing of homes, the curfews and checkpoints – all done in our name. Those of us who demur are labeled 'self-haters'.

But we're not as rare a species as people are led to believe. Indeed prior to the Holocaust, Zionism was a minority trend in world Jewry. In the tradition of the Old Testament prophets (well, some of them), there have always been Jewish voices warning against the siren call of Zionism, with its foundation myth, that Palestine was 'a land without people for a people without land'.

In 1891, the Russian Jewish journalist Ahad Ha'am returned from a visit to Palestine to report that 'in the entire land it is hard to find tillable land that is not already tilled'. He condemned the 'impulse to despotism' over the local people which seemed to have infected the Jewish colonisers, so recently 'slaves in their land of exile'.

In a letter of 1930, Sigmund Freud wrote: 'I can raise no sympathy at all for the misdirected piety which transforms a piece of Herod's wall into a national shrine, thereby challenging the feelings of the natives.' In 1938, Albert Einstein warned of the dangers of seeking to establish a Jewish state – as opposed to a place of Jewish refuge: 'I am afraid of the inner damage Judaism will sustain – especially the development of a narrow nationalism within our own ranks.'

Einstein's fears proved prescient. Today, most Jews remain in denial about the reailties of Israel. And there's a powerful lobby dedicated to keeping them that way. Nonetheless, increasing numbers of Jews find that loyalty to the state ostensibly constructed on their behalf clashes with their humanist ethics. It's hard to look at the 'separation wall' as it cuts through Palestinian land or the roads designated for use by Jews only and reconcile these with a basic sense of decency or a sane strategy for Jewish self-preservation. Groups like European Jews for Just Peace and Jews for Justice for Palestinians or the Israeli 'refuseniks' (who refuse military service in the occupied territories) testify to the fact – deeply uncomfortable for the the Israel lobby – that global Jewish opinion is diverse and in flux.

As a boy I attended Sunday school for eight years. When I was 13, I was bar mitzvah. I liked Passover – a holiday celebrating the ancient Hebrews' emancipation from slavery – but found Yom Kippur too dour. (I was never sure what I was supposed to be atoning for.) I did not attend synagogue last week, thus maintaining a decades long tradition of my own, a tradition that is not so un-Jewish as may seem. Surveys reveal that Jews in the US and UK are less likely to believe in God, less likely to attend religious services, and more likely to intermarry than members of any other religious group.

Nearly 40 years ago, Isaac Deutscher, biographer of Trotsky, wrote a classic essay entitled *The Non-Jewish Jew*. Here he argued that 'The Jewish heretic who transcends Jewry belongs to a Jewish tradition.' He cited Spinoza, who wrote about the contradiction within Judaism between a universal god and a 'chosen people', for which offense the rabbis excommunicated him. Others in Deutscher's lineage included Heinrich Heine, Marx, Rosa Luxemburg, and Freud. In our own day one could add Noam Chomsky and Bob Dylan.

Backward in time, Deutscher traced the tradition to a story in the *Midrash*, a compilation of Biblical commentaries. One Sabbath, Rabbi Meir, a pillar of orthodoxy, is walking with his mentor, a heretic named Elisha ben Abiyuh, called Akher (The Stranger). Meir was so absorbed in Akher's words that, Deutscher tells us, 'he failed to notice that he and his teacher had reached the ritual boundary which Jews were not allowed to cross on a sabbath. The great heretic turned to the orthodox pupil and said: "Look, we have reached the boundary – we must part now; you must not accompany me any farther – go back!" Rabbi Meir went back to the Jewish community, while the heretic rode on – beyond the boundaries of Jewry.'

ECHOES AND ANALOGIES

First published in 2007.

The more I travel, read and study the history of peoples and societies, the more analogies I discover, and at the same time the warier I become of all analogies. History does not repeat itself exactly, but it is full of echoes.

Some analogies are routinely abused, while some are bitterly resisted. Today, the prime example of the latter must be the angry clamour that arises whenever Israel's treatment of the Palestinians is compared to white South Africa's treatment of black people under apartheid. In the US, uttering the 'A-word' in relation to Israel elicits a surfeit of outrage, inevitably accompanied by accusations of anti-Semitism. As Jimmy Carter has found out, even being a widely respected former President of the United States does not shield one from the backlash.

It is true that people throw the word apartheid around incautiously. I was guilty of this when I referred in an article to the segregation of business from economy class passengers at airports as a form of 'social apartheid'. But when it comes to Israel, the analogy is apt and unavoidable. Crucially, it is a spontaneous response from those black South Africans who have visited the occupied territories. What they see there – the Jews-only roads, the 'security fence', the confinement in camps and villages, the checkpoints, the daily harassment – reminds them graphically of the system they once suffered under.

There is, however, at least one major difference, though it's not one that favours Israel. Under apartheid, the dominant whites used the black population as a source of cheap labour; they denied that population basic human rights, but they needed it. In contrast, Zionism has aimed to remove the Palestinian population, to replace Palestinians with Jews. That was the meaning of what Zionists called 'the conquest of labour' (when Jewish settlers campaigned for the non-employment of Palestinians) and it is the ultimate source of the current calls within Israel for 'transfer', the final expulsion of the bulk of the Palestinian population.

In an article I published on the fifth anniversary of the Gujarat pogrom, I referred to the role played by 'the stormtroopers of the Hindu right' – and was rebuked by a correspondent who said that he never trusted writers who invoked the Nazi analogy, because it tended to close rather than open debate. I have some sympathy for his argument. The Nazi analogy is indeed indiscriminately used, as is the word 'fascist', applied too readily to anyone who is authoritarian and racist. It becomes a form of name-calling, a substitute for analysis.

By the way, the prime culprit here is not the left. In my lifetime, every US military action, from Vietnam to Iraq (and now the threat against Iran), has been justified with analogies drawn from World War II. Every enemy is a new Hitler (Nasser, Qadaffi, Noriega, Milosevic, Saddam Hussein, Ahmadinejad) and every call for peace is Munich-style appeasement.

Nonetheless, I stand by my use of 'stormtroopers' in the Gujarat context. The *Sturmabteilung* or SA (German for 'Storm division', always translated as 'stormtroopers') was the paramilitary, street-fighting wing of the Nazi movement, also known as 'brownshirts' because of the colour of their uniforms. Claiming to be the guardians of German national pride, they mounted aggressive public actions whose aim was to spread terror among minorities and political opponents. In November 1938, they played a key role in *Kristallnacht*, ransacking Jewish homes, beating Jews to death, burning down synagogues, destroying Jewish-owned shopfronts with sledgehammers, leaving the streets covered in broken glass from smashed windows (hence the name). Given the similarities with what happened in Gujarat in 2002, it takes an effort to avoid the analogy, and the effect of that effort is to downplay the horror of the Gujarat pogrom.

Of course, the Nazis and the Holocaust represent an acme of inhumanity, an evil so enormous that any comparison seems dubious. Yet if we remove them from history and treat them as *sui generis*, we debar ourselves from learning and applying the broader lessons. When the world discovered the extent of Nazi barbarism in the wake of World War II, the cry was 'Never again!' We cannot turn that cry into a reality; we cannot ensure that nothing even remotely like this happens again, unless we are permitted to draw appropriate analogies from the experience.

League tables of atrocities serve no purpose, or rather, the only purpose they serve is to allow scope for the apologists for atrocities. The holocaust, the enslavement of Africans, the genocide of Native Americans and Australians, the centuries of 'untouchability' in South Asia, the Belgian Congo (where, according to Adam Hochschild's revelatory book *King Leopold's Ghost*, some ten million Africans may have perished in little more than a decade), Stalin's Gulag. All these are distinct historical phenomena, but share in common an institutionalised inhumanity on a mass scale. All are unspeakably, irredeemably horrific; they exemplify that which every human being has an absolute obligation to resist and not to aid, in any way, even by omission.

Which brings me back to the Palestinians. Their suffering is not only analogous to black suffering under apartheid but also to Jewish suffering, and specifically the experience of exile and diaspora. 'We travel like everyone else, but we return to nothing,' writes the marvellous Palestinian poet, Mahmoud Darwish, 'We travel in the chariots of the Psalms, sleep in the tents of the prophets, and are born again in the language of Gypsies... Ours is a country of words. Talk. Talk. Let me see an end to this journey.'

PATHWAYS ACROSS TIME AND SPACE

First published in 2007.

The Internet has helped fuel a genealogy boom. Websites serving the legions of amateur family historians are popular and profitable. As more archives are digitised and more data goes online, the field of research opens wide, a territory criss-crossed with intriguing, unexplored pathways. Half an hour on the web can turn up a link that in former times could only have been unearthed through months or even years spent amidst dusty tomes.

Genealogy has long exercised a particular fascination for North Americans. In a society that envisions its own birth and identity as a radical breach with the Old World, there's a hunger for ancestry, and an industry that caters to it, with specialist services for Irish-, Scottish-, Indian-, African-Americans and others.

Since the US is not only an immigrant but also a geographically mobile society, Americans without upper-class pedigrees can find it hard to trace family history back beyond their grandparents. So in search of their forebears they burrow through census, draft board and social security records, passenger ship lists and business directories. In my own family's case, another useful source has been the FBI, whose (heavily censored) files are available to the public under the Freedom of Information Act.

Thanks to the FBI, I know that in 1943 my maternal grandfather was described by a confidential informant as 'super-sensitive on the Semitic question and always on a Jewish crusade'. This informant advised that hiring him 'in any capacity ... would be a detriment to the Government and the war effort'. I also know that in 1951, a citizen felt public spirited enough to inform J. Edgar Hoover that my father had 'spoken favourably of the Soviet system' in a launderette in Ithaca, New York.

I've got forebears who emigrated from Germany in the wake of the failed democratic revolutions of 1848. And from Poland and Lithuania with the great wave of Eastern European Jewry from 1881 to the eve of the First World War. Plus a lone non-Jew, an Irishman from Cork.

Thanks to a 19th century ancestor I share with a genealogist in Mecklenburg, Germany, I know that I am descended from (among many anonymous others) Yahi'a Ibn Ya'ish, the first Chief Rabbi of Portugal, who was born in Moorish Cordova in the 12th century. I know that one of Yahi'a's descendants fled the Inquisition and established himself as a coin-maker in northeast Germany in the early 17th century. And I know that among the descendants of the coin-maker, those who remained in Germany in 1940 were annihilated by the Nazis. In the database of Yad Vashem, the Holocaust memorial and institute, I can identify scores of names with whom I might have a connection.

Genealogy can be a wonderful introduction to the joys of research as well as a tool for democratising the study of history. But much depends on what people are looking for when they embark on the journey.

Some hope to aggrandise their lineage, to establish a personal link with famous or exceptional human beings. Some want proof of their ethnic authenticity. Oprah Winfrey paid a great deal of money to be told that her DNA showed that she was of Zulu heritage. The problem here is that Oprah's forebears were enslaved in West Africa many years before the formation of the Zulu nation several thousand miles to the southeast. A few years ago Indian Jews queued to have their DNA tested and their link with Judaism confirmed. But what is actually demonstrated by this test is merely that the person has a genetic strand in common with people who lived in ancient Palestine; its presence does not make one a Jew nor does its absence make one a non-Jew.

Genetics is not genealogy. Genealogy, if it isn't to descend into obscurantism, is a social science. Not least because the genealogical chain depends on the testimony of generations of mothers, at least one or more of whom are bound to have been less than frank about the actual parentage of an heir. What's more, the noteworthy ancestor is likely to be radically unrepresentative. The poor leave behind far fewer recorded traces. In rural areas family memory is sustained through oral tradition, but where a great break has occurred – from rural to urban, from Europe, Africa or India to the Western hemisphere – that tradition is often lost. So conscientious family historians must study the ebbs and flows of the broader social groups to which their ancestors belonged, not just hunt out named individuals.

Above all, family historians must distinguish between conjecture and established fact. The temptation to claim a link because it is attractive, because it elevates the researcher's sense of self, has to be resisted. In other words, family history has to be good history – both rigorous and imaginative.

For me, genealogy offers insights into the shifting ties between people and places. It's a study in ironies and contrasts, not a monument to a coherent or definitive inheritance. My great-grandmother who left Lithuania for the US in 1888 was a divorcee fleeing the tyranny of the Rabbis as much as the pressure of anti-Semitism. She was one of five of my great-grandparents who were Yiddish speakers and whose generation enriched the vocabulary of global English. If you've ever heard the word *chutzpah*, it's because of them.

THE REAL THING

First published in 2009.

Something special took place in Durban in February and though the media have rushed past, we should pause. In solidarity with the people of Gaza, dockworker members of the South African Transport and Allied Workers Union refused to unload a ship carrying Israeli cargo. Here was a local intervention in global politics, driven not by national, ethnic or religious affinity but by principle, experience and common humanity.

Significantly, in explaining their action, union leaders and members stressed the similarity between Palestinians' experience of Israeli rule and their own experiences under apartheid. Supporters of Israel object fiercely to this analogy; but they are on thin ground when it is being explicitly drawn by those with most authority to draw it.

The analogy is loathed not only because of the negative light in which it casts Israel, but because of the positive way out it offers Palestinians. Apartheid was overthrown and international support – boycotts and sanctions – played a material role in that overthrow.

Those who dismiss 'international labour solidarity' as a relic of a superseded age need to think again. True, far too often it's empty rhetoric. But what we saw in Durban was international labour solidarity not as a slogan or impossible ideal or bit of wishful thinking but as a living practise, a pointer to the future. Among much else, it exposed the selectivity and superficiality of the 'universalism' promoted by supporters of the war on terror. In a world of over-hyped spectacle, Durban was the real thing.

It was also the crest in a wave of global protest that followed the assault on Gaza. In Britain, students at more than 21 universities (at last count) mounted occupations demanding an end to ties with

Israel. Victories have been secured: scholarships for students from Gaza and in some cases cancellation of contracts with Israeli-based corporations.

The boycott and divestment campaign has, of course, a long way to go. The British government wants to see a significant expansion of trade with Israel. It's also sobering to note that the US Congress supported Israel's actions in Gaza by a majority of 390 to 5.

Nonetheless, for dockworkers, students and many others, Gaza epitomised basic divisions, basic choices. Between the powerful and the powerless; between the 'war on terror' and respect for human rights and human life; between Western interests and the interests of the world majority. Perhaps most piquantly, the choice between passively standing by and actively pursuing justice.

The international response to the horror of Gaza brings hope, but it also highlights our difficulties in rousing opposition to the wars and occupations in Iraq and Afghanistan. Though British soldiers are directly engaged in both conflicts, it's unlikely that at this juncture a demonstration focussed solely on Iraq or Afghanistan would attract the numbers, feelings and focus of the Gaza protests. Withdrawal from both countries enjoys wide public support but it is passive. To the limited extent that these wars are visible in Britain, their course seems dictated by a confusion of forces beyond our control.

In Iraq, the British military role is seen to be nearly negligible. The myth of the 'surge' is widely accepted; Obama is believed to be keeping his pledge to withdraw. The fact remains, however, that Iraq is an occupied country in a state of war and that 35-50,000 US troops will remain there for another two years. Attacks on and by US forces and their Iraqi allies are and will continue to be a daily occurrence. The corporate invasion of Iraq – with British companies in the lead – is only just getting underway.

Meanwhile, the 8-year-old war in Afghanistan grows bloodier, more costly, more futile. Obama has made this war his own. Here, he has declared, is the real front line in the war on terror. Accordingly, tens of thousands of additional US and British troops will intensify and expand what is already a brutal war of counter-insurgency, the burden of which is born by the civilian population. Instead of taming resistance, the occupation has spurred it – something it required no PhD to predict.

We know far less about Afghanistan than about Palestine (partly because there is no Afghan counterpart to the articulate Palestinian diaspora). We hear no one from 'the other side'; we see them only at a distance, in stock footage of turbaned men with mules and Kalashnikovs. In a typical recent BBC feature, talking heads tried to explain why the war seemed so intractable, why so many initiatives had failed. But unexplained and unexamined was the underlying fact – accepted by all – that resistance keeps growing. No one asked why. No one asked who these people are or what they want.

As foretold, the overspill of the Afghan war into Pakistan has had dire results. Again, Obama seems wedded to an aggressive policy. US military mount regular cross-border attacks, by unmanned drones or helicopter lifted special forces, targeting 'terrorists' and terrifying civilians in Pakistani villages.

That this crass violation of sovereignty goes largely un-remarked is a big part of our problem. Critically, the US attacks place Pakistan's fragile democracy in an untenable position: unable to protect its own people from violent assault by an 'ally'. The worse than useless Zardari has found himself cornered, under pressure from the US, from India following the Mumbai attacks and from the Islamist insurgency within.

In response, the government has offered to institute Sharia law in the Swat Valley in the northwest. It's a disastrous concession in every respect, and strongly opposed in Pakistan. As election results have confirmed, the Pakistani majority is both anti-US and anti-Taliban. The 'war on terror' paradigm excludes and silences them – one of its basic flaws.

The attraction of Sharia law is that it promises relief from the corrupt, dysfunctional Pakistani justice system, under which the rich are beyond the law and the poor without redress. It is a false promise, but it highlights once again that it is the failure of the secular order on secular questions that fosters the politics of religious identity. The quest for secularism will not prosper if it is conceived as a battle against religious ideologies and divorced from struggles for social justice and against imperial occupations.

While there is a good deal of activity in relation to Iraq and Afghanistan in Britain, no one can doubt that overall the anti-war movement is becalmed. Part of the problem, as widely noted, is a sense of impotence. In the absence of any electoral punch, what leverage can we exercise? There's no simple recipe for success here. If there is I certainly don't have it.

But as the response to the horror of Gaza has shown, the chemistry of protest is unpredictable. Gaza made many people feel that they had to do something now, not tomorrow, and the boycott campaign offered them an avenue.

Common assumptions about the limits of human solidarity are routinely and excessively pessimistic. It is taken for granted that our loyalties – our willingness to sacrifice – are confined to family and close friends, and beyond that, to ethnic, communal or national groups, somehow also assumed, like the family, to be 'natural' categories. Anything wider is weighed as too abstract, too remote, too theoretical to motivate human activity. In their uncompromising, far-reaching and at the same time concrete universalism, the Durban dockworkers and their global allies have shown that this is not the case.

BIBLE BASHING (LESSONS FOR THE RICH)

First published in 2011.

A body of antiquated dogma and myth, a source of repression, paean to patriarchy, bulwark of hierarchy. That's how many would summarise the Bible, and there are more than enough juicily quotable Biblical passages to justify that view. But there's much more to this book – or rather, this collection of texts by various hands – than either its detractors or devotees often suppose.

Take 1 Samuel, Chapter 8, where the elders of Israel ask the sage-judge Samuel to appoint a king 'to govern us like all other nations.' Samuel, after consulting with God, warns them to be careful what they wish for. Under a king, their sons will be conscripted 'for his chariots and his horsemen' and made to 'to reap his harvest and to make his instruments of war'. Their daughters will be forced to work in the king's kitchens. Their vineyards and olive groves will be seized and given to the king's cronies. To support the army and bureaucracy they will be taxed to the tune of ten per cent of everything they produce. Nonetheless the elders insist on having a king, to be 'like all other nations'.

That the Jews should become like other nations ('normalised', with a territory, state and army of their own) was one of the earliest Zionist shibboleths. But here, at the founding of what many see as the first 'Jewish state', the Biblical author raises troubling questions about the whole idea of statehood. In the work of the prophets, who were mostly critics of the monarchy, these questions would be amplified.

The Hebrew Bible embraces contending voices and visions, even within a single text attributed to a single author. It incorporates 'official' and 'unofficial' narratives, temple orthodoxy and subaltern dissent, laudatory regime chronicles and savage critiques of those regimes. Most of it was composed between 750-500 BCE by authors living in small, poor states in the isolated highlands west of the Jordan – a frontier region between the competing empires of the Nile and Mesopotamia. The strategic situation was perpetually vulnerable and state authority uncertain. Ironically, these weaknesses meant that there was more space for the clash of ideas and for self-critical perspectives than in the monolithic empires to the north, east and south.

Some prophets opposed all imperial entanglements; others urged tactical submission or collaboration. In parts of the Bible, the great empires are depicted as brute instruments of God's judgement. Their capacity for destruction is vividly evoked, but so is their ephemeral nature. In the fate of empires, Biblical authors saw the possibility of an epochal overturning of hierarchies:

> He humbles those who dwell on high, he lays the lofty city low; he levels it to the ground and casts it down to the dust. Feet trample it down – the feet of the oppressed, the footsteps of the poor. (Isaiah 26:5-7)

Although the Bible includes reams of ritual prescription, it also includes criticism of the emptiness and hypocrisy of ritual. Against the legalistic regime of the priests, the best of the prophets posited an ethical and spiritual religion, a credo of social conscience. In Isaiah 58:6-9, God makes clear what kind of worship he prefers:

> Is not this the kind of fasting I have chosen: to loose the chains of injustice and untie the cords of the yoke, to set the oppressed free and break every yoke? Is it not to share your food with the hungry and to provide the poor wanderer with shelter, when you see the naked, to clothe them?

Malachi denounces the 'rulers of Israel, who despise justice and distort all that is right; who build Zion with bloodshed and Jerusalem with wickedness.' Similarly, Micah comes 'to declare to Jacob his transgression, to Israel his sin'. He resists the siren voices of the establishment: 'I will not listen to the music of your harps. But let justice roll on like a river, righteousness like a never-failing stream!'

'Justice' means above all justice for the poor and vulnerable. The greatest criminals, Isaiah argues, are those who 'deprive the poor of their rights and withhold justice from the oppressed of my people, making widows their prey and robbing the fatherless.' New Labour may have been 'intensely relaxed' about the accumulation of great private wealth, but many of the Biblical authors are anything but. Isaiah (3:13-15) cries out: 'What do you mean by crushing my people and grinding the faces of the poor?' And Proverbs 28:11 archly observes: 'The rich are wise in their own eyes; one who is poor and discerning sees how deluded they are.'

Amos excoriates traders for 'skimping on the measure, boosting the price and cheating with dishonest scales.' Israel will be destroyed, he says, because: 'They sell the innocent for silver, and the needy for a pair of sandals. They trample on the heads of the poor as on the dust of the ground and deny justice to the oppressed.' In particular, Amos warns that God will be 'quick to testify' against 'those who defraud labourers of their wages... and deprive the foreigners among you of justice'.

Amos and other prophets influenced the later writers who drew up the social codes contained in the first five books of the Bible. These include restrictions on the rich that would be regarded as intolerable by current economic orthodoxy. 'If you lend money to one of my people among you who is needy, do not treat it like a business deal; charge no interest.' 'The land must not be sold permanently, because the land is mine and you reside in my land as foreigners and strangers.' 'Do not take advantage of a hired worker who is poor and needy, whether that worker is a fellow Israelite or a foreigner residing in one of your towns. Pay them their wages each day before sunset, because they are poor and are counting on it.'

This social vision had its contradictions. Much of the Hebrew Bible takes for granted the justice of collective punishment, extending even into unborn generations. However, in the wake of the final destruction of the ancient Hebrew state and the deportation to Babylon, Biblical authors stressed individual salvation and reshaped their God as a comforter in exile and distress (thus laying the basis for the New Testament).

The Book of Job, composed some decades after the exile, turns the justice debate on its head. Job is a just man who suffers injustice. In his complaint, the suffering of the innocent is laid at God's feet. Job's friends, who come as comforters but speak as defenders of orthodoxy, are appalled: 'Does God pervert justice? Does the Almighty pervert what is right?' Yes, Job insists, he does: 'God has wronged me and drawn his net around me. Though I cry, "Violence!" I get no response; though I call for help, there is no justice.' Job refuses to compromise his 'integrity' by accepting that he is to blame. God's response, 'the voice out of the whirlwind', is a poetic triumph, imagining the cosmos from a non-human perspective. Though it over-awes Job, it really answers none of his questions. In the book's coda, Job is rewarded for speaking the truth as he knew it, for holding on to his integrity, while his friends are punished for offering false comfort.

Like other Biblical texts, Job is puzzling and open-ended. It demands interpretation, calls for a response, even if that response is a rejection of monotheism and its internal contradictions. The best of the Bible writers leap across time and space to question us with intimacy and urgency. What they'd have to say about the deficit-chopping governments of Europe would probably get them pulled from the Internet.

'IF NOT NOW, WHEN?': ON BDS AND 'SINGLING OUT' ISRAEL

First published in 2014.

This is an edited version of a letter I've just sent to a relative in the US who's been trying to figure out the boycott, disinvestment and sanctions [BDS] issue in the wake of the recent onslaught against the American Studies Association's decision to support the academic boycott:

The 'singling out' objection seems to me quite perverse. It's not possible to campaign against any injustice anywhere without 'singling it out'. When people campaigned and boycotted South Africa, they were 'singling it out' – and that accusation was in fact frequently made by apologists for South Africa. 'What about the black dictatorships in Africa?' they would say. This was always an evasive manoeuvre, a poor excuse for allowing gross racial oppression to continue unhindered. Many of those who raise this objection now in relation to Israel would have or indeed did dismiss it when it was raised in relation to South Africa.

There's an implication in these arguments that Israel is really 'not that bad' and somehow deserves a break from criticism. But just how 'bad' does a regime have to get before it's subject to penalties? The facts on the ground day-by-day show without doubt that Israel in its treatment of the Palestinians IS one of the world's worst, most brutal, most racist, most oppressive regimes. There's a huge element of denialism in many pro-Israel arguments and sentiments: something a bit like the denialism of generations of sincere Communists in regard to Stalinism and the Soviet Union. The difference being that in the latter case, the denialism was driven by an ideological identification, whereas in the Israel case it's driven by an ethnic identification. I think what's behind a lot of this is a deep reluctance to believe that 'people like us' could commit such terrible crimes. That attitude has a long and very grim history and needs to be rejected.

Of course Israel is not the only regime worthy of active opposition and censure, and in fact, most people I know in the BDS movement have been and are involved in numerous other international solidarity campaigns (unlike the bulk of their opponents). But there are two factors that make Israel a particular case calling for a particular response.

First, the BDS call has been issued by a wide and representative array of Palestinian civil society organisations, including trade unions, and enjoys strong support from Palestinians in both the occupied territories and Israel itself. There is at the moment no similar call being issued by people engaged in a struggle against other oppressive regimes: the opposition in Burma, for example, has backed a relaxing of sanctions, because they believe that it will strengthen their position. BDS is not a universally appropriate strategy; it's a particular tactic chosen because of its potential effectiveness in a particular situation. And most importantly it's chosen by the people on the sharp end, the people affected by Israel's policies, just as it was in South Africa, when poll after poll revealed that black South Africans overwhelmingly supported the ANC's call for boycott, sanctions and disinvestment – which proved to be a highly effective tactic and one of the major factors in the final defeat of apartheid.

Arguing that one should ignore this specific call for BDS because it is not simultaneously aimed at all other oppressive regimes is like arguing that you should cross a picket line because the union in dispute isn't simultaneously picketing all other bad employers. In fact, I think defying the Palestinian BDS call is very much like crossing a picket line: it shows a contempt for or ignorance of the principle of solidarity.

Secondly, the people who constantly 'single out' Israel are the US and EU and other governments that supply it with military, economic and diplomatic assistance. The repeated use of the US veto in the

Security Council to protect Israel from the consequences of its actions being only one example. The demand of the BDS campaign is not that Israel should be better than other countries but that it should adhere to minimal standards of human rights and human decency. Over the years the West has given Israel an impunity which has made it ever more intransigent in relation to the Palestinians. The BDS campaign is an attempt to end that impunity, that special protected status, and create instead something like a level playing field for the Palestinians.

I have to say I'm puzzled what a 'balanced' account of Israel is supposed to be. What is there that could 'balance out' atrocities and ethnic cleansing – currently ongoing in the West Bank and the Negev? Whatever achievements US society has to its credit, they don't in any way 'balance out', i.e. justify, the extermination of indigenous people or the oppression of African-Americans. Shakespeare, Wordsworth etc. do not 'balance out' the British empire's blood-stained record in Asia, Africa and the Caribbean.

You ask whether Israelis themselves are capable of making this assessment. In fact, there are quite a few Israelis who've written brilliantly and objectively about Israel's history and politics: Ilan Pappe, Michel Warshavksy, Avi Shlaim, Jeff Halper, Shlomo Sand, and the late Tanya Reinhardt, to name only a few (all their books are well worth reading). These dissident intellectuals are for the most part supporters of the BDS movement.

For the Palestinians, the criticisms of BDS carry a particular indignity. For years they've been told by people in the 'international community' to abandon violence and use democratic means to advance their cause. BDS is an attempt to do precisely that: a non-violent, democratic, grass-roots based effort to rouse global public opinion to put some real pressure on Israel to change its policies. Somehow it's still not enough to earn the support of Western liberals.

It's important to remember that what BDS calls for is basically the withdrawal of the current support given to Israel by our governments and institutions. If you invest money in a company that is profiting from the settlement programme in the West Bank, you are investing in ethnic cleansing – and the first thing you should do when you learn that is simply to stop doing it. All the rest is special pleading.

On the academic boycott, the precise formulations and demands have now been worked out in great detail by a serious collective effort among academics themselves. It's not a boycott of individual Israelis and it's carefully targeted. Check out the various explanations on the BRICUP (British Committee for Universities in Palestine) web page.

The reality is that Palestinian academics are asking their counterparts in the US and UK to take a specific form of action to help relieve the intolerable conditions they live under, which include persistent Israeli obstruction of academic freedom. If academics in, say, France or Spain or Egypt or Argentina asked their US/British counterparts for such support, with the same clarity and precision, it would be given without hesitation by many of the people who so bitterly resent the Palestinian call. Sorry, but all I see in that is ethnic bigotry. For some people, it seems, the rights of the Palestinians are always dispensable.

As Rabbi Hillel said, 'If not now, when?'

BDS is beginning to have a serious impact on Israeli society – check out Tzipi Livni's recent warning about the dangers of ignoring it. It's precisely because it is so effective and has such clear moral force that the pro-Israel camp hates and fears it so much and spends so much time and energy smearing its proponents and lying about its content.

I know that many people – not only in the US but in Europe also – simply do not want to acquaint themselves with the realities of Israel's record (past and present). Can I note that in the first three days of 2014, the Israeli army has already killed a 16-year-old and and an 85-year-old in Gaza, plus a three-year-old child on Christmas Eve. That's just the tip of an iceberg. Blocking out that reality or trying to 'balance' it by talking about Israel's 'achievements' is a form of intellectual-emotional bad faith. In a sense, this is itself the biggest problem facing Palestinians and anyone who wants a just and sustainable peace in the Middle East.

The people pressing for BDS in US and Britain have done so in the face of an avalanche of lies, smears and threats. I've been on the receiving end of many of them. So I have to say one of the poorest arguments against BDS is that its supporters do this for fun, for self-promotion, for some kind of 'easy' thrill (see for example Michael Kazan's most recent exercise in self-serving intellectual dishonesty). Campaigning for BDS is anything but easy. You have to challenge a lot of mythology, a host of ingrained prejudices and assumptions backed up by an enormous propaganda machine – virtually the whole of the mainstream media. And you have to be willing to withstand vicious personal attacks. (An extreme Zionist website recently reported to its readers what it called 'the good news' that I have cancer and will die soon.)

Contrary to the view taken by Obama supporters, justice for Palestine isn't some optional extra, a luxury cause reserved for the far left; it's one of the central and decisive moral-political conflicts of our time, as Spain was in the thirties or South Africa in the seventies/eighties. In the future, those who are arguing against BDS now will look as foolish as those who argued for 'neutrality' in Spain or 'constructive engagement' in South Africa.

Anyway, that's my take on it, summarised as briefly as I can. Much, much more could be and needs to be said.

Best,
Mike

9

THE LAST DANCE – A BATTLE FOR HEALTHCARE, NOT FOR HEALTH

AS LONG AS YOU'VE GOT YOUR HEALTH

First published in 2007.

St Bartholomew's Hospital – known to Londoners for generations simply as Barts – has a claim to being the world's longest-established provider of free medical care to the poor. It was founded by a penitent Norman courtier in 1123 as a priory hospital on the edge of the then walled City of London.

Following Henry VIII's dissolution of the monasteries in 1539, the citizenry of London petitioned the king to save the hospital. He granted it to the Corporation of the City of London and it continued as a municipal institution until 1948, when it was absorbed into the new National Health Service.

Having been diagnosed some months ago with an illness that requires frequent visits to hospital for complex treatments, I've been spending much of my life these days at Barts. Not far from St Paul's Cathedral, I enter via the 1702 gateway – a little gem of English baroque – past the unadorned solid square tower of the 13th century Priory Church, under the North Wing with its Hogarth murals, and into the compact 18th century square designed by James Gibbs to provide a cloister-like retreat for patients and staff. It's now an unprepossessing carpark, but will shortly be pedestrianised and returned to its former sober elegance, with the bubbling mid-19th century fountain as light-hearted centrepiece.

The architectural legacy reflects a remarkable medical history. The 17th century scientist William Harvey was a surgeon at Barts when he discovered the circulation of the blood. In the century that followed Barts became a major medical school, and its staff led the way in breaking from the old barbers' guilds and establishing surgery as a modern science. It was one of the first hospitals to employ anaesthetics and pioneered developments in ophthalmology, surgical techniques, pathology, radiotherapy, and the treatment of thyroid disease and cancers. On the negative side, the hospital resisted the introduction of antiseptic procedures and excluded women students until 1947.

The school's most famous student was not, however, renowned for surgical prowess. W G Grace studied here between 1874-1876, years when he was busy revolutionising the game of cricket and had already become one of the most famous names in the realm. Teachers and fellow students expected little from the young celebrity, for whom the medical profession was mainly a sinecure that protected his otherwise dubious status as an amateur cricketer.

Historical intrigue aside, what counts for any patient in any hospital is the quality of treatment. When I was transferred from my general practitioner to Barts I feared I might fall through the cracks at such a large, multi-faceted institution. I was not reassured by the fact that at the moment Barts is something of a building site, as a long delayed and often controversial refurbishment finally gets underway. Despite the confusion caused by temporary access, diversions and scaffolding, the coordination and integration in the inter-disciplinary care I've received – from doctors, nurses, technicians and support staff – has been exemplary.

Here I have benefited from recent sea-changes in best medical practise. The glibness and arrogance for which some sections of the medical profession are noted and resented – across national and cultural boundaries – has given way in some quarters at least to a commitment to transparency and patient involvement. Doctors share with me all the information about my case on their computer screens, from lab reports to x-rays and MRIs. They copy me into correspondence. The various nurses and specialists treating me are kept up to date with all the details of my condition and, importantly, my medication regime. At each stage, I've found an openness to questions and a willingness to address anxieties. Given the pressure on resources, there are sometimes delays, but every effort is made to keep me informed of these and to minimise inconvenience.

All this is delivered with a quiet, caring, un-panicked but thorough efficiency by a staff drawn from all over the world. Only 36 per cent of Barts staff are British and white; 13 per cent come from the Indian subcontinent; ten per cent from Africa, seven per cent from the Philippines and four per cent from the Carribbean. In my experience the diversity is anything but an obstacle to the impressive teamwork.

Most importantly, I am not treated as a lab rat or an ambulatory statistic but as an intelligent and autonomous human being. The more democratic practise yields more effective treatment. I am able to benefit from the high-tech and clinical advances that in other contexts can tear patients into pieces as they cope with uncoordinated, sometimes contradictory information and the diverging dynamics of various specialisms.

My entire treatment, including medication, is free and I receive it by right. It's not charity and it's not conditional on anything but my need for it. I've not only never been issued a bill of any kind for all the numerous services provided; I've never had to fill in a claim or an application or a form (except for consent forms). We take this for granted in Britain but friends in India and the US learn of it with envy. The complete alleviation of the burden and anxiety of finance is an obvious boon for all concerned, and it transforms the ethos with which care is delivered and received. Medical care is surely a human right, like primary education, and India and the US are both societies that can afford to make it a reality for all their citizens. That they have failed to do is the result of vested interests and wrong priorities.

Not that Barts is safe from the relentless pressures corroding the social democratic principles of the NHS. In the early nineties, the Conservative government threatened it with closure (it occupies a piece of prime central London real estate). As in Henry VIII's day, London's populace rallied to Barts' support; more than one million signed a petition to save the hospital. In 1997, the new Labour government promised to refurbish Barts on its historic site. Years of consultation and delay followed. The government insisted that finance for the project should be provided exclusively from the private sector, in keeping with its favoured Private Finance Initiative (PFI), through which consortia of banks, building firms and developers finance, build and supply hospitals which are then leased back to the NHS over 30 or more years at a handsome and guaranteed rate of profit.

As the projected PFI costs for the Barts project soared, in early 2006 the government once again renewed threats to the venerable institution's existence. And once again popular resistance, including an appeal signed by 1,000 doctors, prevented the worst, though at a cost. The scaled-back redevelopment involves a 20 per cent loss of planned bed capacity (250 beds) plus leaving empty several floors of the new buildings, presumably for commercial lease. This will still saddle the Trust that runs Barts with annual re-payments to the PFI consortium of some £55m – more than 11 per cent of its total income – for 35 years.

Inevitably, the patient will pay, as staff and services are squeezed to ensure risk-immune private investors get their promised return.

So the quality of care I've received at Barts is by no means guaranteed for the future. That will depend, as in the past, on the willingness of the people of London and the staff at the hospital to fight to sustain (and expand) its democratic heritage.

EQUALITY: WITHOUT IFS, ANDS OR BUTS

First published in 2008.

Wherever there are inequalities, there will be no shortage of people rationalising or defending them. That's easily explicable. Those who benefit from inequalities enjoy, by definition, greater resources and greater access to the public ear and eye. What's sad for me is that blunt defenders of equality – not equality before the law or equality of opportunity, but practical, material equality – are these days so few and so muted.

By equality I do not mean identity or sameness. Nor am I talking about a world without excellence (without Usain Bolt!), without the surprise of the individual. Just the opposite. My argument for equality is rooted in the reality of human diversity and complexity, which demands that each of us is treated as an irreducible entity, a compound of possibilities (positive and negative) that of right deserves an equal share in the world's goods.

One of the reasons I became a socialist, years ago, was that I could find no justification for the inequalities I saw around me. In the decades since then, as socialism has fallen ever further out of fashion, my increasing awareness of the diversity and multi-dimensionality of human beings has made me more affronted than ever by the injustice of economic and social inequalities. They impose a hierarchy on what is inherently non-hierarchic. Inevitably, those on the wrong side of inequality are denied their full rights as human beings.

Inequalities are endlessly rationalised but at root they are irrational. Over the centuries, they have been seen as the judgement of God, nature, or the market, a measure of individual talent or drive, the product of the hard work of some and the laziness of others, but economic inequality is in fact, everywhere, overwhelmingly inherited; where you start from is the single most influential determinant of where you'll end up.

I'm not aware of any society where there is a general correspondence between wealth and hard work, creativity, perspicacity, determination or contribution to others' welfare. And I'm not aware of any civilised hierarchy of values which could not find offensive the current gulf in the rewards offered to nurses, teachers, train-drivers, farm-workers, street-cleaners, carers for the infirm, on the one hand and, say, financial speculators, arms dealers, management consultants and absentee landlords, on the other. That's a hierarchy that needs to be turned upside down.

But then what hierarchy of reward could reflect the necessary diversity and interdependence of human contributions to human welfare? Even under ideal conditions, meritocracy involves a judgement on each of us, on our relative value, which is at best artificial and one dimensional. It's more of a utopian illusion than the goal of practical material equality. And of course, one of the central drives of those who benefit from a meritocracy is to pass on their acquired advantages to their children.

As for equality of opportunity, vaunted by politicians and theorists as an alternative or means to material equality or what's called 'equality of outcomes', it's a chimaera. Outcomes can be measured with precision, opportunities cannot. When is equality of opportunity supposed to kick in? At age 18? A six-year-old with access to books, computers, travel, a room of their own, etc. is already way ahead of one who doesn't. If you really want equality of opportunity then you have to have a starting point of material equality.

Far from being a necessary accompaniment of democracy, economic inequality compromises it. Power follows wealth, and wealth seeks power to protect itself. In the electoral arena, in the courts, in dealings with the civil service, in the media, wealth gives privileged clout. It undermines formal or legal equality – valuable and necessary though they remain. The history of every democracy confirms this, though it also shows that great wealth can be constrained.

Adam Smith, Thomas Jefferson, Thomas Paine – among other Enlightenment theorists – all regarded excessive disparities in wealth as incompatible with the stability of a rational, democratic society, and notably with a functioning 'free market'. All would have found 21st century Britain, India or the US, permeated by inequalities, utterly alien to their vision of a just society.

Inequality is also environmentally unsustainable. Climate change affects us all, but the poor more than the rich. An unequal society, in which the rich have a massive investment in unsustainable industries and practices, has made it more difficult to address the urgent global crisis. It's obvious that if we enjoyed a more equal economic order – globally as well as domestically – there would be much quicker and more concerted action on the threat, unimpeded by special interests.

We need rewards and incentives, but surely people should not be rewarded for anti-social behaviour, as are large corporations and speculators. And do rewards and incentives need to be solely economic? Isn't that a presumptuous limiting of human nature, in which self-interest and our awareness of it are shaped and reshaped by various ingredients, ideas and experiences?

I don't regard myself as inferior in any way to those who have more money than I do or superior in any way to those who have less. I regard myself as different, unique, and I try to regard others in the same light. To do or believe otherwise would be to subscribe to an illusion. I therefore want to see a social policy that disdains that illusion – rather than, as at present, one that deepens it.

The fear of 'levelling', usually pictured as a levelling downward, is long standing, and in the neo-liberal global order it's been bolstered by the political unchallengeability of 'free enterprise' and the prerogatives of the wealthy. Behind it is, of course, a fear of losing what we have, but also a fear of being exposed to the kind of insecurity and want to which so many of our fellow human beings are exposed. The only answer to that, in the long run, is to end insecurity and want.

It's argued that all attempts at establishing an egalitarian order have ended in disaster of one kind of another: chaos, dictatorship, economic stagnation. Examples are cited from the French Revolution to the Soviet Union to British social democracy in the 1970s. The crises, unexpected reversals and contradictions encountered by egalitarian experiments raise difficult questions, but they are not necessarily unanswerable. It's a principle of the scientific world view that because something is unknown does not make it unknowable, because it has yet to be achieved does not make it unachievable.

It says much about our world that only a tiny fraction of the intellectual effort that's put into rationalising inequalities is put into discussing how equality might be achieved. We won't see each other as we truly are – we won't see ourselves, collectively, for who we truly are – as long as we live in a world divided between rich and poor, or even between the not-so-rich and the not-so-poor.

THE MISBEGOTTEN 'WAR AGAINST CANCER'

First published in 2009.

Obituaries routinely inform us that so-and-so has died 'after a brave battle against cancer'. I'm waiting for the day I get to read one that says so-and-so has died 'after a pathetically feeble battle against cancer...' One thing I've come to appreciate since I was diagnosed with multiple myeloma (a cancer of the blood) two years ago is how unreal both notions are. It's just not like that.

The stress on cancer patients' 'bravery' and 'courage' implies that if you can't 'conquer' your cancer, there's something wrong with you, some weakness or flaw. If your cancer progresses rapidly, is it your fault? Does it reflect some failure of will-power? In blaming the victim, the ideology attached to cancer mirrors the bootstrap individualism of the neo-liberal order, in which 'failure' and 'success' become the ultimate duality, dished out according to individual merit, and the poor are poor because of their own weaknesses.

It also re-enforces the demand on patients for uncomplaining stoicism, which in many cases is why they're in bad shape in the first place. Late diagnosis leads to tens of thousands of avoidable deaths in the UK each year. It also accounts for much of the discrepancy between UK cancer survival rates and those in France. And for those who are diagnosed and undergoing treatment, a reluctance to complain inhibits the vital flow of information between patient and doctor and thereby obstructs recovery.

Earlier this year, Barack Obama vowed to 'launch a new effort to conquer a disease that has touched the life of nearly every American'. In so doing, he was intensifying and expanding a 'war on cancer' first declared by Richard Nixon in 1971. For all the billions subsequently spent by the US, British and other governments, progress in that 'war' has been fitful. The age-adjusted mortality rate for cancer is about the same in the 21st century as it was 50 years ago, whereas the death rates for cardiac, cerebrovascular and infectious diseases have declined by about two-thirds. Since 1977, the overall incidence of cancer in Britain (discounting increases caused by an ageing population) has shot up by 25 per cent.

The 'war on cancer' is as misconceived as the 'war on terror' or the 'war on drugs'. For a start, why must every concerted effort be likened to warfare? Is this the only way we are able to describe human cooperation in pursuit of a common goal? And who are the enemies in this war? Cancer cells may be 'malignant' but they are not malevolent. Their 'abnormality' is as much a product of nature as the 'normality' of other cells. Like the wars on 'drugs' and 'terror', the war on cancer misapplies the martial metaphor to dangerous effect. It simplifies a complex and daunting phenomenon – making it ripe for political and financial exploitation.

In the war on cancer, the search for the ultimate weapon, the magic bullet that will 'cure' cancer, overshadows other tactics. Nixon promised 'a cure for cancer' in ten years; Obama promises one 'in our times'. But there is unlikely to be a single 'cure for cancer'. There are more than 200 recognised types of cancer and their causes are myriad. As a strategic objective, the search for the ultimate weapon distorts research and investment, drawing resources away from prevention and treatment, areas where progress has and can be made.

Thanks to collusion between industries and scientists, it took decades for the truth about tobacco and asbestos to come out; for the same reason it will probably take many more years for us to learn the truth about other cancer-causing agents in our environment. In 2007, six per cent (10,000) of cancer deaths in the UK were caused by occupational exposure to carcinogens. In cases like this, what's needed is a revolution in our tawdry health and safety regime, not new drugs.

As for 'lifestyle' factors, they are part of the wider environmental and social background of cancer – not a separate category applying to individuals with inadequate will-power. The context of any 'lifestyle' choice is a mix of opportunity and deterrence, economics and culture, personal circumstances and social conditions. A real general attack on the causes of cancer would require industrial, consumer and environmental reforms on a vast scale, not scapegoating those perceived as shirkers and deserters in a holy war.

Thankfully, as the incidence of cancer has risen, so has our ability to treat it. Survival rates have doubled in the past 30 years, with almost half of those diagnosed with cancer living for five years or more. This is less about drug breakthroughs than early diagnosis, improvements in care, and refinements in existing treatments. Today, what's preventing cancer patients from living longer and more happily is mainly a failure to apply existing best practises universally. The biggest single boon for people living with cancer would be the elimination of inequalities in healthcare. In England and Wales, over the period 1986-99 the 'deprivation gap' in survival between rich and poor became more marked for 12 out of 16 male cancers and nine out of 17 female cancers examined.

Like other wars, real and imagined, the 'war on cancer' is a gift to opportunists of all stripes. Among the vultures are travel insurers who charge people with cancer ten times the rate charged to others, the publishers of self-help books and the promoters of miracle cures, vitamin supplements and various 'alternative therapies' of no efficacy whatsoever.

But most of all, there's the pharmaceutical industry, which manipulates research, prices and availability of drugs in pursuit of profit. And with considerable success. The industry is the UK's third most profitable sector, after finance and tourism, with a steady return on sales of some 17 per cent, three times the median return for other industries. Their determination to maintain that profitability has seen drug prices rise consistently above the rate of inflation. The cost of cancer drugs, in particular, has soared.

The industry claims high prices reflect long-term investments in R&D. But drug companies spend on average more than twice as much on marketing and lobbying as on R&D. Prices do not reflect the actual costs of developing or making the drug but are pushed up to whatever the market can bear. Since that market is comprised of many desperate and suffering individuals, it can be made to bear a great deal.

The research that this supposedly funds is itself warped by the industry. When it comes to clinical trials of their products, pharmaceutical companies engage in selective publication and suppression of negative findings and are reluctant in the extreme to undertake comparative studies with other products.

Exorbitant drug prices are at the root of recent cancer controversies over NICE approval of 'expensive' cancer drugs (notably Revlamid, a therapy that can extend life in the later stages of a number of cancers, including mine) and top-up or 'co-payments' (allowing those who can afford it to buy medicines deemed too expensive by the NHS). 'We are told we are being mean all the time but what nobody mentions is why the drugs are so expensive,' said NICE chairman Michael Rawlins. 'Pharmaceutical companies have enjoyed double-digit growth year-on-year and they are out to sustain that, not least because their senior management's earnings are related to the share price.'

Many cancer therapies are blunt instruments; they attack not only cancer cells but everything else in sight. This is one reason people fear cancer: the treatment can be brutal. Making it less brutal would be a huge stride for people with cancer. And that requires not a top-down military strategy, with its win or lose approach, but greater access to information, wider participation in decision-making (across hierarchies and disciplines) and empowerment of the patient.

Because I live in the catchment area for Barts Hospital in central London, I find myself a winner in the NHS postcode lottery. The treatment is cutting-edge and the staff are efficient, caring and respectful. What's more, I live close enough so that I can undergo most of my treatment as an outpatient, a huge boon.

Cancer treatment involves extensive interaction with institutions (hospitals, clinics, social services, the NHS itself). Even in the best hospitals, the loss of freedom and the dependence on anonymous forces can be oppressive. Many cancer patients find themselves involved in a long and taxing struggle for autonomy – a rarely acknowledged reality of the war on cancer, in which the generals call the shots from afar.

As Susan Sontag noted, in the course of the 20th century cancer came to play the role that tuberculosis played in the 19th century; it is a totem of suffering and mortality, the dark shadow that can blight the sunniest day. But the ubiquitousness of cancer in our culture is of dubious value to those living with the disease. The media love cancer scares and cancer cures; they dwell on heroic survivors (Lance Armstrong) and celebrity martyrs (Jade Goody), but as Ben Goldacre has shown in his essential 'Bad Science' column in the *Guardian*, they grossly misrepresent research findings, conjuring breakthroughs from nothing and leaving the pubic panicked, confused or complacent.

For those living with cancer, now and in the future (and that's one in three of the UK population), the biggest threat is the coming public spending squeeze. Cuts in NHS budgets and privatisation of services will mean more people dying earlier from cancer and more people suffering unnecessarily from it. Even better survival rates will become a curse, as responsibility for long-term care is thrown back on families. A real effort to reduce suffering from cancer requires a political struggle against a system that sanctifies profit – not a 'war' guided by those who exploit the disease.

THE CANCER DANCE AND THE RITES OF POSITIVITY

Completed December 2014, previously unpublished.

The media relish cancer stories. They like to trumpet news about causes and cures. But they especially like to focus on celebrities – Angelina Jolie, Lance Armstrong, Stephen Sutton – famous people who can be presented as taking a heroic stand against their illness, battling it with bravery, remaining relentlessly positive before either tragically succumbing or joyously prevailing. The cancer dance sweeps up patients in its rites and rhythms. The triumph of the individual will seems ubiquitous: entrepreneurs, athletes, game show contestants, cancer patients.

As a sufferer of multiple myeloma for more than seven years now, this way of approaching the story of cancer leaves me profoundly uneasy. It seems to put enormous pressure on people already under great strain. It amounts to a call for a triumph of the will, a mastery of the individual over their environment, an assertion that obstacles, however daunting, can be overcome by individual desire and determination. The implication is that those of us who cannot achieve this mastery, whose cancers do not respond to our positivity, who are lacking in determination, are somehow lazy, deficient and weak.

I think part of my discomfort with this approach comes from witnessing the death of my father. My dad was addicted to positivity. One of his most cited sooths was that one 'should never pay for it twice', that the initial loss of whatever it was, a lost or stolen possession, a business venture that went awry, or one's health, was bad enough without duplicating the sorrow through prolonged regret. This stratagem evolved into a kind of ban on loss and grief in any form.

When he acquired the brutal kidney disease that was to consume his final years, his personal credo – positive thinking, being grateful for what you had rather than lamenting what you didn't – crumbled before the solid advancing wall of the disease. That unyielding reality would not bend to his will, to the form of magical thinking he had relied on throughout his lifetime. When he was first diagnosed, he was full of great hopes for a medical solution and enthusiasm for his doctors who he lauded as potential miracle workers. When they failed to produce the miracle or, in the end, even reduce the pain, he grew bitter. As death loomed large, he was bereft of positive spirit of any kind.

There's an element of reassuring those who are closest to the sick and ailing in this emphasis on being positive. By remaining hopeful we, those who are sick, can demonstrate to those not afflicted that we're doing all we can to help ourselves and that, in any event, 'life goes on'. We can offer them comfort by displaying dignity in suffering, and ultimately, dying well. Cancer patients in this way are viewed as sources of inspiration; it's expected that we will make the affirmative gesture for the benefit of those we care about and who care for us.

But the positivity mantra also infects the carers, a huge army, many of whom have had no real choice in the role they now play. What does positivity mean to them? Are they to deny the irritations and inconvenience caused by their spouse, child, parents, sibling or friend? Those of us who are sick may not be easy to live with, we can be changeable and inconsistent, impatient and sulky. It turns out that being depended on is as awkward and demanding as being dependent.

The reassurances of positivity, though, are primarily to be directed inward. And it's evident that many sufferers do derive solace and strength by taking a positive attitude towards their illness. Stressing optimism over pessimism, counting one's blessings rather than dwelling on misfortune, is evidently helpful for many, and, in itself, a good thing. There's no argument for everyone being permanently po-faced about cancer, that the only note to be sounded is one of tragic misery.

There's plenty of dark humour, slapstick even, irony and gratitude attached to being ill. The joy of relief from pain is tangible. Emphasizing these aspects of illness is of course legitimate. People in extremis have every right to pursue whatever approach works for them; they should be free to deal with their illness as they see fit.

No, I'm not advocating negativity or pessimism, which are as one dimensional as their positive counterparts. The negatives of illness do not kill off the positives of beauty, justice and kindness, just as the existence of the beautiful is not disproved or annulled by the existence of the ugly. I still find enough that is beautiful, stimulating, exciting in life and the world outside that I am bitter, resentful about increasingly losing access to it. It is precisely the positive here that constitutes the negative: it is losing out on, missing that which is valued – at more or less that same moment.

The alternative to positivity is not negativity but candour and truth. And yet the pressure to remain brave and optimistic is often impossible to resist. It's amazing how it clicks in automatically: a knee-jerk response when you're asked about your cancer and its progression. You find yourself talking down the negative and talking up whatever happy news there is, supplementing any report you give by noting something that has been positive in some way.

But for me and, I suspect, many others, none of these positive thoughts can annul the pain and discomfort and fear that accompanies my cancer. Positivity is a crude one size fits all model; its reassurance is ultimately hollow. I don't doubt that there is a psychological dimension to illness. Subjective elements surely play a role in the progress of disease and response to treatments. But that part is far from the simple notion that remaining positive counters illness. It is complex and multi-dimensional, not susceptible to a bare breakdown into two opposed categories.

Species of magical thinking abound in an age in which technological sophistication often remains the preserve of the wealthy and powerful. But despite repeated tests over many years, there is no evidence that positive thinking improves survival rates. Cancer has a brutal indifference and icy impersonality. I know that my own prolonged survival of multiple myeloma has little to do with any effort I made on my own behalf. I know I cannot think myself well. The experience has been all about the power and limitations of modern science.

The tyranny of positive thinking breeds anxiety on a mass scale. But there's nothing to be ashamed of in cancer patients feeling despair or frustration or bitterness. I know of course that my illness is a random misfortune, not the result of a conspiracy. But that doesn't stop me, when things get rough, from crying out against this dreadful burden, against the injustice of it all. I can't imagine anything I've done heinous enough to deserve this cruel manhandling.

To wall yourself off from these feelings is damaging. Anger is something we're taught to be ashamed of, to restrain as wasteful and self-indulgent. But it is a necessity and sometimes a virtue. We need our anger to motivate and defend ourselves. Accepting the realities of illness and of modern medicine does not mean banishing anger or suspending protest. It's not true that anger produces only more anger, pace Gandhi. The process of social change inevitably involves large numbers of people becoming angry about the same issue at more or less the same moment.

What we need, and rely on every day, is not the magic of positivity but a different kind of miracle, the miracle of mutual service, co-operation, interdependence, of collective human labour and ingenuity. Whenever I'm treated at an NHS facility, I'm touched by the ethos of care and cooperation; in escaping momentarily from the cash nexus, I experience a little taste of utopia.

But another side of healthcare has also been evident. It has centred on the power and limitations of modern science. It's not been about counterposing 'scientific' evidence-based treatments vs 'holistic' alternatives. In Big Pharma the crux is about politics and economics, about corporate self-interest and democracy. Obvious echoes of neo-liberalism in cancer and illness issues. The field is saturated in appeals to individualism, ceaseless injunctions to celebrate, to consume. In the face of this, it's political thinking not positive thinking that's needed.

Cancer may not be much susceptible to will-power, but it is demonstrably related to income, housing, diet, and poverty. The poorer you are the more likely you are to get cancer and the less likely to survive. Survival is presented as a triumph of the will when it is really a triumph of collective endeavour.

This is not to say that politics is the only optic through which to view cancer, or that it's sufficient when cancer enters your life. For me it's one of several necessary approaches. But the cult of positivity is politically dis-empowering. NHS cuts and privatisation are not a subjective battle. That fight happens out there, on the public battlefield of politics, ideology and mass demonstrations.

SONG OF THE BESIEGED

From Saved by a Wandering Mind, *2009. An earlier version was a prize-winning* Poetry Life *entry in spring 1998.*

Drink yourself silly tonight, the news is bad;
riots have broken out among the rich and famous,
they're heading our way in a raucous rabble,
they're heading our way seeking revenge.

Let's have a pint and a chaser each,
count our offences and prepare to amend
whatever it is that's maddened the pack,
whatever it is makes them slaver and growl.

It's dark outside but in here there's beer,
fags in the machine and nothing to lose,
the only complaint the price of a double,
the only sound the hubbub that soothes.

So what if somewhere in this city tonight
troubled millionaires go red in the face,
form posses in search of a good night's sleep,
form victim support groups and beg for relief?

Have you ever noticed how sensitive they are,
the famously famous, to wisecracks and quips,
how quick to react to a fall in the pound,
how adept at assessing the stranger's kiss?

Poor darlings! Having to remember
the innumerable names of unfamiliar friends,
having to remember to speak for us all
yet never speak ill of the lame or the dead.

So the news is bad, they're lonely and mean,
the rich and famous from *Hello* magazine.
Our betters are demented but after one more short
we forgive their excesses and turn to the sport.

PUBLISHING HISTORY

'Egypt', first published in *Street Music: Poems by Mike Marqusee*, Clissold Books, 2012.

'A victim of America: Muhammad Ali and the war against terrorism', first published in *Red Pepper*, March 2002.

'The politics of Bob Dylan', first published in *Red Pepper*, November 2003.

'1968: the mysterious chemistry of social change', first published in *Red Pepper*, April 2008.

'The voice within: a pilgrimage to Walden Pond', first published in *The Hindu*, September 2006.

'Thomas Paine: restless democrat', first published in *Red Pepper*, June 2009.

'Streets of the imagination', first published in *Red Pepper*, October 2011.

'Time to talk utopia', first published in *Red Pepper*, June 2011.

'1792: this is what revolution looks like', first published in *Red Pepper*, October 2012.

'For love of the game', first published in *New Statesman*, March 1996.

'Triumph and travail: the subcontinental story', first published in *Frontline*, April 1996.

'Pathways of memory', first published in *The Hindu*, March 2006.

'Branding the nation', first published in *The Hindu*, June 2006.

'The privatisation of cricket', first published in *The Hindu*, March 2008.

'A level playing field?: global sport in the neoliberal age', first published in *Red Pepper*, June 2014.

'India's tryst with the death penalty', first published in *The Hindu*, October 2006.

'Life-changing happenstance: discovering India', first published in *The Hindu*, February 2009.

'Free speech and the war on terror', first published in *The Hindu*, December 2005.

'Imperial whitewash', first published in *The Hindu*, August 2006.

'Multi-culturalism and the politics of white identity', first published in *The Hindu*, October 2006.

'A lovely, worldly quirk: Madeira's north coast', first published in *The Hindu*, February 2009.

'Contesting white supremacy', first published in *Red Pepper*, June 2010.

'Small country, big struggle', first published in *Morning Star*, August 2010.

'"The greatest nation on earth"? Obama's victory speech viewed from overseas', first published in *The Hindu*, November 2012.

'White Supremacy alive and well in Britain', first published in *Red Pepper*, August 2013.

'...And all those against', first published in *New Statesman*, October 1995.

'All because he loves you: a Christmas tale', first published in *New Statesman*, December 1995.

'Alternative campaign diary', first published in *Labour Left Briefing*, June 1997.

'The sleep of reason breeds monsters', first published in *Labour Left Briefing*, October 1997.

'Mistaken priorities', first published in *The Hindu*, January 2006.

'Politics and "the art of the possible"', first published in *Red Pepper*, February 2010.

'Riots, reason and resistance', first published in *Red Pepper*, August 2011.

'Politics, our missing link', first published in *Red Pepper*, August 2012.

'Success, failure and other political myths', first published in *Red Pepper*, December 2013.

'Thatcherism's resistible rise', first published in *Red Pepper*, June 2013.

'Why I am an unrepentant Bennite', first published in *Red Pepper*, March 2014.

'Rocking for revolution', first published in *Red Pepper*, November 2004.

'A rasika's tribute', first published in *The Hindu*, December 2006.

'Matchless feast', first published in *The Hindu*, March 2008.

'Not pop as we know it: flamenco and the quest for authenticity', first published in *Red Pepper* in February 2010.

'John Ford: melancholy democrat', first published in *Red Pepper*, October 2010.

'My fantasy career (or why there is no such thing as world music)', first published in *The Hindu*, January 2011.

'"Life is possible on this earth": the poetry of Mahmoud Darwish', first published in *Red Pepper*, March 2011.

'1200 BC: The world's first industrial action...rescuing the past for the future', first published in *Red Pepper*, April 2013.

'Past visions, future dreams', first published in *Red Pepper*, February 2014.

'Some crucial distinctions', first published in October 2005.

'Echoes and analogies', first published in *The Hindu*, March 2007.

'Pathways across time and space', first published in *The Hindu*, June 2007.

'The real thing', first published in *Red Pepper*, April 2009.

'Bible bashing (lessons for the rich)', first published in *Red Pepper*, March 2011.

'If not now, when?: on BDS and "singling out" Israel', first published in *Red Pepper*, January 2014.

'As long as you've got your health', first published in *The Hindu*, August 2007.

'Equality: without ifs, ands or buts', first published in *The Hindu*, September 2008.

'The misbegotten "war on cancer"', first published in *Red Pepper*, October 2009.

'The cancer dance and the rites of positivity', previously unpublished, December 2014.

ACKNOWLEDGEMENTS

Friends at *Red Pepper*, James O'Nions and Hilary Wainwright, first suggested this anthology. They worked on it, suggesting articles, discussing themes etc. along with Huw Richards, Rob Steen and Megan Hiatt. James collected a large number of *Red Pepper* articles. Paul Field meticulously scoured back editions of *Labour Briefing* to find Mike's earlier writing. Thanks also to Mike Phipps, Jeff Marqusee and Sarah White for comments on the introduction. Tom Walker has resurrected Mike's website and ensured that Mike has a virtual presence.

Colin Robinson was, as he always is, publisher extraordinaire. He published several of Mike's books. He was ably assisted by Alex Doherty and Christopher O'Brien. Aditya Sarkar understands Mike's interests and can navigate his way through the twists and turns of Mike's thoughts.

Lachlan Stuart, Kevin Flack and my family were all part of this project. Thanks to all. Any omissions are my responsibility. Some of these articles, along with more information about Mike's books and other articles, can be found at http://www.mikemarqusee.co.uk/.

Liz Davies
London, December 2017